AN
ESSAY

ON

NAVAL TACTICS,

SYSTEMATICAL and HISTORICAL.

WITH

EXPLANATORY PLATES.

IN FOUR PARTS.

By JOHN CLERK, Esq. of Eldin,
FELLOW OF THE SOCIETY OF SCOTISH ANTIQUARIES,
AND OF THE ROYAL SOCIETY OF EDINBURGH.

SECOND EDITION.

The Naval & Military Press Ltd

Published by the
The Naval & Military Press
in association with the Royal Armouries

© 2008

Unit 10 Ridgewood Industrial Park,
Uckfield, East Sussex, TN22 5QE
Tel: +44 (0) 1825 749494
Fax: +44 (0) 1825 765701

MILITARY HISTORY AT YOUR FINGERTIPS
www.naval-military-press.com

ONLINE GENEALOGY RESEARCH
www.military-genealogy.com

ONLINE MILITARY CARTOGRAPHY
www.militarymaproom.com

ROYAL
ARMOURIES

The Library & Archives Department at the
Royal Armouries Museum, Leeds, specialises
in the history and development of armour
and weapons from earliest times to the
present day. Material relating to the
development of artillery and modern
fortifications is held at the Royal
Armouries Museum, Fort Nelson.

For further information contact:
Royal Armouries Museum, Library, Armouries Drive,
Leeds, West Yorkshire LS10 1LT
Royal Armouries, Library, Fort Nelson, Down End Road, Fareham PO17 6AN

Or visit the Museum's website at
www.armouries.org.uk

*In reprinting in facsimile from the original, any imperfections are inevitably reproduced
and the quality may fall short of modern type and cartographic standards.*

Printed and bound by CPI Antony Rowe, Eastbourne

ADVERTISEMENT

TO THE FIRST EDITION.

A FEW copies of this FIRST PART of an *Essay on Naval Tactics* being printed in 1782, were handed about among Friends. But, although the Author has been flattered with many letters of approbation, not only from Gentlemen of literary fame, but from Naval Officers of diftinguifhed merit, and of the higheft rank, while others have taken the trouble to make copies in manufcript ; and although, fince that time, he has been occafionally employed in making additions, and, he hopes, fome improvements, it is not without folicitude that his Work is now fubmitted to a more public examination.

The reft of the Work is in great forwardnefs, and will be publifhed as foon as it is finifhed. In the mean time, it was thought proper no longer to delay the publication of this FIRST PART.

EDINBURGH, *January* 1790.

PREFACE.

THOUGH a fuperior degree of knowledge in naval affairs be evidently of the utmoſt confequence to the inhabitants of this iſland, yet the ſubjeɛt of Naval Taɛtics had long remained among us in a very rude and uncultivated ſtate. Of this I was convinced at an early period of life, and I had long applied to this ſtudy before I ventured to communicate my thoughts upon it to the Public.

Since the appearance of the following ſyſtem in print, about twenty-two years ago *, it has been a ſource of the greateſt ſatisfaɛtion to me to obſerve a total change in the mode of conduɛting engagements with great fleets, on the part of our gallant Britiſh Admirals. The ſpirit, perſeverance, and ſuperior ſkill of our

ſeamen,

---

* The firſt impreſſion of Part Firſt conſiſted of a few copies, not for ſale, but to be given away.

feamen, uniformly difplayed in clofe engagements in the cafe of
fingle fhips, but which, from the dexterous manœuvres of the
enemy, could not formerly be brought into proper effect, on
account of a total neglect of the ftudy of Naval Tactics, have at
laft been exhibited alfo in the cafe of great battles with numerous
fleets, in a manner which has led to naval victories that muft
ever appear with the greateft luftre in the Britifh annals.   The
letters of approbation which I have received, not only from men
of learning, but from naval officers of diftinguifhed ability and
of the higheft rank *, and the numerous compliments that have
of late been paid to me, might exempt me from the imputation
of vanity, if I fhould now conclude, that my work, however im-
perfect, has effentially contributed to the fervice of my country.

As I never was at fea myfelf, it has been afked, how I fhould
have been able to acquire any knowledge in Naval Tactics, or
fhould have prefumed to fuggeft my opinions and ideas upon
that fubject.   The following detail, which I truft I fhall now be
excufed for entering upon, will, it is hoped, obviate every prejudice of this kind.

I had acquired a ftrong paffion for nautical information,
when almoft an infant.   At ten years old, before I had feen a
fhip,

* I was, in particular, much flattered by the decided approbation of my
Effay, by Lord Duncan and other naval officers at Portfmouth, conveyed by his
Lordfhip, then Captain Duncan, in a letter to my relation, Sir John Clerk, fo
long ago as October 4. 1785 ; in which is mentioned alfo the attention paid to
my work by his Royal Highnefs the Duke of Clarence.

ſhip, or even the ſea, but at a diſtance of four or five miles, I
formed an acquaintance at ſchool with ſome boys who had come
from a diſtant ſea-port, and who inſtructed me reſpecting the
different parts of a ſhip from a model which they had procured. After this apprenticeſhip, I had frequent opportunities
of ſeeing and examining ſhips at the neighbouring port of Leith,
which increaſed my paſſion for the ſubject; and I was ſoon in
poſſeſſion of a number of other models, ſome of them even of
my own conſtructing, which I often ſailed on a piece of water
of ſome ſize in my father's pleaſure-grounds, where there was alſo a boat with ſails, which furniſhed me with much employment.
Beſides this, I had ſtudied Robinſon Cruſoe, and had read a number of voyages. A deſire of going to ſea could not but be the
conſequence of all this. Checked it was, however, at all times
by my family, who already had ſuffered heavy loſſes in both ſea
and land ſervice.

During the courſe of two long wars, the firſt of which commenced about this time, I had the advantage of the converſa-
tion of many of my own near relations, who had been bred
to the ſea-ſervice. Beſides this, I had at all times courted a
connexion with other profeſſional ſeamen and ſhipbuilders, of
all ranks and capacities, wherever they were to be met with, as
at London, and in almoſt all the other ſea-ports round the iſland.
At the ſame time, I was unwearied in my attention to the many
valuable experiments of the ingenious and liberal-minded Mr
PATRICK MILLER of Dalſwinton; to whom, whether in ſhip-
building or in conſtructing artillery, both muſketry and great guns,

b

his

have put to fea, an anxiety inexpreffible laid hold of my mind; and the defire of being prefent at the meeting of the hoftile fleets was fo great, that, could my private concerns in any way have admitted of it, or rather had I not been at fuch a diftance from Portfmouth, from whence the armament on the part of Britain was fitted out, I certainly fhould have been on board fome one fhip of Lord KEPPEL's fleet.

The rencounter which followed on the 27th of July 1778, became the fubject of two other long trials; the firft that of Lord KEPPEL the Admiral; the fecond that of Sir HUGH PALLISER, the fecond in command, which, far from giving fatisfaction, proved only frefh caufe of difquiet among the officers of the Navy. The fubject was new—an attack from the leeward: it had never oc- curred before, at leaft in thefe later times; and therefore it was the lefs wonderful that it might be fubject to animadverfions, or that the moft able officers might differ in opinion with refpect to the manner of conduct. But it is remarkable, that not only in the courfe of thefe two long trials, but alfo in the courfe of the two trials formerly mentioned, of Admiral MATTHEWS in 1744, or that of Admiral BYNG in 1756, not one fingle hint has efcaped, from any one concerned, that it was poffible any thing defective could be attributed to the fyftem of the attack itfelf, or that any kind of improvement fhould be attempted *.

The

P. 124. Sect. II.
P. 132.

* Alluding to what has fince been put in practice—the cutting the enemy's line afunder—the directing the greater part of the force of a fleet againft a few fhips, either in the van or the rear, or even making prize of the flower-failing, or crippled fhips of the enemy.

The inveftigation, however, of many things in this engagement, which to me feemed to be palpable blunders, and moft important, roufed a defire which could not be refifted, and hurried me on to put in writing a number of ftrictures, accompanied with drawings and plans, containing fketches of what might have been attempted in this new kind of rencounter of fleets upon contrary tacks, more particularly applicable to this attack, as it was from the leeward, which, after communicating to friends, naval officers, and others in my neighbourhood, copies were fent to London.

The next example of a fea-engagement which followed, was that of Admiral BYRON off the ifland of Grenada, July 6th 1779. The attack was from the windward, and fimilar both to that of MATTHEWS and that of Admiral BYNG. Thefe attacks, together with this of Lord KEPPEL, made four cafes, in which it appeared to me, that neither the difficulty of bringing on an engagement, nor that of purfuing the enemy, arofe from any abatement in the fpirit of the feamen, nor of any defect in the fhipping, on the one fide, nor even from any fuperiority of failing on the other; but muft be attributed alone to the unfkilful manner in which the feveral attacks were conducted.

P. 54. No. 73.

In January 1780, when I was in London, being fully impreffed with the importance of the naval ideas which long had been working in my imagination, and in confequence of the ftrictures on Lord KEPPEL's engagement fent the year before, fome appointments, for the purpofe of farther communication on this

fubject,

subject, were made by my friends. Among the first of these, was an appointment with Mr RICHARD ATKINSON, the particular friend of Sir GEORGE RODNEY, who was then in London, and was immediately to set out to take the command of the fleet in the West Indies. At this meeting, the whole of my acquisitions on the subject of Naval Tactics, for many years back, was discussed. I communicated to Mr ATKINSON the theories of attack from both the windward and the leeward; the first as contained in the first part of this Essay; the last as contained in the second part, now published a second time. I particularly explained my doctrine of cutting the enemy's line, &c. as set forth in both first and second parts. I also produced the paper of strictures on Lord KEPPEL's rencounter of the 27th of July, which contained all my general ideas on the subject of Naval Tactics. All this Mr ATKINSON undertook to communicate to Sir GEORGE RODNEY, which he could have no difficulty in doing, as I left in his custody sketches made according to my usual method of demonstration, together with the necessary explanations.

P.104. No.115.

From the best authority, I have been informed that Lord RODNEY himself at all times acknowledged the communication; and having, from the first, approved of my system, declared, even before he left London, that he would strictly adhere to it in fighting the enemy.

Soon after this, Admiral RODNEY sailed with a strong fleet for the West Indies. Off Cape Finisterre, he fell in with and captured a number of Spanish transports; and off Cape St Vincent, meeting with a Spanish squadron, he took several ships, and made prisoner Don LANGUARA the commander. Proceeding to the

West

West Indies, on the 16th April 1780, he came in sight of the French fleet, to the leeward of the Pearl Rock, west end of the island of Martinico. On the 17th, the French were still to leeward; and Admiral RODNEY brought on an action, by an attack from the windward. In his official despatches describing the battle, there is the following remarkable passage: ' At forty-five minutes after six Page 78.
' in the morning, I gave notice, by public signal, that my inten-
' tion was to attack the enemy's rear with my whole force. '

This was a language altogether new, either from Admiral RODNEY, or any of his predecessors; and as it was the first in-stance in which a British Admiral had ventured to deviate from the old practice, I could not help immediately ascribing it to the communications I had made to Mr ATKINSON, as mentioned be-fore. Elated as I was by the above passage, I was disappointed by another in the same letter. ' At fifty minutes after eleven A. M., Page 79.
' I made the signal for every ship to bear down, and steer for her
' opposite in the enemy's line, agreeable to the 21st Article of the
' Additional Fighting Instructions. '

Afterwards on the 15th May, and again on the 19th, Admiral RODNEY came to actions with Count de GRASSE; but I was ex-tremely mortified, that although, on both occasions, he met the enemy on contrary tacks, and from the leeward, he shewed no Page 93. intention whatever of attempting to cut asunder the enemy's line, or even of separating, or cutting off a single ship from the rest of the line, although this could have been accomplished with the most perfect ease.

P. 104. No. 115.

In

In four other engagements which followed, 1. That of Admiral ARBUTHNOT, on the 16th March 1781, off the mouth of the Chesapeak; 2. That of Admiral HOOD on the 29th April, off Port Royal, Martinico; 3. That of Admiral PARKER, on the 5th August, on the Dogger Bank; 4. That of Admiral GREAVES, on the 5th September, off the mouth of the Chesapeak, the former practice was still continued; and accordingly, our fleets did not take a single ship from the enemy, and completely failed to accomplish the purpose of their destination. And though I must take notice, that on the 16th of March 1781, Admiral ARBUTHNOT had much merit, in disappointing the intentions of the French upon the Chesapeak, that officer knew nothing beyond the old erroneous system of Tactics; and, very soon after, the French entirely succeeded in their purposes in that quarter, to the great mortification of the British.

Having convinced myself of the effects that would follow a change of system, every fresh despatch from our fleets gave me new pain. The fatal errors, to which our want of success was to be attributed, still prevailed.

In the mean time, so often as despatches with descriptions of these battles were brought home, it was my practice to make animadversions, and criticise them, by fighting them over and over again, by means of the foresaid small models of ships, which I constantly carried in my pocket; every table furnishing sea-room sufficient on which to extend and manœuvre the opponent fleets at pleasure; and where every naval question, both with respect to situation and movement, even of every individual ship, as well

as

as the fleets themfelves, could be animadverted on ;—in this way not only fixing and eftablifhing my own ideas, but alfo enabling many landfmen to form a judgment with refpect to the fubject of Tactics as well as myfelf.

Often, on thefe occafions, I had been preffed to publifh my ideas, and had certainly done fo long before, had it not been for two objections, both of which were of great weight with me. 1. Not being a profeffional man, and having even to learn many of the fea terms, I thought fuch a work from me would come very ill recommended; 2. Having always employed my mind in mechanical ftudies, and in drawing only. I found myfelf extremely deficient, too, in the art of writing. I had therefore wifhed to find fome profeffional feaman, who, approving of my ideas, would either communicate them to the public, or fail upon means of getting them attended to in the Navy.

At laft, however, I found myfelf irrefiftibly impelled, by the melancholy accounts of the tranfactions which followed the 5th September 1781; when Admiral GREAVES, inftead of entering Page 7. the Chefapeak, and relieving Lord CORNWALLIS, which he could have done with perfect eafe, unadvifedly followed Count de GRASSE to fea, and, after making an attack not lefs feeble and undecifive, than any which had preceded it, found himfelf obliged to retire, leaving Lord CORNWALLIS and his fine army to their fate; which was followed with confequences not lefs important, but far more dreadful, than thofe that happened on the lofs of the ifland

c of

of Minorca, when abandoned by the unfortunate Admiral BYNG in 1756.

P. 103. 105. 176.

P. 23. & 24.

P. 27.

P. 44. 110. &c.

In profecution of my tactical ideas at the time, put in motion by the ftrictures upon Lord KEPPEL's engagement, on the 27th of July 1778, now twenty-fix years ago, I had made confiderable progrefs in forming diagrams for illuftrating the attack from the leeward, as appearing to me to be both new, and a manœuvre of greater ingenuity than the attack from the windward; when it occurred that, in compofing an Effay on Naval Tactics in general, it would be neceffary to begin by faying fomething, 1. On the method of attack in the cafe of fingle fhips; 2. On the mode of bringing a number of fhips, or that of great fleets, to action: and I had, by way of illuftration, made a collection of engagements which had formerly taken place, fuch as that of Admiral MATTHEWS in 1744, that of Admiral BYNG in 1756, and of Lord KEPPEL's in 1778, &c.; to which were added, plans, with obfervations, founded upon defpatches from the feveral Admirals. And laying hold of an opportunity to read this Effay to a number of gentlemen affembled on purpofe, it was fo much approved of, that I was encouraged to finifh it immediately, that, being publifhed, it might be of fome ufe in the very critical fituation we were brought into by this laft misfortune and difgrace of our fleets in the mouth of the Chefapeak.

P. 148.

The attack from the leeward, it is true, was the firft begun to be wrote. But as the materials of the attack from the windward were

were in greater forwardnefs, it was determined that this part of the fubject, the attack from the windward, fhould be firft executed; and accordingly, after getting it finifhed with as great fpeed as poffible, it was publifhed by the 1ft of January 1782. A few copies, only 50 in number, were printed, and handed about among friends: fome copies I took the liberty to prefent to profeffional men. Very foon, however, I found that my fyftem, fo far as it then went, had excited a good deal of attention; and I was much gratified by the many flattering letters of approbation which I received, not only from men of letters, but from naval officers of diftinguifhed merit, and of the higheft rank. Thus encouraged, I was advifed to fend copies to his MAJESTY's Minifters at the time, which was in Spring 1782; and my opinions, if juft, no doubt deferved the immediate attention of Government.

Our affairs at fea foon after took a different turn; and I have fince had the great fatisfaction to fee, by the adoption of my fyftem, a decided and permanent fuperiority given to our fleets. I fhall fay nothing, in this place, of the brilliant enterprife of Lord HOOD for the relief of St Chriftophers, the account of which arrived about this time. The public joy on this glorious occafion had not fubfided, when intelligence came of the memorable and glorious victory gained by Lord RODNEY, upon the 12th April P. 248. 1782; a victory far more decifive and important than any which had been gained by our fleets during the laft century. The general exultation was exceffive; and I flattered myfelf I could diftinctly perceive, even from the firft accounts of the engage-

c 2 ment,

CONTENTS.

PART I.

SEC-

SECTION IV.

EXAMPLES.

INTRODUCTION

SECTION I.

Of engagements, the Britiſh fleet being to windward 43

SECTION II.

I. Ad-

MODE OF ATTACK PROPOSED.

SECTION I.

SECTION II.

SECTION III.

b

SECTION IV.

SECTION V.

SECTION VI.

SECTION VII.

SECTION VIII.

SECTION IX.

SECTION X.

APPENDIX.

PART II.

INTRODUCTION　　-　Page 167

SECTION I.

SECTION II.

SIMPLE ATTACK.

SECTION III.

CROSS ATTACK.

SECTION IV.

PART

PART III.

Application

PART IV.

INTRODUCTION   -   -   -   227

Line

CONTENTS.

TO

TO THE BINDER.

The Plates to be placed facing the refpective pages of the Work marked upon the top of each Plate ; and fo folded, that they may turn out to the right hand, and the Engravings be al! beyond the margin of the letter-prefs.

NAVAL TACTICS.

PART I.

INTRODUCTION.

UPON inquiring into the transactions of the British Navy, during the two last wars, as well as the present *, it is remarkable, that, when single ships have encountered one another, or when two, or even three, have been engaged of a side, British seamen, if not victorious on every occasion, have never failed to exhibit instances of skilful seamanship, intrepidity, and perseverance; yet, when ten, twenty, or thirty great ships have been assembled, and formed in line of battle, it is equally remark-

B able,

---

* By the present war is understood the American war; this Tract being written in October 1781, immediately after the surrender of Lord Cornwallis's army, the consequence of Admiral Greaves's unsuccessful rencounter with the French fleet off the mouth of the Chesapeak. A few copies only were printed, and at that time distributed among friends.

able, that, in no one inftance, has ever a proper exertion been
made, any thing memorable achieved, or even a fhip loft or won
on either fide *.

Whoever ftudies the hiftory of the times, will be convinced of
the truth of both thefe affertions. But many, without properly
attending to the firft, acknowledge, and endeavour to account for,
the laft, by infinuating, that as our feamen, whatever they were
in former times, are now, in no refpect, preferable to thofe of
our rivals, it would be abfurd to expect from them a greater
degree of exertion ; and that the fhips of our enemies, being better conftructed, have had it always in their power to avoid an
engagement, by outfailing us. As thefe opinions, unhappily,
have already had too much influence, even among feamen, it
will be partly the bufinefs of the following Treatife to fhow, that
they are ill-founded; and that it is neither to any abatement of
fpirit in our men, nor even to any fault in the conftruction of
our fhipping, that the want of fuccefs in the late great fea-battles
ought to be attributed.

From our infular fituation, we are led to avail ourfelves of a
naval force, in fome fuch manner, as that in which all animals
are directed to make ufe of the weapons or talents with which
nature has furnifhed them, whether for fupport or defence.

Why

---

* Neither the gallant manœuvres off St Chriftophers, nor the memorable
12th of April, took place till the fpring following.

Why the effect of this propensity to sea affairs was not more conspicuous in the earlier part of our history, may be accounted for likewise from our insular situation. Occupied with disputes, while divided into two kingdoms, our attention was withheld from the rest of Europe ; and, separated as an island, we were much less the object of foreign interference : But, as soon as these internal disputes began to subside, which in a great measure they did, from the influence that the hope of succeeding ELIZABETH had upon MARY Queen of Scots, and her son JAMES, this naval disposition broke forth with irresistible force ; and, cherished by successive improvements in commerce, every obstruction being removed by the Union of the two kingdoms, it has produced effects which have been the admiration of the world.

It is obvious that, from the greater extent of coast, number of bays, dangerous ferries, and from the various sea-carriage which our produce consequently requires, a greater portion of our people must be bred to a seafaring life than is necessary in other nations. From these causes, as well as from the tempestuous nature of our seas, rapidity of our tides, and inconstancy of our climate, it may be expected, that our seamen, besides being numerous, ought at the same time to acquire courage and dexterity sufficient to encounter the difficulties to which they must unavoidably and constantly be exposed ; and that, from a combination of all these circumstances, a national character will arise, distinguished by a hardy and persevering intrepidity, which, without such causes, can never exist.

A prepoſſeſſion in favour of one's countrymen is both natural and commendable; but, where they have undertaken and uniformly ſucceeded in great and glorious enterprizes, it does not require the influence of national prejudices to conclude that they are diſtinguiſhed by an extraordinary character. Whether this may have ariſen entirely from the cauſes above enumerated, or in ſome degree alſo from the nature of our government, is not the object of our preſent inquiry: it is ſufficient, for the purpoſe of this Eſſay, that ſuch a character is actually found to exiſt in this iſland.

During the reign of ELIZABETH, not to dwell upon the famous expeditions of DRAKE, CAVENDISH, NORRIS, and the Earl of CUMBERLAND, for which we refer to our beſt hiſtorians *, where can a more illuſtrious example of naval ſkill be met with, than the conduct diſplayed in the deſtruction of the SPANISH ARMADA? in which we may obſerve that the prudence of ſuſtaining a defence, by ſuffering that immenſe armament to waſte its force in a contention with the winds and waves, was no leſs conſpicuous than the intrepidity with which the repeated attacks were made.—SIR MARTIN FROBISHER's exploits and death before the harbour of Breſt reflect additional glory on his countrymen.—Neither ought the ſpirited behavour of JAMES LANCASTER before Fernambuco, in the Brazils, to be forgotten. Seeing the ſhore lined with great numbers of the enemy, he ordered his men to row their boats with ſuch violence againſt the ſhore, as to ſplit

them

---

* See Hume's Hiſtory, Chap. 51. 52. and 53. 4to edit.

them in pieces. By this bold action he both deprived his men of all hope of returning, unlefs by victory, and terrified the enemy, who fled after a fhort refiftance.—We may alfo mention the fecond enterprife at Cadiz, when ESSEX threw his hat into the fea. —But the true character of the Britifh failor is fo juftly difplayed in the obftinate refiftance made by SIR RICHARD GREENVILLE, in a fingle fhip, againft a numerous Spanifh fleet, as defcribed by Mr HUME, that an account of the action fhall here be given in the very words of that great hiftorian.

" LORD HOWARD being fent with a fquadron of feven fhips
" to intercept the Weft India fleet, was attacked by a Spanifh
" fquadron of fifty-five fail. By the courageous obftinacy of
" SIR RICHARD GREENVILLE the Vice-Admiral, who refufed
" to make fail with the reft of the fquadron, one fhip was taken,
" being the firft Englifh man of war that had fallen into the hands
" of the Spaniards. This action of SIR RICHARD GREENVILLE
" is fo fingular as to merit a more particular defcription. He
" was engaged alone with the whole Spanifh fleet, of fifty-five
" fail, which had ten thoufand men on board ; and from the
" time the fight began, which was about three in the afternoon,
" to the break of day next morning, he repulfed the enemy fif-
" teen times, though they had continually fhifted their veffels,
" and boarded with frefh men. In the beginning of the action,
" he himfelf received a wound, but he continued doing his duty
" above deck till eleven at night, when, receiving a frefh wound,
" he was carried down to be dreffed.

" During this operation, he received a fhot in the head ; and
" the

" the furgeon was killed by his fide. The Englifh began now
" to want powder ; all their arms were broke or become ufelefs :
" of their number, which was but a hundred and three at firft,
" forty were killed, and almoft all the reft wounded ; their mafts
" were beat overboard, their tackle cut in pieces, and nothing
" but a hulk left, unable to move one way or other. In this fi-
" tuation, Sir Richard propofed to the fhip's company to truft to
" the mercy of God, not to that of the Spaniards, and to deftroy
" the fhip, with themfelves, rather than yield to the enemy. The
" mafter-gunner, and many of the feamen, agreed to this defpe-
" rate refolution ; but others oppofed it, and obliged GREENVILLE
" to furrender himfelf prifoner. He died a few days after ; and
" his laft words were, " Here die I RICHARD GREENVILLE,
" with a joyful and quiet mind, for that I have ended my life as
" a true foldier ought to do, fighting for his country, his Queen,
" religion, and honour. My foul willingly departing this body,
" leaving behind the lafting fame of having behaved as every
" valiant foldier is in duty bound to do." The Spaniards loft in
" this fharp, though unequal action, four fhips, and about a
" thoufand men ; and GREENVILLE's veffel herfelf perifhed foon
" after, with two hundred Spaniards on board *. "

It would be endlefs to enumerate every achievement, where
the capture, almoft of every fhip, muft have furnifhed materials
for a particular panegyric. Mr HUME, in treating of this fubject, expreffes himfelf in the following manner : " In every
" action, the Englifh, though they had long enjoyed domeftic
" peace, difcovered a ftrong military difpofition ; and the Queen,
" though herfelf a heroine, found more frequent occafion to
" reproach

---

* See Hume's Hift. ch. 43. firft edit. 4to.

" reproach her Generals for encouraging their temerity, than for
" countenancing their fear or caution." However much ELI-
ZABETH might wifh to temper the ardour of her fubjects on
fome occafions, on others fhe does not feem to be wanting in
her endeavours to roufe their fpirit fufficiently; for, in a harangue
before Parliament, when fpeaking of the *Spanifh Armada*, fhe
faid, " But I am informed, that when he, Philip, attempted this
" laft invafion, fome upon the fea-coaft forfook their towns, fled
" up higher into the country, and left all naked and expofed
" to his entrance; but I fwear unto you, by God, if I knew
" thofe perfons, or may know of any that fhall do fo hereafter,
" I will make them feel what it is to be fo fearful in fo urgent a
" caufe." *

Notwithftanding the great attention which ELIZABETH gave
to the Navy, yet, at her deceafe, it confifted of forty fmall fhips
only, of which number four did not exceed forty guns,
and but two of thefe amounted to a thoufand tons; twenty-
three others were below five hundred tons: of the reft, fome
were of fifty, and fome even did not exceed twenty tons; and
the whole number of guns belonging to this fleet was 774. If
fuch brilliant and glorious actions were performed by fo inconfi-
derable a force, what might we not expect from our navy in its
prefent ftate? For the honour of the Englifh at that time, it muft
be remarked, that, while the Royal Navy confifted of thefe forty
fhips only, fo great was the national fpirit, and fo much was it
united, that an infinite number of other fhips of war was foon
fitted out, as well by private gentlemen, at their own expence, as

by

---

* Hume's Hift. *ubi fupra.*

by the different fea-ports. Thus, the ill concerted *, but formidable attempt of the *Spanifh Armada*, by farther exciting the refentment, and affording the greater occafion of gratifying the military genius of the nation, now about this period firft ferioufly exerted in naval enterprife, may be faid to have laid the foundation for that renown, which, ever fince, has been maintained with fo great fpirit.

One would have thought, however, that the Naval force fhould not have increafed much during the reign of ELIZABETH's fucceffor JAMES, when it is confidered, that the practice of the Englifh merchants then was to carry on their trade in foreign bottoms; yet, from the 1582, when the number of feamen, upon a computation, amounted to 14,295, until the year 1640, at the beginning of the domeftic troubles, that number was found to be tripled.

After an interval of twelve years, the Dutch war was the next occafion of a farther difplay of our Naval character. But, it muft be obferved, that, while the Englifh feamen had been fo often engaged, and generally fuccefsful, in the leffer battles, or rather enterprifes, yet, till now, they had never been tried in the greater, where a number of fhips were affembled together. However, their wonted intrepidity, far from forfaking them on this new and unexperienced occafion, feemed to be augmented, or rather exalted to a ftate of enthufiaftic fury, which

was

---

* See Note A.

was fupported with an unremitting perfeverance during the courfe of three dreadful wars; in the firft of which we had nine pitched battles; in the fecond five; and in the third not lefs than five alfo; making in all nineteen general engagements; in one of which the fight was renewed for three additional days fucceffively; in another for two days; and in a third for one day; which may fairly be ftated for other fix engagements; making, when taken together, twenty-five days of general actions. And, what would now be confidered as ridiculous and impracticable, many of the officers appointed to the command of thefe fleets had never been in fea-fervice till they were paft the age of forty, and fome even of fifty years. Of the laft number was BLAKE, who, although renowned for the many obftinate battles he had been engaged in, particularly that in the Downs, where he had no more than fifteen fhips, did not refufe the combat when attacked by forty-two fhips of the enemy, led on by the great VAN TRUMP. Yet for nothing was he more confpicuous than for his patriotic virtue. When in oppofition to the party then in power, " It is ftill our duty, " faid he to the feamen, " to " fight for our country, into whatever hands the government " may fall. "

In all of thefe enterprifes, whether with the Spaniards or the Dutch, whether in making the attack on caftles, fhips in harbours, or encountering fhip with fhip in clofe action, and formed in line of battle, we fhall find the Britifh feamen, whether equal or inferior in number, victorious or worfted, invariably fired with fuch enthufiaftic courage, that thefe battles, though not always

C decifive,

decifive, were conftantly marked with ftrong effect; ten, twenty, thirty, or more fhips, being taken or deftroyed, two thoufand men killed, and as many taken prifoners.

Therefore, without derogating from the gallant behaviour of the Dutch, which was equally difplayed in thofe wars, we are bound, from thefe proofs and examples, to believe, that Britifh feamen are, by nature or habit, endued with a peculiar extraordinary character. And, though the fpirits of the people might have been, for a little time, depreffed by the unfortunate battles of Beachy-head and Bantry-bay, which were fought fome time after; yet the natural impreffions, fo juftly in favour of our feamen, foon recovered our confidence; which was fo much increafed by the battle off La Hogue, that, many years afterwards, the victories off Malaga and Meffina were things to be expected of courfe.

The long intervals between thefe actions, and that of the war 1743, nowife abated the fanguine impreffions refpecting our feamen. Much effect was expected from the powerful fleet fent into the Mediterranean under the command of MATTHEWS and LESTOCK, who encountered the combined fleets of France and Spain on the 11th of February 1744. But, intending afterwards to give a more particular defcription of this affair, we fhall only add, that MATTHEWS, who commanded, accompanied with the Marlborough and Norfolk, his two feconds a-head and a-ftern, together with the Berwick in another place, broke out from the line of battle, got within a proper diftance, and fought with great bravery; but, being ill fupported by the reft of the fleet, little more

was

was done, than to fhow what cannon-fhot, at a reafonable diftance, might effect. The two Admirals mutually accufed each
other; and MATTHEWS, in confequence of a trial, was broke.
But the late King, without attending to the nice diftinctions which
had determined the Court-martial, and being fatisfied that the
Admiral had behaved like a brave man, refufed to confirm the
fentence.

Happily fome other more favourable opportunities offered,
during the courfe of this war, in which, having a greater fuperiority, we were more fuccefsful. Thefe were, the capture of the
May fleet by Admiral HAWKE; the voyage round the world by
Lord ANSON; his bold attack of the Acapulco fhip, fo much
his fuperior in force; his capture of fix French fhips of the line
and Indiamen in October.

Thefe, with the unremitting exertions in the many leffer fea-
combats, removing the evil impreffions made by the mifcarriage
in the Mediterranean, we ftill flattered ourfelves that the glory
of the Britifh flag was yet untarnifhed.

But, be that as it may, we could not, without fome emotion,
recal to mind thofe tremendous and glorious battles with the
Dutch, in which the fpirited and *united* exertions of our feamen
had been fo juftly celebrated, that, when the laft war broke out,
our minds were fo prepoffeffed with enthufiaftic partiality, that
there were but few of our countrymen who did not firmly believe
and truft, that, if one Britifh failor was not a match for two of
the enemy, he was at leaft a very fuperior being.

How

How great, then, was the difappointment of the nation, when it was known, that Admiral BYNG, commanding a Britifh fleet of fupcrior force, in a general engagement with the French, without lofing a fhip, almoft without the lofs of a man, half of his fleet not having fired a fhot, had acknowledged himfelf worfted, by flying to Gibraltar, abandoning Minorca, and leaving the garrifon at the mercy of the enemy, who were then mafters of the fea !

Meanwhile, it is with aftonifhment that we muft remark the innumerable leffer conflicts during the courfe of this war, where examples of perfevering courage and daring intrepidity were invariably exhibited in private as well as public fervice, and generally of fuch effect, that one or other of the combatants, of neceffity, was obliged to ftrike. A complete catalogue of which, however acceptable, would be too great for the bounds of this work.

It muft be owned, indeed, that feveral fortunate and important occafions occurred during the courfe of this war, where numbers of fhips were affembled, particularly that of HAWKE with CONFLANS ; but then the enemy, though nearly equal, after difcovering great want of determination, fairly ran away, without coming to an engagement. But, as we had a great fuperiority on all thefe occafions, excepting the one now mentioned, the decifion that took place, by means of that fuperiority, will never deftroy the force of the general obfervation.

Again, while we remark the wonderful exertions, and conftant fuccefs, attending the leffer conflicts; while we remark
                                                                how

how much, and how often, our ſhips have been put to ſevere trial, by being expoſed, in all weathers, during the ſtorms of winter, the enemy not daring to ſet out their heads * ; when, after recollection, we remark, that, to the numerous, bold, and ſucceſsful enterpriſes, *coups de main*, performed during the laſt 250 years, and that our enemies have only the ſingle diſgrace, which befel us at Chatham to counterbalance ſo great an account, ſhould we not at the ſame time remark, that this boaſted intrepidity, this perſevering courage of Britiſh ſeamen, has never once been brought to trial, where it would have been of the greateſt importance ; that is, in the greater engagements ; of which, becauſe this ſuperiority has never had an opportunity of being diſplayed, the reſult has always been the ſame, namely, that, in ſuch actions, our fleets, in the two laſt wars and the preſent, have been invariably baffled, nay worſted, without having ever loſt a ſhip, or almoſt a man ?

While we remark theſe circumſtances, is it not evident, and will it not be admitted, that one of three things muſt be the fact, either that our enemy, the French, having acquired a ſuperior knowledge, have adopted ſome new ſyſtem of managing great fleets, not known, or not ſufficiently attended to by us ? or that, on the other hand, we have perſiſted in following ſome

old

---

* Alluding to the ſquadron of Britiſh ſhips kept in the Bay of Biſcay during the courſe of laſt war, to watch over the motions of the enemy, in winter as well as in ſummer.

old method, or inſtructions, which, from later improvement, ought to have been rejected ?   Or, laſtly, that theſe miſcarriages, ſo often, and fatally repeated, muſt have proceeded from a want of ſpirit in our ſeamen ?

But as, from the many inſtances given, both of public and private exertion, the mind muſt revolt at this laſt ſuppoſition, it follows, that theſe repeated miſcarriages muſt have proceeded from one or other of the two firſt, or from both ?

During the courſe of the wars with the Dutch, before men- tioned, much improvement was made, particularly in the inven- tion of ſignals.   But the naval inſtructions then framed, al- though founded upon experience and obſervation, and though they might be admirably fitted for fighting in narrow ſeas, where theſe battles were fought ; yet, from later experience, it will be found, that they have been but ill qualified for bringing on an action with a fleet of French ſhips, unwilling to ſtand a ſhock, having ſea-room to range in at pleaſure, and deſirous to play off *manœuvres* of defence, long ſtudied with the greateſt atten- tion.

But if it were poſſible that there could have remained a doubt of the truth or force of theſe obſervations before the breaking out of the preſent war, will not this doubt be reſolved, if they ſhall be confirmed by every caſe that has followed ſince ; whe- ther we conſider the intrepidity and exertion ſo conſpicuous in the leſſer conflicts, or the defect of conduct and addreſs, ſo pal-

pable

pable in moſt of the greater engagements, although, at the ſame
time, our Admirals, whether by good fortune, by ſkilful ſeamanſhip, or by permiſſion of the enemy, have never failed, on every
occaſion, to acquire their wiſh, *viz.* the circumſtance of being to
windward ; excepting, indeed, on thoſe occaſions, where the
FRENCH have choſen to keep ſuch an advantage, without avail-
ing themſelves of it ; a circumſtance which is plainly a confirmation that their ſyſtem or mode is different from ours, and
that they are uniformly determined never to be brought to make
the attack, if it can be avoided.

From all which theſe three concluſions will naturally follow :
1ſt, That, in bringing a ſingle ſhip to cloſe action, and in conduct
during that action, the Britiſh ſeamen have never been excelled :
2dly, That the inſtructions, (by which is meant the method hitherto practiſed of arranging great fleets, ſo as to give battle, or to
force our enemy, the French, to give battle upon equal terms),
after ſo many and repeated trials, having been found unſucceſsful,
muſt be wrong : And, *laſtly,* that, on the other hand, the French
having repeatedly and uniformly followed a *mode* which has
conſtantly the effect intended, they therefore muſt have adopted
ſome new ſyſtem, which we have not diſcovered, or have not
yet profited by the diſcovery.

But, it may be aſked, Have the French ever effected any
thing deciſive againſt us ? Have they ever, in any of theſe
rencounters, taken any of our ſhips ? Have they ever, preſuming

upon

upon their fuperior fkill, dared to make the attack?—No. But, confident in their fuperior knowledge in Naval Tactics, and relying on our want of penetration, they have conftantly offered us battle to leeward, trufting that our headlong courage would hurry us on to make the cuftomary attack, though at a difadvantage almoft beyond the power of calculation; the confequences of which have always been, and always will be, the fame, as long as prejudices prevent us from difcerning either the improvements made by the enemy, or our own blunders.

To be completely victorious cannot always be in our power; but, to be conftantly baffled, and repeatedly denied the fatisfaction of retaliation, almoft on every occafion, is not only fhameful, but, in truth, has been the caufe of all our late misfortunes.

Before concluding this part of the fubject, it may be proper further to obferve, That, though our apprehenfions of fuffering in character and importance, as a Naval Power, might have been very great at the breaking out of the war with the Colonies, from an idea that the recent increafe of that importance had arifen alone from the growth of thefe Colonies; yet, from experience, from the great exertions made, and from the continuance of the war itfelf, it has been clearly proved, that that increafe muft have arifen from other refources, which will every day more and more be found to exift in the Mother Country herfelf. At the fame time, from that fuperior exertion, fo conftantly and glorioufly exhibited by our feamen in the leffer conflicts,

flicts, as well during the courfe of the prefent as of the two laft wars, we may reft fatisfied that the character of the Britifh tar is not in the leaft debafed, but ftill as predominant as formerly.

Hence, if the American Colonies fhall accomplifh their wifhed-for feparation, Britain, by her force being more collected, and with thefe refources, will yet be more powerful than ever.

D   N A V A L

NAVAL TACTICS.

Of the ATTACK from the WINDWARD.

DEMONSTRATIONS*.

SECTION I.

METHOD OF ATTACK IN THE CASE OF SINGLE SHIPS.

1. SUPPOSE a fingle fhip to windward at B (Plate I. fig. 1.), difcovering an enemy's fhip to leeward at F, Is it the practice for B, in making the attack, to bear directly down, end-wife, on F? No. Becaufe, if B did fo, the cafe would ftand thus: Suppofe the two fhips of eighty guns each, the receiving

fhip

---

* As it is by the influence of the wind alone that all the movements of fhip-ping are performed, for this reafon, as well as for rendering the following de-monftrations more fimple, we have made the courfe of the wind to proceed from the top of the page in the plans prefented in this Work.

N. B.

fhip F, by lying-to (as in fig. 2.), would prefent a broadfide of
forty heavy guns bearing upon B, during a courfe of two miles,
in which every fhot might take effect, while B, in this pofition,
(Plate I. fig. 2.), has it only in her power to bring the two light
guns of her fore-caftle, or bow-chafe, to bear on F, a difadvantage
greatly exceeding twenty to one. But the receiving fhip F, by lying broadfide to, will have all her mafts and rigging more open,
and, confequently, will allow fhot to pafs with lefs effect; her men,
alfo, will be lefs expofed to the impreffion of fhot, as it muft take
the breadth of the fhip only; whereas the fhip B, coming end-
wife down, muft be greatly affected by every fhot that may take
place in the extenfive area of her hull and rigging; the mafts and
fhrowds, from being feen in a line, and the whole fpace, from the
fituation, being quadruply darkened with rigging, a fhot taking
place in that area, therefore, muft carry away fomething of confiderable confequence; and a fhot taking place in the hull muft rake
the men from one end of the fhip to the other: Which fituation,
or pofition of B to F, is underftood to mean, that the fhip B is
raked by the fhip F; and the confequence would be, that B
would be difabled in her rigging, &c. long before fhe could arrive

---

N. B. In what follows, we have confined ourfelves more particularly to the
attack from the Windward; referving what relates to the attack from the Leeward for an after part of the Work.

The Britifh fhips are diftinguifhed by a red colour, and letters of reference
beginning with the alphabet and ending at E; and the fhips of the enemy are
diftinguifhed by a black colour, with letters beginning at F.

rive at a proper pofition for annoying F; and, when fhe has attained this pofition, F, by being entire in her rigging, will have it in her power to fight, or make off at pleafure.

2. The method then is, B having the wind, will run down aftern, as per dotted line, and getting into the courfe, or near the wake of F, or a pofition that will bring her parallel to the courfe of F, at a proper diftance, fhe will then run up clofe along fide of F, upon equal terms (as in fig. 3.); or, otherwife, on fhooting a-head, fhe will wear, and run down on the weather bow of F (as in fig. 4.), till fhe fhall force F to bear away to leeward, keeping clofe by F on equal terms; but, during the courfe, in both cafes, carefully watching that F fhall not have it in her power to bring her broadfide to bear upon B, without retaliation.

SECTION II.

COMPARISON OF THE EFFECT OF SHOT DIRECTED AGAINST THE RIGGING OF A SHIP, WITH ITS EFFECTS WHEN DIRECTED AGAINST THE HULL.

3. It having been often faid, that the French have made it a rule to throw the whole effect of their fhot more particularly into the rigging of their enemy, and that the Britifh, on the other hand, have been as attentive to point the force of their fire againft the

hull

hull of the fhip, it may be proper here to ftate the two cafes, and compare the effect.

4. Let us fuppofe a fhip of eighty guns wifhing to avoid the effects of a clofe engagement, but, at the fame time, lying-to, as at F (Plate I. fig. 5.), intending to receive, with every advantage, an enemy, B, of equal force, coming down with an intention to fight her; and let us fuppofe that F, by aiming her fire at the rigging of B, fhall have carried away any of the principal ftays, eight or ten windward fhrowds, or a fore-top maft, or any other rigging, though of much lefs confequence, but, at the fame time, without having wounded a fingle man of the fhip B; and fup-pofe a fecond fhip, confort to F, receiving fuch another fhip as B, and by firing at her hull only, fhall, without other damage, have killed thirty or forty of her men :———

5. In this critical juncture, when F and her confort are defir-ous of avoiding a clofe engagement, which of the two fhips of B will be moft difabled from following after, and clofing with the enemy? Is it not evident, that it muft be the fhip which has loft part of her rigging; for, as fhe will not be able to make fufficient fail, till after having been repaired, this neceffary ftoppage muft be of greater confequence at this time than if fhe had loft a hun-dred, or even two hundred of her complement of men; the re-mainder being always fufficient to navigate the fhip.

6. Again, let the comparative bulk of the two objects be con-fidered: The hull of a fhip, taken by itfelf, on the one fide, and

the

Plate 1. Part I. p. 26.

Fig. 1.

B

Fig. 2.

F

B

Fig. 3.

F

B

F

Fig. 4.

B

F

Fig. 5.

B

F

the whole area of the mafts, rigging, and hull, taken on the other; and, as the killing and deftroying of men may be the principal view in firing at the hull, fuppofe, for example, a fhip of feventy-four guns, which has two decks, the breadth, or rather the height, of the line expofed, which will comprehend both thefe decks crowded with men, cannot exceed twelve feet, which fum, multiplied by 120, the length of the fhip, will give 1440 feet, the whole area of the vulnerable mark: But the area, comprehending the rigging and hull, of fuch a fhip, will give a furface of twenty times thefe dimenfions.

SECTION III.

OF BRINGING GREAT FLEETS TO ACTION.

And, 1ft, A preliminary cafe, fhewing, that any one fhip, in her ftation in the line of battle, muft be at a confiderable diftance to admit of being expofed to the fire of three or more fhips, bearing upon her at one and the fame time, extended, as they muft be, in the line of the enemy.

7. As it has alfo been often faid, that fome particular fhip has been expofed, in battle, to the cannonade of three, four, or even five fhips, all extended in the enemy's line, and all bearing upon

on her at one and the fame time, figure 1. of Plate II. is intended
to prove, that this fhip muft have been at a very great diftance before fhe could have been expofed to the fire of even three fhips,
fuppofing them to be extended in line of battle a-head, and at one
cable's length afunder.   Suppofe a line of battle, in which four
or five fhips are extended, as I, H, F, H, I, the fpaces between
each fhip to be two hundred and forty yards, or one cable's
length, and the length of each fhip to be forty yards, fo that the
whole fpace between head and head, of any two fhips, is two
hundred and eighty yards; and let the perpendicular line F K,
proceeding right out from the beam of the middle fhip F, be divided into a fcale of fix cables length, making in all a diftance of
1440 yards: Quere, At what diftance may any oppofite fhip of
an enemy be expofed to the fire of three fhips bearing upon her
at one and the fame time? and let H, F, H, be the three fhips
lying-to, and extended in line of battle a-head; and let the opponent fhip be ftationed in any of the lines drawn through the
points E, C, G, and parallel to the line I, I.

8.   From infpection, it will be evident, that the opponent fhip,
ftationed at the point E, 720 yards diftant, cannot, for any length
of time, be expofed to the fire of more than the centre fhip F.
For the fhip H a-head, in *lying-to* in line of battle, will not be
able to bring her head fo much nearer the wind as to admit of
her broadfide to bear on E.   But, fuppofing this to be practicable,
will fhe not diforder her own line by being thrown out of her
ftation, and alfo leave her head expofed to a raking fire from her
oppofites in the enemy's line?

9.   Neither

9. Neither will it be more proper for H, the ſhip a-ſtern, to bring her broadſide on E; for, in doing this, ſhe will run to leeward, and expoſe her ſtern to be raked by her oppoſites.

10. But if the opponent ſhip cannot well be expoſed to the fire of the two ſhips, H, H, at the point E, ſhe muſt be ſtill leſs expoſed at the point C, 480 yards diſtant; and it will be almoſt impoſſible for the ſhips H, H, to touch her at the point G, 240 yards, or one cable's length diſtant.

11. But one cable's length aſunder is too ſmall an allowance for accidents that may happen to ſhips extended in line of battle a-head. Therefore, let us ſuppoſe I, F, I, to be the three ſhips extended at two cables length aſunder, or 480 yards between each of the three ſhips:

12. Then it will be evident, if the opponent's ſhip could not be much expoſed, at the point E, to the fire of the three ſhips, when at one cable's length aſunder, that, proportionally, ſhe would not be more expoſed at the point K, from the fire of the three ſhips now, when at two cables length aſunder, which is double the diſtance, or 1440 yards.

13. But as ſhips cannot well be kept in line of battle at a leſs allowance than one and a half cable's length aſunder, it follows, that a ſhip muſt be at leaſt 1080 yards diſtant, before ſhe can be expoſed or annoyed by a cannonade from three ſhips extended

E

in

in line of battle, and bearing upon her at the fame time, which let be fuppofed at L.

14.　Hence, it may be concluded, that, when it has been faid, that any fhip has been expofed to the fire of five, four, or even three fhips of the enemy's line, that fuch fhip has been at a very great diftance.　For, from what has been faid, it will not be ad-mitted, that either of the fhips I, I, or H, H, a-head and a-ftern of the principal, F, will have time to bring their broadfides to bear directly upon the fhip in queftion; their attention, as is fuppofed, being too much engroffed by their oppofite fhips in the enemy's line, at the points B, B, B, B, who affuredly would take the ad-vantage then offered, and rake them fore and aft.

━━━━━━━━

SECTION IV.

OF THE PRINCIPLES NECESSARY TO BE KNOWN FOR ENA-BLING US TO JUDGE OF THE DIFFERENT MODES OF BRINGING GREAT FLEETS TO ACTION.

15.　Let us fuppofe a fleet of ten, twenty, thirty, or more fhips, of eighty guns each, extended in line of battle to leeward, and *lying-to* at F (Plate III. fig. 1.), with the intention of avoiding an attack; and fuppofe another fleet at B, of equal number and

force

Plate II. Part I. *p. 30.*

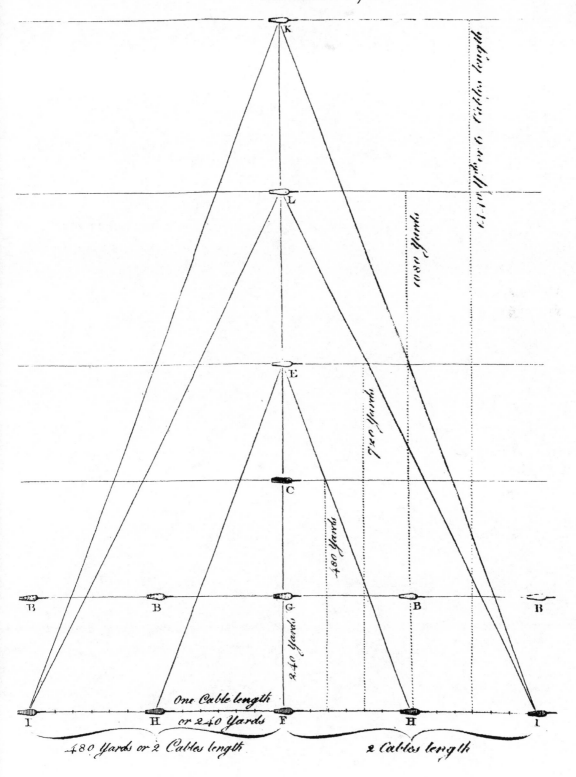

force of fhips, alfo extended in line of battle, three or four miles to windward, and defirous of making an attack, and coming to clofe action, on equal terms, with the faid F :

16. From the nature of the attack on a fingle fhip, (fee Plate I.) it muft be evident, that, if the fleet B fhall attempt to run down headlong, fhip for fhip, upon the fquadron F, (as reprefented in Plate III. fig. 2.) each individual fhip of B, having been expofed, during a courfe of two miles, to a cannonade, at a difadvantage of above twenty to one, muft be difabled long before it can reach fuch a point of diftance from F, as properly may be termed clofe-action, or even to reach a fituation proper for annoying her antagonift in the line F.

17. Again, let it be fuppofed that B, though much difabled in his rigging, while in his courfe a, a, a, from the windward, has made his fhips bring to, at a diftance from whence he can hurt F, (Plate III. fig. 3.) Is it to be expected that F, whofe defire has always been to avoid a clofe engagement, and has already difabled the fhips of B, will patiently lye ftill, or wait until B fhall have time fufficient to difable him in his turn? Is it not evident that F, while unhurt, before he may feel the effects of a cannonade from B, and while enveloped in his own fmoke, as well as that of the enemy, will withdraw himfelf, by bearing away to leeward to attain a new fituation, where he may be out of reach of cannon-fhot, outfailing B, who would be obliged to repair his rigging, before he can be in order to follow, and make a fecond attack?

E 2   18. Again,

18. Again, fuppofe that B, in place of going headlong, and endwife down, fhall attempt to run down in an angular courfe, or lafking, as it has been called, (as in Plate III. fig. 4.) Is it not evident that this will be a means of protracting the courfe of B, and, confequently, the duration of the unequal cannonade from F, with the certainty of having his headmoft fhips expofed to more than their fhare of the damage?

19. But it is alfo evident, (from fig. 5.) that, fhould any fhip B in this angular line come to be crippled, her way, being ftopped, may, of confequence, occafion a confufion amongft the fhips that are next a-ftern, fome running to leeward, while others are endeavouring to get to windward of the difabled fhip; and, while this point is fettling, the time may be loft, and, of confequence, the neceffary fupport to the fhips a-head, now fo far feparated, may be too long retarded, as in the cafe of Mr Byng. But as it may be faid, that a ftoppage of one fhip a-head will not neceffarily produce a ftoppage in every fhip a-ftern, becaufe they may go to leeward of the difabled fhip: We anfwer, That it is precifely what happened to Mr Byng, to be afterwards illuftrated by the cafe of the *Intrepide*, when we come to give a defcription of that gentleman's engagement. Befides, by the fuppofition, the fhips a-head, in the van A, (Plate IV. fig. 1.) may be now engaged, and, of confequence, not having much headway, may be faid to be ftationary; therefore, every fhip a-ftern, if fhe fhall attempt to bear down, as at D, D, from being confined to a determined courfe, muft be brought into the pofition of being raked, when coming down before the wind,

(as

(as in fig. 2. Plate III.), and, confequently, of being completely difabled long before fhe can get clofe enough along-fide of the enemy.

20. Again, the headmoft fhips, or van of B, having attained their ftation at A, that is, a-breaft of the van of F, (as in Plate IV. fig. 1.), and having begun the cannonade, may we not fuppofe that F, whofe conduct, or defire, has always been to fave his fhips, has inftructed, that, fo foon as any of his fhips, particularly the van, fhall begin to feel the effect of a cannonade, they fhall immediately withdraw from danger?

21. And we are alfo to fuppofe, that, fo foon as they have thrown in their fire upon the van of B, each fhip, one after another, as inftructed by F, fhall bear away in fucceffion, as at H, to form a new line at I I, two or three miles to leeward. Now, Is it not evident, from this cautious conduct, that F, feeing the embarraffment of B, and that his fhips are difabled, and his van unfupported, will, by making a crowd of fail, endeavour to range paft B, fhip by fhip, in fucceffion, till his whole fquadron has poured in their fire upon the van of B; and that he, F, will then bear away to join his headmoft fhips, and form a new line of battle to leeward, at I I, to be in readinefs to receive a fecond attack, if B fhall be fo imprudent as to attempt it?

22. Is it not alfo evident, that, if any one or more fhips of the fquadron of F fhall be crippled, they will have it in their power

to

to quit their ftation, being covered with fmoke, at any time, and
to fall to leeward, as at G, where they will be in fafety? As a
farther part of the fyftem of manœuvre fuppofed to be adopted,
it may be conceived, that fhips in this manner fhall be made to
withdraw from battle, leaving intermediate fhips as a cover, to
keep up a good countenance in the line, and amufe the enemy.
But, by the fuppofition and demonftration, the fhips of the fquadron B muft be crippled, and much feparated, long before they
can get to their ftation, whether the attack fhall have been made
in the perpendicular direction, (as in Plate III. fig. 2.), or in the
lafking manner, (as in fig. 4. and 5.); therefore, in both cafes,
B's van muft inevitably be expofed to the effect of the laft defcribed movement, which was, that F, perceiving the fhips of B
in diforder, unfupported, and difabled from following him, will
make fail, and difcharge the fire of his whole line upon the van
of B, fhip by fhip, as they pafs in fucceffion, and will form a
new line to leeward, to be prepared, if another attack fhall be
made upon them.

<hr>

A FARTHER ILLUSTRATION.

23. Again, let B (Plate IV. fig. 2.) reprefent a fleet putting
before the wind, each fhip with an intent, when brought to, at a
determined diftance at A, to take up her particular antagonift in
the line of the enemy F, to leeward; and, for argument's fake,
let F be fuppofed at reft, without any motion a-head whatever.

24. From

Plate III. Part I. p. 34.

Fig. 1.

B

Fig. 2.

F

B

Fig. 3.

F

a   a   a

B

F *first position*

2 Miles

F *second position*

Fig. 4.

B

F

Fig. 5.

B

A

24. From what has been faid, (No. 22.), it may be admitted, that alternate fhips of F's line, under cover of the fmoke, being made to withdraw from battle, as at G G; the intermediate fhips left behind them in the line will be fufficient to amufe even the whole of B's fleet, while the fhips G fhall be forming a new line H H, as a fupport, from the leeward: That, in fuch cafe, B, after being difabled, as he muft be, and not having forefeen the ma-nœuvre, will neither be able to prevent thefe intermediate fhips from bearing away to join their friends, nor, were he able, would it be advifeable to follow them; for the fame manœuvre, with equal fuccefs and effect, can again and again be repeated.

25. In order to fhow the relative movements of both fleets, with refpect to each other, Plate V. is divided, by a fcale, into fquares of a mile each, in which let F (fig. 1.) reprefent a fleet to leeward, with motion a-head, as required for good fteerage, each fhip having fufficient to keep her under command of the rudder, and let it confift of twelve fhips occupying a fpace of two miles, as extended in line of battle, at one cable's length afunder*; and F's motion through the water, if at the rate of

four

---

* The length of a fhip of 74 guns is about   -   -   54 yards
Interval between two fhips at one cable's length afunder   -   240

The fixth part of a mile   294
   6

Six fhips, formed in a line of battle a-head, will extend about
a mile in length, or 1760 yards   -   -   -   1764
And four large fhips, when at 1¼ cable's length afunder, may
form another fcale fufficiently correct for a mile.

four miles per hour, may be expreſſed by the ſpace comprehended by the perpendicular lines marked by F and G on the ſcale
below.   Theſe four lines comprehended by F and G will alſo
expreſs the time in which any fleet, B, may perform his courſe,
when coming down to the attack from the windward.

26. Let B be the opponent fleet, conſiſting alſo of twelve
ſhips, and four miles to windward ; and let the point A be 440
yards, or one quarter of a mile right to windward of the point G.

27. Then B, by putting before the wind, if he ſhall arrive at
the point A, in the ſame time that F, the fleet to leeward, has
arrived at the point G, his motion will have been at the rate of
$5\frac{1}{2}$ miles per hour, as muſt be evident from the ſcale of miles
placed at the top of the figure ; and his courſe, as deſcribed by
the lines B A and C D, will be ſlanting or diagonal, forming an
angle of 43 degrees with B C, his line a-head, and nearly 4
points large from the wind.

28. Again, if F, (Plate V. fig. 2.), by carrying more ſail, ſhall
move at the rate of ſix miles per hour, that is, from F to G ; then
B, having his courſe made thereby the more ſlanting, will have juſt
ſo much the greater difficulty of keeping his ſhips in line a-breaſt
while coming down to the attack.   For the leading ſhip meeting
with no obſtruction in her courſe, will puſh on, whereas every accident of obſtruction accumulating, as it happens to each ſhip pro-
greſſively, the rear, being affected in the greateſt degree, will, for
that reaſon, be left the farther a-ſtern.   But, from the very form
of

Plate IV. Part I. p.36.

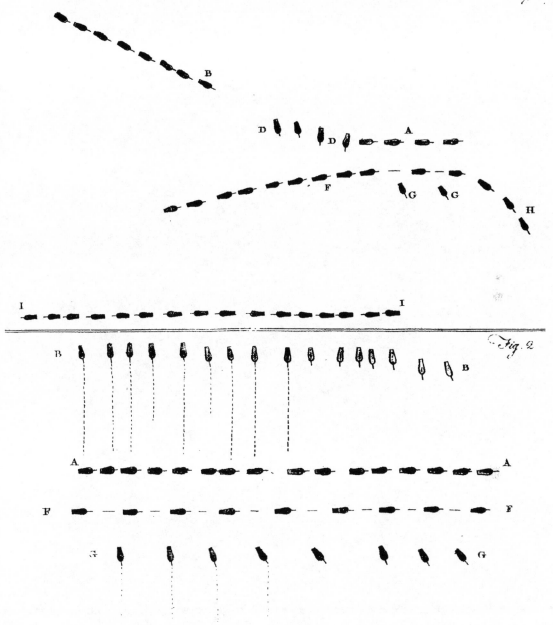

Fig. 1.

Fig. 2.

of this flanting courfe, every fhip a-ftern will be apt to get into the wake of the fhip a-head. Therefore, the whole fleet of B, van and rear, will not arrive in the fame time at the line A D, fo as to be in a perfect line a-breaft, and parallel with the fleet to leeward, but will have affumed the lafking form, as reprefented at the points M, N, and O, in the different parts of the courfe.

29. And again (in Plate V. fig. 3.), if the fleet to leeward fhall keep his wind, fo as to lie up one point, as per line of courfe F G, making an angle of $11\frac{1}{4}$ degrees with his former line of courfe K F K: Then the rears of the two fleets will thereby be removed at a much greater diftance, and the van A, of confequence, muft be fooner up with the enemy's van, and evidently fo much the farther from fupport, while F, by bringing up his fhips in fucceffion, will have it in his power to difable the van A, (No. 21.) and will afterwards bear away as at H, unhurt, and at pleafure; while B, at this time, by the fuppofition, being crippled, or having his rear, D, obftructed, and at a diftance, will be unable to prevent him. And, in all the three cafes, it is evident that the fleet B, fo foon as he fhall approach within reach of gun-fhot, muft be expofed to the fire of F's whole line, for he will be a-breaft of B continually in every part of his courfe.

30. But the difficulty of bringing the rear of the windward fleet to action will ftill be more increafed, if the fternmoft fhips of the fleet to leeward, in place of keeping their wind, fhall bear away occafionally, as at M L, (fig. 3.)

F   31. All

31.   All which being admitted, the difficulty of bringing opponent fleets to clofe engagement may be accounted for, without
being obliged to have recourfe to that fuppofed inferiority, in point
of failing, imputed to our fhips, compared to thofe of the French,
our enemy.

32.   Hence it appears, that a fleet, B, to windward, by extending his line of battle, with a defign to ftop and attack a whole
line of enemy's fhips to leeward, muft do it at a great difadvantage, and without hope of fuccefs :   For the receiving fleet, F, to
leeward, unqueftionably will have the four following advantages
over him, which will be more particularly proved when we come
to examine the real practice.

33.   *Firft*, The fuperiority of a fire, above twenty to one,
over the fleet B, while coming down to attack.

34.   *Secondly*, That, when the fhips of B are brought to at
their ftation, if it blows hard, the fhot from F, by the lying along
of the fhips, will be thrown up into the air, and will have an effect at a much greater diftance ; whereas, on the other hand, the
fhot from B, from the lying along of the fhips alfo, will be
thrown into the water, and the effect loft.

35.   *Thirdly*, That F will have the power of directing, and
applying at pleafure, the fire of his whole line againft the van of
B, who is now unable to prevent it, his fhips being difabled, feparated, and, therefore, unfupported.

36.   *Fourthly*,

36. *Fourthly*, That F will alfo have a greater facility of withdrawing from battle, the whole, or any one of the difabled fhips of his line.

37. If, then, after a proper examination of the late fea engagements, or rencounters, it fhall be found, that our enemy, the French, have never once fhown a willingnefs to rifk the making of the attack, but invariably have made choice of, and earneftly courted a leeward pofition : If, invariably, when extended in line of battle, in that pofition they have difabled the Britifh fleets in coming down to the attack : If, invariably, upon feeing the Britifh fleet difabled, they have made fail, and demolifhed the van in paffing : If, invariably, upon feeling the effect of the Britifh fire, they have withdrawn, at pleafure, either a part, or the whole of their fleet, and have formed a new line of battle to leeward : If the French, repeatedly, have done this upon every occafion : And, on the other hand, if it fhall be found that the Britifh, from an irrefiftible defire of making the attack, as conftantly and uniformly have courted the windward pofition : If, uniformly and repeatedly, they have had their fhips fo difabled and feparated, by making the attack, that they have not once been able to bring them to clofe with, to follow up, or even to detain one fhip of the enemy for a moment ; Shall we not have reafon to believe, that the French have adopted, and put in execution, fome fyftem, which the Britifh either have not difcovered, or have not yet profited by the difcovery ?

F 2   NAVAL

Plate V. Part I. p. 40.

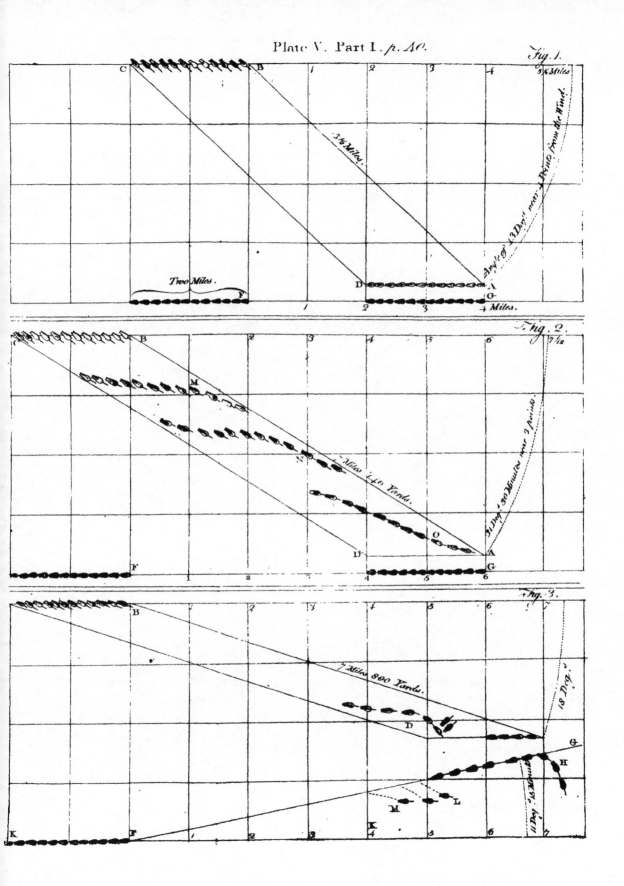

Fig. 1.

Fig. 2.

Fig. 3.

NAVAL TACTICS.

EXAMPLES.

INTRODUCTION.

IT is propofed to illuftrate the preceding DEMONSTRATIONS by EXAMPLES taken from late Engagements ;—of which the following is a Catalogue, according to the order of time in which they happened.

ENGAGEMENTS IN FORMER WARS.

1. Admiral MATTHEWS' engagement with the combined fleets of France and Spain, off Toulon, February 11. 1744.

2. Admiral BYNG's engagement with the French fleet, off Minorca, May 20. 1756.

ENGAGEMENTS OF THE LATE WAR ;—TWELVE IN NUMBER.

1. That of Admiral KEPPEL, off Ufhant, July 27. 1778.
2. Admiral BYRON, off Grenada, July 6. 1779.
3. Admiral BARRINGTON, at St Lucia.

4. Sir

4. Sir GEORGE BRIDGES-RODNEY captures the Spanish tranſports off Cape Finiſterre, takes the Spaniſh men of war off Cape St Vincent.

5. His engagement with the French fleet, off the Pearl Rock, Martinico, April 17. 1780.

6. His rencounter with the ſame fleet, to windward of Martinico, May 15. 1780.

7. His ſecond rencounter, about the ſame place, May 19. 1780.

8. Admiral ARBUTHNOT, off the Cheſapeak, March 16. 1781.

9. Sir SAMUEL HOOD, off Fort Royal, Martinico, April 29. 1781.

10. Admiral PARKER, on the Dogger Bank, Auguſt 5. 1781.

11. Commodore JOHNSTON, Porta Praya, iſland of St Julian.

12. Admiral GREAVES, off the Cheſapeak, September 5. 1781.

From this Catalogue, that the propoſed Illuſtration may be made with the greater advantage, we ſhall begin with thoſe engagements the moſt applicable to the ſubject, ſelected without attending either to the dates, or order in which they took place.

SECTION

SECTION I.

Of Engagements, where the British fleets being to windward, by extending their line of battle, with a design to stop, take, destroy, or disable, the whole of the ships of the enemy's line to leeward, have been disabled before they could reach a situation from whence they could annoy the enemy;—and, on the other hand, where the French, perceiving the British ships in disorder, unsupported, and thus disabled, have made sail, and, after throwing in their whole fire upon the van of the British fleet, ship by ship, as passing in succession, have formed a line to leeward, to be prepared if another attack should be made.

1. Admiral BYNG's engagement with the French fleet, off Minorca, May 20. 1756.

2. That of Admiral BYRON, off Grenada, July 6. 1779.

3. Admiral ARBUTHNOT, off the Chesapeak, March 16. 1781.

4. Admiral GREAVES, off the Chesapeak, September 5. 1781.

5. Admiral Sir GEORGE BRIDGES-RODNEY, off the Pearl Rock, west end of Martinico, April 17. 1780.

I. *The*

I. THE DESCRIPTION OF ADMIRAL BYNG'S ENGAGEMENT WITH THE FRENCH FLEET, OFF MINORCA, MAY 20. 1756. *

38. B. (Plate VI. fig. 1.) The Britifh fleet, about one o'clock afternoon, upon the ftarboard tack, and after they had weathered the French fleet, F, then upon the larboard tack.

39. B. (Plate VI. fig. 2.) The Britifh fleet edging or lafking down to attack the enemy, F, lying to, to receive them. (Vide No. 18. 28. and 29.)

40. A. The van of the Britifh obeying the fignal, by bearing away two points from the wind, but each fhip fteering upon her oppofite in the enemy's line.

41. A. (fig. 3.) The five headmoft fhips of the Britifh line *brought to*, and engaged in a fmart cannonade, but not till after having greatly fuffered in their rigging by three broadfides received from the enemy, during a courfe of fome miles, while, at the fame time, they had it not in their power to make retaliation. (No. 17.)

42. G. The fourth fhip of the enemy having received fome little damage, or being fo inftructed, as Mr Weft has conjectured, bore away, that is, quitted the line, and, in a very little time after, the

* Britifh, 13 fhips, 4 frigates, 1. floop.   French, 12 fhips, 5 frigates.

the fifth ship, H, then the two headmoft, I, and, after them, the third ship, for the fame reafon, it is prefumed, followed their ex-ample, and quitted the line alfo; each ship, as she went off, occa-fioning repeated huzzas from the Britifh Tars, who conceived that the fuperiority of their fire had beat thefe ships out of their line; and, laftly, about the fame time, but in another part of the line, the third ship a-ftern of the French Admiral, (the ship againft which the Ramillies more particularly directed her fire), quitted the line likewife, and withdrew from battle. (NO. 20. and 24.)

43. While matters were going on after this manner in the van, the Intrepid, the fixth ship of the Britifh line, at B, having loft her fore-top maft, was fo taken a-back, that her courfe was ftopped. This, of confequence, produced a diforder and ftoppage to the ships next a-ftern, fome defigning to go to leeward, and others endeavouring to get to windward of the diftreffed ship, as at B. (No. 19.) *.

44. (Fig. 4.) Meanwhile, the centre and rear of the French, who, though at a great diftance, had been bufy firing random shot, perceiving this diforder in the Britifh line, (at B. fig. 4.), made-fail, and with impunity, threw in the fire of their whole line, each ship as she ranged paft the van of the Britifh; after which they bore away in fucceffion to join their own van, and form a new line of battle three miles to leeward, (as in fig. 5.), to be prepared, should the Britifh Admiral have any thought of making a fecond attack. (No. 21. and 22.).

G

OBSER-

---

* The rate at which the ships were fuppofed to move through the water at this time, having their fore-fails and fore-top-fails fet, might be full three miles per hour; and, with all their fails fet, near fix miles. *Admiral Byng's Trial, p. 45.*

————————

OBSERVATIONS.

45. This engagement of the unfortunate Mr BYNG, whether we fhall confider the Britifh mode of making the attack, or the French mode of avoiding the attack, while it offers an example ftrictly applicable to the principles laid down (Sect. IV.), is alfo a proof, that neither the one mode nor the other is a new practice, but is of a date as far back as the former war 1756.

46. The Britifh fleet being to windward, in running down to the attack in an angular courfe, and extending their line of battle, with a defign to ftop, take, deftroy, or difable, the whole of the fhips of the enemy's line, by having their headmoft fhips the longer expofed to an unequal cannonade, and therefore to a greater fhare of the damage, have been difabled before they could reach a fituation from whence they could annoy the enemy.

47. That a fingle fhip, in their line of courfe (No. 28.), to make the attack, the Intrepid (No. 19.) having loft her fore-top maft, and her way by that means being ftopped, occafioned a diforder among the fhips immediately a-ftern, fome endeavouring to pafs her to windward, and fome to leeward ; by which accident of lofing a maft, how much foever impoffible it is to guard againft it, much time was loft, and fupport to the fhips a-head retarded at a time the moft neceffary, when far feparated from the reft of the fleet, and while obliged to fuftain a fire from almoft every fhip in the enemy's line in paffing. (No. 21.)

48. On

48. On the other hand, that the enemy, from their pofition to leeward, perceiving the effects of that fuperiority of fire, which undoubtedly they had over the Britifh fleet, coming down to make the attack, whether it was in the mode of running end-ways right before the wind, as it was faid the van did for fome part of their courfe, or lafking, as was the form in the approach of the centre and rear divifions, laying hold of the advantage, that is, of the diforder occafioned in confequence, and without lofs of time, or remaining till they might be crippled themfelves in their turn, crowded fail, and, in the mean time, made fure of difabling a part of the Britifh fleet, that is, the van ; and whether it might, or might not, have been practicable for the enemy to have cut off any one, or more, of thefe headmoft fhips, now fo far feparated and unfupported, is not difputed ; but, as they could not hope to fucceed in an attempt of this kind without fuftaining fome damage, they, wifely preferring a more cautious conduct, kept their fhips unhurt, to be the better prepared when formed in a new line of battle to leeward (No. 21.), to give the Britifh Admiral a proper reception, fhould he again think of re-peating the like attack, or fhould he afterwards attempt to throw in relief to the Caftle of St Philips, or moleft their troops em-ployed in the fiege, their particular object.

49. It has been faid, that firft the fourth fhip from the head of the enemy's line foon bore away, quitting the line ; then the fifth fhip ; afterwards the two headmoft ; and then the third fhip, after that, followed their example ; and, laftly, the third fhip aftern of the Admiral, and about the fame time, quitted the line alfo. This, as a manœuvre, no doubt makes a part of their fyftem, that alternate

fhips

ſhips ſhall be made to withdraw from battle (No. 24.), leaving
intermediate ſhips, as a cover to ſuſtain the line, and in this way
to amuſe the enemy in the mean time :—And it was not in conſequence of the ſuperior fire of the Britiſh van; for theſe ſhips
of the French that withdrew, as deſcribed, had received no damage, and were in no way diſabled.   One gentleman, a witneſs
in the long trial which followed this action, has theſe words :
' The French fourth or fifth ſhip from the van, ſeemed to me
' to have bore up from the fire of our ſhips in the van, and
' very ſoon afterwards the three headmoſt of the enemy, but
' none of them appeared to me to be diſabled ; ſo that, whether
' it was to avoid action, or by a ſignal from their commander
' in chief, I know not ; I ſhould rather imagine the latter, as I
' had not obſerved any ſuch cloſe * engagement, to oblige ſhips
' of their ſeeming force to avoid an action †.'

50.   Another witneſs in the trial, the commander of the
Portland ‡, the ſecond ſhip of the van, being aſked, ' Did you
' beat away the ſhip oppoſed to you by yourſelf, without the
' aſſiſtance of any other ſhip ?' anſwered, ' No ; I can't ſay that :
' She was a very heavy ſhip the ſecond ſhip, of greater force
' than

---

* The diſtance, on this occaſion, between van and van of the opponent fleets,
docs at no time ſeem to have been leſs than four hundred yards. By many of
the witneſſes on Mr BYNG's trial, it ſeems to have been underſtood, that no-
body had been killed or wounded on board the fleet by muſketry, not even in
the van.   On board the Defiance, the leading ſhip of the Britiſh ſquadron, ſmall
arms were, for ſome time, made uſe of ;—as alſo by the enemy, as was conceived
by ſome ;—but without effect on either ſide, as it would appear ; for they were
ſoon laid aſide.   † Admiral Byng's Trial, p. 38.   ‡ Ditto, p. 58.

' than the Portland, and the third still greater, which must be a
' seventy-four gun ship: Neither did I expect they would have
' bore away so soon; but their fourth and fifth ships bearing
' away before, from the Captain and Buckingham, they bore
' away also, really to our great surprise. '

51. Here it might be proper to observe, alluding to what was premised in the Introduction (Page 6.), that neither was the usual spirit of British seamen any way deficient on this occasion, nor could the cause of miscarriage be attributed to any fault of construction in our ships. For the only opportunity given, by which any comparison could be made, in point of sailing, was when our fleet weathered that of the enemy, at one o'clock, immediately before the engagement. And this circumstance, if it was not a proof that the British ships were the better sailers of the two fleets, showed plainly, on the other hand, that the French, in their giving up the contest about the wind, were not only unwilling to hazard the danger of making the attack, but indeed preferred the leeward situation, from whence they could with the greater certainty disable their adversary's ships, while they might preserve their own unhurt. (See Introd. page 19.)

ADMI-

ADMIRAL BYRON'S ENGAGEMENT WITH THE FRENCH FLEET, OFF GRENADA, THE 6TH OF JULY 1779.

EXTRACT OF A LETTER FROM ADMIRAL BYRON, RELATIVE TO HIS ENGAGEMENT.

' It being my intention, from this intelligence, to be off St
' George's Bay foon after day-break, I drew the fhips of war
' from among the tranfports, leaving only the Suffolk, Vigi-
' lant, and Monmouth, for their protection, under the orders of
' Rear-Admiral ROWLEY, who was intended to conduct the de-
' barkment of the troops; but he was to join me with thefe
' fhips if I faw occafion for their fervice. One of the enemy's
' frigates was very near us in the night, and gave the alarm of
' our approach. Soon after day-light, (on Tuefday the 6th),
' the French fquadron was feen off St George's, moft of
' them at anchor, but getting under way, feemingly in great
' confufion, and with little or no wind. The fignal was imme-
' diately made for a general chafe in that quarter, as well as
' for Rear-Admiral ROWLEY to leave the convoy; and as not
' more than fourteen or fifteen of the enemy's fhips appeared
a ' to be of the line, from the pofition they were in, the fignal
' was made for the fhips to engage and form as they could get
' up: In confequence of which, Vice-Admiral BARRINGTON
' in the Prince of Wales, with Captain SAWER in the Boyne,
' and Captain GARDNER in the Sultan, being the headmoft of
' the

' the Britifh fquadron, and carrying a prefs of fail, were foon
' fired upon, at a great diftance, which they did not return till
' they got confiderably nearer.   But the enemy getting the *b*
' breeze of wind about that time, drew out their line from the
' clufter they were lying in, by bearing away, and forming to
' leeward, on the ftarboard tack, which fhewed ther ftrength
' to be very different from our Grenada intelligence; for it was
' plainly difcovered they had thirty-four fail of fhips of war,
' twenty-fix or twenty-feven of which were of the line, and
' many of thefe appeared of great force.   However, the general
' chafe was continued, and the fignal made for clofe engage-
' ment; but our utmoft endeavours could not effect that; the
' enemy induftrioufly avoiding it, by always bearing up when
' our fhips got near them; and I was forry to obferve, that
' their fuperiority over us, in failing, gave them the option of *c*
' diftance, which they availed themfelves of, fo as to prevent
' our rear from ever getting into action; *and, being to leeward,*
' *they did great damage to the mafts and rigging, when our fhot*
' *could not reach them.*   The 'fhips that fuffered moft were 'thofe *d*
' *the action began with,* and the Grafton, Captain COLLING-
' WOOD, the Cornwal, Captain EDWARDS, and the Lion, Cap-
' tain CORNWALLIS.   The fpirited example of Vice-Admiral
' BARRINGTON, with the former three, expofed them to a fe-
' vere fire in making the attack; and the latter three happen-
' ing to be to leeward, fuftained the fire of *the enemy's whole*
' *line, as it paffed on the ftarboard tack.*   The Monmouth like- *e*
' wife fuffered exceedingly, by Captain FANSHAW's having bore
' down, in a very gallant manner, *to ftop the van of the enemy's*
                                                        ' *fquadron.*

f ' *squadron, and bring it to action.*   But, from the very smart, and
  ' well-directed fire kept up by these ships, and others that were
  ' engaged, I am convinced they did the enemy great damage,
  ' although *their masts, rigging, and sails, appeared less injured*
  ' *than ours* *.   The four ships last mentioned, with the Fame,
  ' being so disabled in their masts and rigging as to be totally in-
g ' capable of keeping up with the squadron, and the Suffolk ap-
  ' pearing to have received considerable damage in an attack made
h ' by Rear-Admiral ROWLEY upon the enemy's van, I took in
  ' the signal for chase, but continued that for close engagement;
  ' formed the best line which circumstances would admit of; and
  ' kept the wind, to prevent the enemy from doubling upon us,
  ' and cutting off the transports, which they seemed inclined to
  ' do, and had the latter very much in their power, by means of
  ' their large frigates, independent of ships of the line.   The
  ' French squadron tacked to the southward, and I did the same,
  ' to be in readiness to support the Grafton, Cornwal, and Lion,
  ' that were disabled, and a great way a-stern.   But the Lion
  ' being likewise much to leeward, and having lost her main and
  ' mizen top-masts, and the rest of her rigging and sails being
  ' cut in a very extraordinary manner, she bore away to the west-
  ' ward when the fleets tacked, and, to my great surprise, no ship
i ' of the enemy was detached after her.   The Grafton and Corn-
  ' wal stood toward us, and might have been weathered by the
  ' French, if they had kept their wind, especially the Cornwal,
                                                          ' which

---

* A strong proof of the advantage of demolishing an enemy's rigging, in preference to the killing his men, or striking the hull of his ship. (No. 4th, 5th,
and 6th.

Plate VI. Part I. p. 52.

Fig. 1.

Wind

B

F

Admiral Byng's Battle
Mediterranean 20th May 1756

Fig. 2.

B

A

F

Fig. 3.

B

A

H G I

Fig. 4.

B A

F

Fig. 5.

B A

F

'which was fartheft to leeward, and loft her main top-maft,
'and was otherwife much difabled; but they perfevered fo
'ftrictly in declining every chance of clofe action, notwithftand-
'ing their great fuperiority, that they contented themfelves with
'firing upon thefe fhips, when paffing barely within gun-fhot,
'and fuffered them to rejoin the fquadron, without one effort to
'cut them off. The Monmouth was fo totally difabled in her
'mafts and rigging, that I judged it proper to fend directions, in
'the evening, for Captain FANSHAW to make the beft of his
'way to Antigua; and he parted company accordingly.

'When we were clofe in with St George's Bay, the French co-
'lours were feen flying upon the fort, and other batteries; which
'left no doubt of the enemy being in full poffeffion of the
'ifland. To diflodge them was impracticable, confidering the
'ftate of the two fleets. I therefore fent orders to Captain
'BARKER, the agent, to make the beft of his way with the
'tranfports to Antigua or St Chriftophers, whichever he could
'fetch, intending to keep the King's fhips between them and
'the French fquadron, which, at the clofe of the evening, was
'about three miles to leeward of us, and, I had no doubt, would
'at leaft be as near in the morning: For, although it was
'evident from their conduct throughout the whole day, that
'they were refolved to avoid a clofe engagement, I could not
'allow myfelf to think, that, with a force fo greatly fuperior
'the French Admiral would permit us to carry off the tranfports
'unmolefted: however, as his fquadron was not to be feen next
'morning, I conclude he returned to Grenada.

H

'It

'It is my duty on this occasion to reprefent, that the behaviour
'of the officers and men of his Majefty's fquadron was fuch
'as became Britifh feamen, zealous for the honour of their
'country, and anxious to fupport their national character.
'The marines, likewife, and troops that were embarked, with
'their officers, in the King's fhips, behaved as brave foldiers;
'and, from the exemplary good conduct of thofe who got into
'action; from the vifible effect which the brifk and well-directed
'fire had upon the enemy's fhips, and from that cool, deter-
'mined refolution, and very ftrong defire of coming to a clofe
'engagement, which prevailed univerfally throughout the fqua-
'dron, I think myfelf juftifiable in faying, that the great fupe-
'riority in numbers and force would not have availed the enemy
'fo much, had not their advantage over us in failing enabled
'them to preferve a diftance little calculated for deciding fuch
'contefts.'

———————

THE DESCRIPTION OF ADMIRAL BYRON's BATTLE OFF
GRENADA, JULY 6. 1779, TAKEN FROM THE FOREGOING
LETTER *.

52.　F, (Plate VII. fig. 1.) The French fleet, as they were feen
at day-light off the town of St George, moft of them at anchor,
but

———————

* Britifh, 21 fhips, 1 frigate, with a fleet of tranfports.
French, 26 fhips, 7 frigates.

but getting under way, and feemingly in confufion, with little wind.

G, Frigates on the out-look.

B, The Britifh fleet difcovering them from windward.

53. B, (fig. 2.) The Britifh now extended in line of battle a-head.

A, The three headmoft fhips under Vice-Admiral Barrington, carrying a prefs of fail, in confequence of the fignal for general chafe, were foon fired upon by the enemy, which fire was not returned till he got confiderably nearer.

F, The enemy having now got the breeze of wind, are feen drawing out their line from the clufter they were lying in, and forming to leeward on the ftarboard tack.

54. B, (fig. 3.) The Britifh fleet after the fignal for clofe engagement, which, with their utmoft endeavours, they could not effect; the enemy induftrioufly avoiding it, by always bearing up when our fhips got near them, as at F. Their fuperiority over us in failing gave them the option of diftance, which they availed themfelves of, fo as to prevent our rear from ever getting into action; *and being to leeward, they did great damage to the mafts and rigging, when our fhot could not reach them.* Though the three headmoft fhips, A, were expofed to a fevere fire in making the attack, yet the Grafton, the Cornwal, and Lion, being farther to leeward, at C, and confequently nearer the enemy, fuffered moft, *having fuftained the fire of the enemy's whole line as it paffed them, to leeward,* upon the ftarboard tack. The

Mon-

Monmouth, D, alfo fuffered confiderably, by Captain Fanfhaw's having gallantly *bore down to ftop the enemy's van, and bring it to action;* as did the Suffolk, in another attack upon the enemy's van.

55.   B, (fig. 4.) The Britifh fleet forming the beft line that circumftances would admit of, to prevent the enemy from doubling back upon us, and cutting off our tranfports, which they feemed inclined to do, by means of their large frigates, as well as their fhips of the line.

C, The Grafton and Cornwal left far a-ftern.

E, The Lion, being much fhattered, making off to leeward.

56.   F, (fig. 5.) The enemy, having tacked to the fouthward, and upon the larboard tack.

B, The Britifh, after having immediately got upon the fame tack, to be in readinefs to fupport the Grafton and Cornwal, who were difabled, and had been left a great way a-ftern, as at C. But the Lion, being much more fhattered, had bore away to the weftward, as at E; and, to our great furprife, no fhip of the enemy had been detached after her.

57. The fimilarity of this battle with that of Mr BYNG, already defcribed, is fo great, that, whether the mode in which the Britifh made the attack, or the mode in which the Fr nch avoided it, fhall be confidered, we have no doubt of fhowing, that the circumftances in either cafe were equally effected by the principles laid down (Section IV.); but as the importance of

the

the subject requires that this should be done in the most satis-
factory manner, the observations made shall be supported by extracts from the Admiral's letter.

I.

OBSERVATIONS ON THE BRITISH MODE OF ATTACK.	EXTRACTS FROM THE ADMIRAL'S LETTER IN SUPPORT OF THESE OBSERVATIONS.
58. That the Admiral by extending his line of battle, in an attempt to stop the van of the enemy, and bring it to action, it may be admitted, that it was with the intent of taking, destroying, or disabling every opponent ship.	' The Monmouth likewise suffered exceedingly, by Captain Fanshaw's having bore down in a very gallant manner to stop the van of the enemy's squadron, and bring it to action (e).—And the Suffolk appearing to have received considerable damage in an attack made by Rear-Admiral Rowley upon the enemy's van;' (g.)
59. In this attempt, however, the ships in the van, by the nature of the course they were obliged to take (No. 27. 28.), were exposed, for a long time, to a heavy fire, which they could not return, or did not return.	' The signal was made for the ships to engage and form as they could get up; in consequence of which, the Prince of Wales, the Boyne, and the Sultan, the headmost ships of the British, and carrying a press of sail, were soon fired upon, at a great distance, which they did not return till they got considerably nearer. ' (Vid. a.)

60. That

'The

60. That by this courfe, which muft have been in the flanting or lafking form (No. 28.), the fhips of the van having got far a-head of the rear, were therefore the fooner in with the enemy; but being difabled by the fire they received in coming down, and becoming in a manner immoveable, or ftationary, compared with the enemy, they were obliged to fuftain the continued fire of their whole line, fhip by fhip, as they paffed in fucceffion, without having it in their power to ftop the van, as intended, or even to bring a fingle fhip of them to action.

' The fhips that fuffered moft, were thofe the action began with, the Grafton, Captain Collingwood, the Cornwal, Captain Edwards, and the Lion, Captain Cornwallis. The fpirited examples of Vice-Admiral Barrington, with the former three, expofed them to a fevere fire in making the attack; and the latter three happening to be to leeward, fuftained the fire of the enemy's whole line, as it paffed on the ftarboard-tack.' (Vid. *d.*)

61. That the rear, by the nature of this courfe alfo, not from any inferiority in point of failing, compared with the enemy, being at firft left far a-ftern by the van (No. 28.), and afterwards, as may be fuppofed, having met with obftruction from difabled fhips a-head, might have been prevented from carrying fupport to the van, in like manner as was occafioned by the Intrepid in Mr Byng's action, fhips a-ftern endeavouring to go to windward of the difabled fhip, but fome for certain paffing to leeward; for how, otherwife, can we account for the fituations of the Grafton, Cornwal, and Lion, or for the gallant attempt of Captain Fanshaw to ftop the van of the enemy, and bring it to action?

' Their fuperiority over us in failing gave them the option of diftance, which they availed themfelves of, fo as to prevent our rear from ever getting into action.' (Vid. *c.*)

H,

II.

OBSERVATIONS ON THE FRENCH MODE OF RECEIVING THE ATTACK.

62. The French, on the other hand, feeing the British fquadron coming down to attack them, drew out their line of battle by forming to leeward; of necef-fity on this occafion, but admirably fitted for their manner of fighting, which pe-culiarly might be faid to confift in an addrefs qualified for faving their own fhips, while they fhould have it in their power to difable thofe of their enemy. According to this fyftem, then, fo foon as the British fquadron approached with-in what might be thought the greatest poffible range of cannon-fhot, and while it was coming down before the wind, the French, from their whole line, kept up a heavy fire; but, as foon as any of the British fhips had brought-to, and they, in their turn, began to be annoyed by the British fire, the fhips the moft expofed bore away, and withdrew from battle (No. 20.) And whether this was in the van or centre, moft probably it was in the

EXTRACTS FROM ADMIRAL BYRON'S LETTER CONTINUED.

' The enemy getting the breeze of wind about that time, drew out their line from the clufter they were lying in, by bearing away and forming to leeward on the ftarboard-tack, which fhowed their ftrength to be very different from our Grenada intelligence; for it was plainly difcovered they had 34 fail of fhips of war, 26 or 27 of which were of the line, and many of thefe of great force. However, the general chafe was continued, and the fignal made for clofe engagement; but our utmoft endeavours could not effect that, the enemy induf-trioufly avoiding it, by bearing up when our fhips got near them.' (Vid. *b.*)

' From

the manner as reprefented in Plate IV. fig.
2. that alternate fhips fhould withdraw,
while intermediate fhips fhould be left to
fill up the intervals, and fupport the line,
(No. 49.); while the rear, to avoid every
poffibility of being forced into action,
kept bearing away (as at H, fig. 3. Plate
VII.) in like manner as before defcribed
(No. 30. and Plate V. fig. 3.)

63. And now again taking advantage
of the difordered condition of the Britifh
fquadron, (for, at that time, feveral of
the headmoft fhips, from the fevere fire
received in coming down, lay crippled,
while the Grafton, the Cornwal, and the
Lion, having got confiderably to leeward with the intention of covering their
friends, were therefore the more expofed)
the French, I fay, laying hold of the opportunity, and without delay, or remaining till they might be difabled themfelves' (No. 48.), made fail, and fhip by
fhip, as many as could reach in paffing,
threw in upon the above fhips the whole
of their fire, when, having formed again,
for the fecond time, to leeward, they were
prepared again and again to play the fame
manœuvre, fo often as the like attack
fhould be repeated. (No. 21. 22. 48.
and 49.)

64. Whether it might, or might not
have been practicable to cut off either of
thefe

' From the very fmart and *well-directed
fire kept up by thefe fhips, meaning the
Prince of Wales, the Boyne, and the Sultan,
and afterwards the Grafton, the Cornwal,
and the Lion, with the Monmouth* and
others that were engaged, I am convinced they did the enemy great damage,
although their mafts, rigging, and fails,
appeared lefs injured than ours, the four
fhips laft mentioned, with the Fame,
being fo difabled in their mafts and rigging, as to be incapable of keeping up
with the reft of the fleet; and the Suffolk appearing to have received confiderable damage,' &c. (Vid. *f.*)

' The Grafton and Cornwal ftood toward us, and might have been weathered
by

these ships, the Grafton, Cornwal, or Lion, is not disputed; but, as they did not think they could succeed in that attempt, without sustaining some damage, they, as usual, preferred a conduct more cautious, and kept their fleet intire, that the reduction of the island Grenada, their particular object, might be carried on with the greater certainty of success. (No. 48.)

by the French, if they had kept their wind, especially the Cornwal, which was farthest to leeward, and lost her main-top mast, and was otherwise much disabled; but they persevered so strictly in declining every chance of close action, notwithstanding their great superiority, that they contented themselves with firing upon these ships, when passing, barely within gun-shot, and suffered them to rejoin the squadron, without one effort to cut them off.' (Vid. *i.*)

65. The damage received by the French ships must have been but trifling; for, otherwise, the British Admiral would not have had reason to express an apprehension that they might be able to double upon him and cut off his transports, which were, at the time, a considerable way to windward.

' I took in the signal for chase, but continued that for close engagement; formed the best line which circumstances would admit of; and kept the wind, to prevent the enemy from doubling upon us, and cutting off the transports.' (Vid. *h.*)

66. On this occasion, the whole of the French system seems to have been as completely followed out as in the former affair, that of Mr BYNG; they preserved their own ships entire, while they disabled those of their enemy; and so intent were they in keeping their main object in view, the making themselves masters of the island, that they cautiously avoided every chance that could lead them into a scrape, which a close engagement possibly

' The French squadron tacked to the southward, and I did the same to be in readiness to support the Grafton, Cornwal, and Lion, that were disabled, and a great way a-stern; but the Lion being likewise much to leeward, bore away to the westward, and having lost her main and mizen topmasts, and the rest of her rigging and sails being cut in a most extraordinary manner, she bore away to the westward, when the fleets tacked; and,

I

possibly might have been, even when opportunities offered, apparently fortunate,
such as the cutting off the transports,
or the capture of those fore-mentioned
ships, the Grafton and Cornwal, or the
Lion.

and, to my surprise, no ship of the enemy was detached after her.

'For although it was evident, from
their conduct throughout the whole day,
that they were resolved to avoid a close
engagement, I could not allow myself
to think, that, with a force so greatly
superior, the French Admiral would
permit us to carry off the transports un-
molested.' (Vide *k*.)

66. But besides the causes mentioned for retarding the rear of
a fleet to windward, from getting into action with a fleet to leeward, there is another, which, being a manœuvre of course, may
therefore have taken place on this occasion, although not taken
notice of by Mr Byron in his letter.——For illustration's sake,
——If the opponent fleet to leeward, as extended in line of battle,
shall lie up but one single point to the wind (No. 29.) the vans
of the two fleets must mutually approximate, and get within
fighting distance ; while the two rears, of consequence, may still
be some miles asunder ; and the more numerous the two fleets
are, and the more they are extended, each of them in their proper line of battle, the greater will this proportional distance be :
For, if two squadrons, consisting of twelve ships each, (as represented in Plate V. fig. 3.), shall make this distance between the
two rears amount to one mile and a half ; in this engagement
of Mr Byron's, where the two squadrons, each of them, con-
sisted of 21 ships, even the least numerous, it follows, that the
distance between the two rears, according to the same ratio,
might,

might, by this reason alone, have amounted to 4620 yards, or $2\frac{5}{8}$ miles.

67. Again, should the ships in the rear of the fleet to leeward, at the same time, keep bearing away, (as represented in Plate V. fig. 3. at L and M, or in Plate VII. fig. 3. at G and H), and which undoubtedly they did in this engagement, then the space between the two rears will be still more increased.

68. From all which, the several advantages which a fleet to leeward has over an extended fleet making an attack from the windward, *as formerly enumerated*, are so fully confirmed, that in recapitulating them, we are obliged to make use of almost the same words as are made use of by Mr BYRON himself in his letter.

69. 1*st*, By their superiority of fire, the ships in the van were disabled in coming down to the attack; *and, before they were brought-to, in a situation from whence they could annoy the enemy*, (No. 33.)

70. 2*dly*, By being to leeward, the enemy, he says, did great damage to our masts and rigging, while our shot could not reach them, *by being thrown into the water*. (No. 34.)

71. 3*dly*, The Cornwal and Lion, part of the van, from being separated and unsupported, or being farther to leeward, as he says, suffered most, having sustained the fire of the enemy's whole line as it passed to leeward. (No. 35.)

72.　*4thly*, And is it not evident, as well from his letter, as from the defcription, that the enemy, from their leeward fituation, laid hold of that advantage, by ftealing away at pleafure? (No. 36.)

73.　*Laftly*, From the letter it is clearly demonftrated, that the difficulty of getting the rear of the fleet brought into action, did arife from the nature of the attack itfelf, not from any abatement of fpirit in the feamen, nor from any defect of the fhipping on the one fide, or even from any degree of fuperiority on the other.

III.

Plate VII. Part I. *p. 04.*

Admiral Byron off Granada
6 July 1779.

Wind

B

Fig. 1.

G

F

Fig. 2.

B

A

F

Fig. 3.

B

A

C

D

F   F

G   H

Fig. 4.

B

C

F

E

Fig. 5.

B

C

F

E

III. ADMIRAL ARBUTHNOT'S ENGAGEMENT WITH THE FRENCH FLEET OFF THE MOUTH OF THE CHESAPEAK, THE 16TH MARCH 1781.

EXTRACT OF A LETTER FROM ADMIRAL ARBUTHNOT, 20TH MARCH 1781, LINNEHAVEN BAY.

74. ' On the 16th, at fix A. M. the Iris made the fignal for
' difcovering five ftrange fail, to the N. N. E. and foon afterwards
' hailed, that they were large fhips fteering for the Capes of Vir-
' ginia, and fuppofed to be diftant about three miles. I imme-
' diately concluded it muft be the enemy I was in fearch of, and
' accordingly prepared the fquadron for battle, by forming the
' line a-head a cable's length afunder, on a wind which was then
' frefh, and proceeding towards them with a prefs of fail. At
' this time Cape Henry bore S. W. by W. diftant about 14
' leagues, wind at Weft; the French bearing from us, N. N. E.
' the weather fo hazy, that the length of the Britifh line could
' fcarcely be difcerned.

' At a quarter of an hour after eight A. M. the wind veered to
' N. W. by W. and foon after to N. by W. which gave the enemy
' the advantage of the weather-gage. About this time feveral of
' the enemy's fhips were difcovered to windward, manœuvring
' to form their line.

' At

' At twenty-five minutes after eight, the Guadaloupe ranged
' up under our lee, bringing the fame intelligence with that al-
' ready given by the Iris, and was ordered to make fail, and en-
' deavour to keep fight of the enemy.

' At thirty-five minutes after eight, I directed the Iris, by
' fignal, to make fail a-head, and keep fight of the enemy, as
' the haze appeared to thicken.   The Britifh line was by this
' time completely formed, and clofe hauled on the larboard tack.

' At twenty minutes after nine, the headmoft of the French
' fhips tacked, as did the reft in fucceffion, and formed the line
' on the ftarboard tack.

' At thirty-five minutes after nine, the weather being very
' fqually, I formed the line a-head, at two cables length afunder.

' At a quarter of an hour after ten, I made the fignal for the
' fquadron to tack, the headmoft and weathermoft firft, and gain
' the wind of the enemy.

75. ' At a quarter of an hour after eleven, the headmoft of the
' French line tacked; but one of them having miffed ftays, the
' reft wore, and formed the line on the larboard tack.

' At forty minutes after eleven, I re-formed my line, at one
' cable's length afunder.

                                                        ' At

' At twelve o'clock, there being a profpect of the van of my
' line reaching the enemy, the whole of my line tacked by fig-
' nal, the van firft, and the leading fhip continued to lead on the
' other tack.

' At one o'clock, the French fquadron having completed their
' form in a line a-head, confifting of eight two deckers, bore
' E. by S. the Britifh line clofe hauled, fteering E. S. E. wind at
' N. E.

76. ' At half an hour after one o'clock, the enemy being very
' apprehenfive of the danger and inconvenience of engaging to
' windward, from the high fea that was running, and fqually
' weather, wore, and formed their line to leeward of the Britifh
' line.

77. ' At two o'clock, the van of my fquadron wore in the line;
' and, in a few minutes, the Robuft, which led the fleet, and
' afterwards behaved in the moft gallant manner, was warmly
' engaged with the van of the enemy. The fhips in the van and
' centre of the line were all engaged by half an hour paft two,
' and by three o'clock the French line was broke; their fhips be-
' gan foon after to wear, and to form their line again, with their
' heads to the South-eaft into the ocean.

78. ' At twenty minutes after three, I wore, and ftood after
' them. I was forry to obferve the Robuft, Prudent, and Europe,
' which were the *headmoft* fhips, and received the whole of the
' *enemy's*

' *enemy's fire* at their rigging, as they *bore down*, so entirely *disa-*
' *bled*, and the London's main-top sail yard being carried away,
' the two first unmanageable, lying with their heads from the e-
' nemy, as to be incapable of pursuit, and of rendering the ad-
' vantage we had gained decisive.

79. ' At half an hour after four, the haze came on so very thick,
' as entirely to intercept the enemy from my view.   The Medea
' joined me soon after, which I directed to follow, and observe
' the route of the enemy, while I proceeded with the squadron
' to the Chesapeak, in the hope of intercepting them, should they
' attempt to get in there. '

THE DESCRIPTION OF ADMIRAL ARBUTHNOT'S BATTLE OFF THE CHESAPEAK, 16TH MARCH 1781 *.

F, (Plate VIII. fig. 1.) The French fleet to windward, formed
in line of battle, on the larboard tack.

B, The British fleet to leeward, on the same tack, at twelve
o'clock, and in hopes that their van would be able to reach the
enemy, (No. 75.)

F,

---

* British, eight ships and three frigates.
  French, eight ships and four frigates.

F, (Fig. 2.) The French fleet now formed to leeward, at half after one, having quitted their windward pofition G, from an apprehenfion of the danger and inconvenience there would be in engaging to windward, from the high fea that was running, and the fqually weather. (No. 76.)

B, The Britifh fleet in chafe, keeping their wind.

F, (Fig. 3.) The French extended in line of battle, and receiving the attack, by firing upon the van of the Britifh, as they came down before the wind.

B, The Britifh, who had wore at two o'clock, left their pofition at C; are now attempting to ftop the van, and fteering every fhip upon his oppofite of the enemy.

Mr ARBUTHNOT fays, ' At two o'clock, the van of my fquadron were in the line; and, in a few minutes, the Robuft, which led the fleet, and afterwards behaved in a moft gallant manner, was warmly engaged with the van of the enemy.'

(Fig. 4.) The fhips in the van A, and the centre B, of the line, were all engaged by half paft two, and by three o'clock the French line was broke at FF.

Their fhips began foon after to wear, and form their line again, with their heads to the fouth-eaft, into the ocean, as at G, Fig. 4. (No. 77.)

80. (Fig. 5.). ' At twenty minutes after three, I wore and ftood after them, (as at B, Fig. 5.); but was foon forry to obferve the

K

Robuft,

Robuſt, Prudent, and Europe, which had been the headmoſt, now the ſternmoſt at A, as they had received the whole of the e-nemy's fire at the rigging, as they *bore down*, ſo entirely diſabled, as was alſo the London, who had her top-ſail yard carried away, that we were incapable of purſuit.'   (No. 78.)

OBSERVATIONS.

81. Mr ARBUTHNOT, by this battle, having defeated this firſt attempt of the enemy to acquire a footing in the Cheſapeak; and having relieved us of our apprehenſions for the little army under General ARNOLD, that is, having had the ſingular merit of ac-compliſhing, in the fulleſt manner, the principal object of his deſtination, it is much to be regretted, that an equal degree of praiſe is not due to the action itſelf. For, by this mode of at-tack (Section IV.), as well as by the attempt to ſtop the van of the enemy, his headmoſt ſhips were ſo diſabled, that they could neither get into cloſe action, nor purſue; whereas, on the other hand, the enemy being unhurt, and perceiving the diſorder of the Britiſh fleet, that they were diſabled from following them, —to avoid the effects of their fire, made ſail, *wore*, and formed a new line of battle to leeward, (No. 77.), where they were pre-pared to receive a new attack, ſhould the Britiſh Admiral attempt to make it.

82. This engagement, however, is diſtinguiſhnd from the two former, by a manœuvre peculiar to itſelf; and muſt be of ſome

weight

weight in fupport of what has been advanced with refpect to French ideas. For, quitting the windward fituation, which they were poffeffed of, and affuming their poft to leeward, as they did, (No. 76.), they plainly fhowed, that they were confident in their fuperior knowledge in naval tactic ; that they relied on our want of penetration ; and, getting to leeward, that they trufted our irrefiftible defire would hurry us on to make the cuftomary attack, (Introd. page 20.) though at a difadvantage almoft beyond the power of calculation ; by which, the Britifh Admiral, having his fhips crippled in the firft onfet, never after was able to clofe with, follow up, or even detain one fingle fhip of them for one moment. (No. 37.)

IV. ADMIRAL GRAVES'S ENGAGEMENT WITH THE FRENCH FLEET OFF THE MOUTH OF THE CHESAPEAK, THE 5TH OF SEPTEMBER 1781.

EXTRACT OF A LETTER FROM VICE-ADMIRAL GRAVES, AUGUST 31ST 1781, OFF SANDYHOOK.

83. ' I beg you will be pleafed to acquaint my Lords Com-
' miffioners of the Admiralty, that the moment the wind ferved
' to carry the fhips over the bar, which was buoyed for the pur-
' pofe, the fquadron came out ; and Sir Samuel Hood getting
' under fail at the fame time, the fleet proceeded together, on the
' 31ft of Auguft, to the fouthward.

K 2   ' The

' The cruifers which I had placed before the Delaware could
' give me no certain information, and the cruifers off the Chefa-
' peak had not joined.   The wind being rather favourable, we
' approached the Chefapeak the morning of the 5th of Septem-
' ber, when the advanced fhip made the fignal of a fleet.   We
' foon difcovered a number of great fhips at anchor, which feem-
' ed to be extended acrofs the entrance of the Chefapeak, from
' Cape Henry to the middle ground : They had a frigate cruifing
' off the Cape, which ftood in and joined them ; and, as we ap-
' proached, the whole fleet got under fail, and ftretched out to
' fea, with the wind at N. N. E.   As we drew nearer, I formed
' the line firft a-head, and then in fuch a manner as to bring his
' Majefty's fleet nearly parallel to the line of approach of the e-
' nemy ; and, when I found that our van was advanced as far as
' the fhoal of the middle ground would admit of, I wore the fleet,
' and brought them upon the fame tack with the enemy, and
' nearly parallel to them, though we were by no means extend-
' ed with their rear.   So foon as I judged that our van would be
' able to operate, I made the fignal to bear away and approach,
' and, foon after, to engage the enemy clofe.   Somewhat after
' four, the action began amongft the headmoft fhips, pretty clofe,
' and foon became general, as far as the fecond fhip from the
' centre, towards the rear.   *The van of the enemy bore away, to*
' *enable the centre to fupport them*, or they would have been cut
' up.   The action did not entirely ceafe till a little after fun-fet,
' though at a confiderable diftance ; for the centre of the enemy
' continued to bear up as it advanced ; and, at that moment,

' feemed

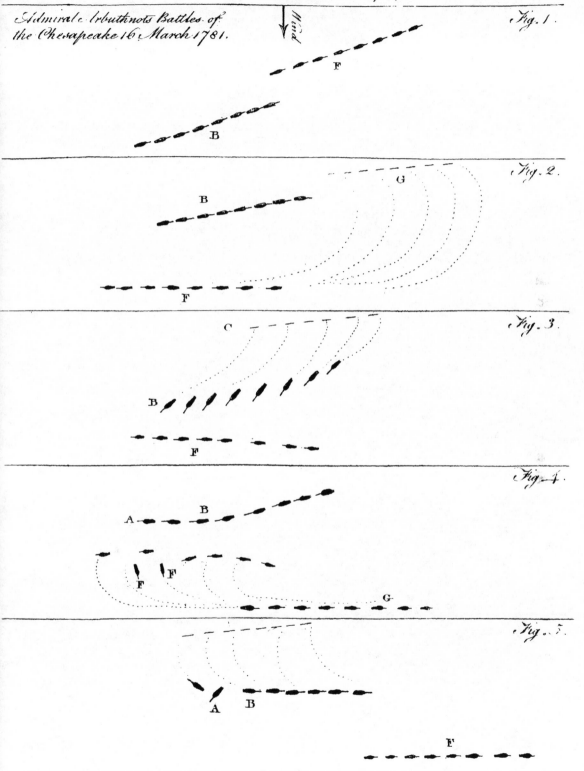

Plate VIII. Part 1. p. 72.

Admiral Arbuthnots Battles of
the Chesapeake 16 March 1781.

Wind

Fig. 1.

Fig. 2.

Fig. 3.

Fig. 4.

Fig. 5.

' feemed to have little more in view, than to fhelter their own
' van, as it went away before the wind.

' His Majefty's fleet confifted of nineteen fail of the line ; that
' of the French formed twenty-four fail in their line. After
' night, I fent the frigates to the van and rear, to pufh forward
' the line, and keep it extended with the enemy, with a full in-
' tention to renew the engagement in the morning ; but, when
' the frigate Fortune returned from the van, I was informed,
' that feveral of the fhips had fuffered fo much, that they were
' in no condition to renew the action until they had fecured their
' mafts : we, however, kept well extended with the enemy all
' night. '

' We continued all day, the 6th, in fight of each other, repair-
' ing our damages. Rear-Admiral DRAKE fhifted his flag into
' the Alcide, until the Princefs had got up another main-top maft.
' The Shrewfbury, whofe Captain loft a leg, and had the firft
' Lieutenant killed, was obliged to reef both top-mafts, fhifted
' her top-fail yards, and had fuftained very great damage. I or-
' dered Captain Colpoys of the Orpheus to take command of her,
' and put her into a ftate for action.

' The Intrepid had both top-fail yards fhot down, her top-mafts
' in great danger of falling, and her lower mafts and yards very
' much damaged, her Captain having behaved with the greateft
' gallantry to cover the Shrewfbury. The Montague was in great
' danger

' danger of lofing her mafts; the Terrible fo leaky as to keep all
' her pumps going; and the Ajax alfo very leaky.

' In the prefent ftate of the fleet, and being five fail of the line
' lefs in number than the enemy, and they having advanced very
' much in the wind upon us during the day, I determined to tack
' after eight, to prevent being drawn too far from the Chefapeak,
' and to ftand to the northward.'

THE DESCRIPTION OF ADMIRAL GRAVES'S ENGAGEMENT OFF THE CHESAPEAK, THE 5TH OF SEPTEMBER 1781. *

84.   (Plate IX. fig. 1.)   The French fleet at anchor, and extended acrofs the entrance of the Chefapeak, from Cape Henry
to the middle ground, who, as foon as they perceived the Britifh
fleet approaching, got under fail, and ftretched out to fea upon
the larboard tack, as at G.

B,   The Britifh fleet advancing to the middle ground, but not
till after the French had left it, formed in a line nearly parallel to
that of the French at G.

B, (fig. 2.)   The Britifh fleet, after having advanced as far as
the fhoal upon the middle ground, as per courfe A, wore; and
having

British, 19 fhips, 7 frigates, and a fire-fhip.   French, 24 fhips.   Frigates.

having ſtood after the enemy, are now upon the larboard tack, extended in line of battle a-head, and almoſt a-breaſt of them.

(Fig. 3.) Mr GRAVES ſays: ' So ſoon as I judged that our ' van would be able to operate, I made the ſignal to bear away, ' and approach as at B; and, ſoon after, to engage the enemy ' cloſe. '

(Fig. 4.) ' Somewhat after four, the action began amongſt ' the headmoſt ſhips, pretty cloſe, and ſoon became general, as ' far as the ſecond ſhip from the centre, towards the rear. The ' van of the enemy bore away,' as at G, ' to enable their centre ' to ſupport them,' as at F, fig. 4. ' or they would have been ' cut up.
' The action did not entirely ceaſe till after ſunſet, though at ' a conſiderable diſtance; for the centre of the enemy continued ' to bear up as it advanced; and, that moment, ſeemed to have ' little more in view than to ſhelter their own van, as it went ' away before the wind. '

85. Mr GRAVES might have added, that the French fleet, by making this movement, not only covered their own van as it went off, but they completely diſabled the van of the Britiſh, now ſeparated and unſupported, and who had been before greatly hurt in their rigging, by making the attack as they did, infomuch, that hardly a ſhip was able to ſtand after, and prevent the enemy from forming a new line to leeward. (No. 16. to 37. incluſively.)
The

The fleets continued in fight of each other for five days fucceffively, and, at times, were very near; but ours had not fpeed enough, in fo mutilated a ftate, to attack them, and they fhowed no inclination to renew the action; but they generally maintained the wind of us, yet did not make ufe of that power *.

87. The anxiety of the French to avoid a battle on this occafion, and their manœuvres in confequence, that they might not again be prevented in their defigns upon the Chefapeak, in which they had been difappointed by Mr ARBUTHNOT, are fo much alike to what has already been defcribed in two engagements, the one with the unfortunate Admiral BYNG, and the other with Admiral BYRON off Grenada, that the obfervations then made being equally applicable in this cafe, it will be unneceffary to repeat them.

V.

---

* Certain French Officers on board their own fleet, it is faid, having received an invitation from the Admiral to dine with him, on feeing the Britifh fquadron approaching the Chefapeak in the morning, and dreading they might be attacked before they could be prepared for action, pleafantly faid to a gentleman, then prifoner on board, We have received an invitation from the Admiral to dine with him to-day, but it muft have been from your Admiral, not our own;—expreffing, by this, an apprehenfion that they might lofe their fhip, and be taken prifoners.

V. SIR GEORGE BRIDGES-RODNEY'S ENGAGEMENT WITH THE FRENCH FLEET OFF THE WEST END OF MARTINICO, APRIL 17. 1780.

EXTRACT OF A LETTER FROM ADMIRAL SIR GEORGE BRIDGES-RODNEY, 26TH APRIL 1780, OFF FORT-ROYAL, MARTINICO.

88. ' In this fituation both fleets remained till the 15th inftant, ' when the enemy, with their whole force, put to fea in the mid- ' dle of the night; immediate notice of which being given me, ' I followed them; and, having looked into Fort-Royal Bay, ' and the road of St Pierre's, on the 16th we got fight of them, ' about eight leagues to leeward of the Pearl Rock. A general ' chafe to the north-weft followed; and, at five in the morning, ' we plainly difcovered that they confifted of twenty-three fail ' of the line, one fifty gun fhip, three frigates, a lugger, and a ' cutter. When night came on, I formed the fleet in a line of ' battle a-head, and ordered the Venus and Greyhound frigates ' to keep between his Majefty's and the enemy's fleets, to watch ' their motions, which was admirably well attended to by that ' good and veteran officer Captain Ferguffon.

L   ' The

' The manœuvres the enemy made, during the night, indicated
' a wish to avoid battle, which I was determined they should not,
' and therefore counteracted all their motions.

' At day-light, in the morning of the 17th, we saw the enemy
' distinctly beginning to form the line a-head.   I made the signal
' for the line a-head, at two cables length distance.   At forty-five
' minutes after six, I gave notice, by public signal, *that my in-*
a ' *tention was to attack the enemy's rear with my whole force;*
' which signal was answered by every ship in the fleet.   At seven
' A. M. perceiving the fleet too much extended, I made the sig-
' nal for the line of battle at one cable's length asunder only.
' At thirty minutes after eight A. M. I made a signal for a line
' of battle a-breast, each ship bearing from the other N. by W.
b ' and S. by E. and bore down upon the enemy.   This signal was
' penetrated by them, who discovered my intention, wore, and
' formed a line of battle on the other tack; I immediately made
' the signal to haul the wind, and form the line of battle a-head.
' At nine A. M. made the signal for the line of battle a-head, at
' two cables length, on the larboard tack.

' The different movements of the enemy obliged me to be very
' attentive, and watch every opportunity that offered of attacking
' them to advantage.

' The manœuvres made by his Majesty's fleet will appear to
' their Lordships by the minutes of the signals made before and
' during the action.   At eleven A. M. I made the signal to pre-
' pare

' pare for battle, to convince the whole fleet I was determined to
' bring the enemy to an engagement. At fifty minutes after eleven
' A. M. I made the fignal for every fhip *to bear down, and fteer for*
' *her oppofite in the enemy's line*, agreeably to the 21ft article of
' the additional Fighting Inftructions. At fifty-five minutes after
' eleven A. M. I made the fignal for battle; a few minutes after,
' the fignal that it was my intention to engage clofe, and, *of*
' *courfe, the Admiral's fhip to be the example*. A few minutes
' before one P. M. one of the headmoft fhips began the action.
' At one P. M., the Sandwich in the centre, after having received
' feveral fires from the enemy, began to engage. Perceiving fe-
' veral of our fhips engaging at a diftance, I repeated the fignal
' for a clofe action. The action, in the centre, continued till fif-
' teen minutes after four P. M., when Monfieur Guichen in the
' Couronne, in which they had mounted ninety guns, *the Tri-*
' *umphant and Fendant, after engaging the Sandwich for an hour*
' *and a half, bore away.* The fuperiority of the fire from the
' Sandwich, and the gallant behaviour of her officers and men,
' enabled her to fuftain fo unequal a combat; though, before at-
' tacked by them, *fhe had beat three fhips out of their line of battle*,
' had entirely broke it, and was to leeward of the wake of the
' French Admiral.

' At the conclufion of the battle, the enemy might be faid to
' be completely beat; but fuch was the diftance of the van and
' rear from the centre, and the crippled condition of feveral
' fhips, particularly the Sandwich, who, for twenty-four hours,
' was with difficulty kept above water, that it was impoffible to

L 2   ' purfue

' purfue them that night without the greateft difadvantage.
' However, every endeavour was ufed to put the fleet in order ;
' and I have the pleafure to acquaint their Lordfhips, that, on
' the 20th, we again got fight of the enemy's fleet, and, for three
' fucceffive days, purfued them, but without effect, they ufing
' every endeavour poffible to avoid a fecond action, and endea-
' voured to pufh for Fort-Royal, Martinico : We cut them off.
' To prevent the rifk of another action, they took fhelter under
' Guadaloupe.

' As I found it was in vain to follow them with his Majefty's
' fleet in the condition they were in, and every motion of the
' enemy indicating their intention of getting into Fort-Royal
' Bay, Martinico, where alone they could repair their fhattered
' fleet, I thought the only chance we had of bringing them again
' to action, was to be off Fort-Royal before them, where the fleet
' under my command now is, in daily expectation of their arrival.
' I have defpatched frigates to windward and to leeward of every
' ifland, to give me notice of their approach. '

THE

Plate IX. Part I. p. 80.

Admiral Graves's Battle off the
Chesapeake 5 Sept.r 1781.

Fig. 1

Wind

Cape Charles

Middle Ground

Chesapeake

F

Cape Henry

B

G

Fig. 2

Cape Charles

A

A

A

B

F

Fig. 3

B

F

Fig. 4

B

F

G

THE DESCRIPTION OF SIR GEORGE BRIDGES-RODNEY'S BAT-
TLE OFF THE WEST END OF MARTINICO, THE 17TH OF
APRIL 1780 *.

89. F, (Plate X. fig. 1.) The French fleet to leeward, at day-
light, diftinctly feen forming the line a-head, and upon the ftarboard tack.

B, The Britifh fleet to windward, thirty minutes after eight,
formed in line of battle a-breaft, and bearing down on the enemy,
and after Sir George had given notice, by public fignal, that his
intention was to attack the enemy's rear with his whole force,
which fignal was anfwered by every fhip in his fleet. (Vid. *a*.)

F, (fig. 2.) The French fleet in the act of wearing, and forming upon the larboard tack, having penetrated Sir George's fignal. (Vid. *b*.)
B, The Britifh fleet ftill in line a-breaft, bearing down.

B, (fig. 3.) The Britifh fleet formed in line of battle a-head,
at two cables length afunder, on the larboard tack, the fignal to
haul the wind being previoufly made at nine o'clock.
F, The enemy lying-to to receive the attack.

B,

---

* Britifh, 20 fhips of the line, 1 fifty, and 4 frigates.
French, 25 fhips, 8 frigates.

B, (fig. 4.) The Britiſh fleet, fifty minutes after eleven o'clock, every one of which bearing down, and ſteering for her oppoſite in the enemy's line, agreeable to the 21ſt article of the additional Fighting Inſtructions, according to the ſignal made for that purpoſe, (vid. *c.*) and after Sir George's ſignal to prepare for battle, which was intended to convince the whole fleet that he was determined to bring the enemy to an engagement. In five minutes after, the ſignal for battle was given ; and, in a few minutes after this laſt, the ſignal that it was his intention to engage cloſe, *and, of courſe, the Admiral's ſhip*, B, *to be the example.* (Vid. *d.*)

A, The Britiſh fleet extended in line of battle. A few minutes before one o'clock, one of the headmoſt ſhips at D began the action, and at one, the Sandwich, the Admiral's own ſhip, after having received ſeveral fires from the enemy, began to engage at C.

F, The enemy lying-to as before.

(Fig. 5.) The action continued above three hours, when Monſ. Guichen in the Couronne, mounting ninety guns, the Triumphant, and the Fendant, after engaging the Sandwich, B, for an hour and a half, bore away, as at F, the ſuperior fire from the Sandwich enabling her to ſuſtain ſo unequal a combat, though, before ſhe was attacked by them, ſhe had beat three ſhips, G, out of the line of battle, had entirely broke it, and was to leeward of the wake of the French Admiral. At the concluſion of the battle, the enemy might be ſaid to be completely beat. But ſuch was the diſtance of the van D, and rear A B, from the centre,

and

and the crippled condition of feveral fhips, particularly the Sand-wich, that we could not purfue the enemy.

90. Though Sir George had the merit of great perfonal cou-rage upon this occafion, yet, it muft be admitted, that the attack, as put in execution, being the fame, was, of courfe, attended with the like want of effect, which, unfortunately, has uniformly marked all our other fea-battles. For, notwithftanding all that has been faid, he could not prevent the wary Frenchman from fliding away from him almoft unhurt, (in like manner as defcribed in No. 23. 24. and Plate IV. fig. 1. and 2.) ; while he got his fhips fo greatly difabled that he could not *follow up*, or even detain a fingle fhip of the enemy for one moment. It is in vain, there-fore, to lay the blame of this mifcarriage upon the fuppofed dif-tance of the van and rear ; for, if both had been completely clofed with the centre, from our hypothefis, as well as from the examples given, we have a right to conclude, that the van and rear of the French fleet might, as ufual, have flid away with the fame eafe as the centre had done (vid. *c*), as foon as they perceived themfelves in any danger of being hurt.

91. Sir George has firft told us, that he had given notice, by public fignal, that his intention was to attack the enemy's rear with his whole force (vid. *a*) ; and then he afterwards fays, at eleven o'clock A. M. I made the fignal for every fhip to bear down, and fteer for her oppofite in the enemy's line. (Vid. *c*.) Why did Sir George change his refolution ?

92. Had he carried the intention of his firſt ſignal into execu-tion *, it is more than probable that he might have taken or de-ſtroyed ſix or eight ſhips at leaſt of the enemy's rear †; but, by carrying down his whole line, every ſhip ſteering upon his op-poſite, according to the intention of the laſt ſignal, from the ex-perience of former engagements, he might have been aſſured of getting every ſhip ſo diſabled by the raking fire of the enemy, as to be incapable of any future purſuit.

93. That the Sandwich, the Admiral's own ſhip, in particular, was crippled, is not ſurpriſing ; for, after having beat three other ſhips of the enemy, ſhe had obliged the Couronne, the Trium-phant, and the Fendant, to bear away and withdraw from battle. But, in the manœuvre of theſe ſix ſhips of the enemy quitting the line, as they did on this occaſion, it is impoſſible not to per-ceive a reſemblance to what has been before explained in the caſe of the alternate ſhips, &c. (No. 24. Plate IV. fig. 1. and 2.) ; or in the caſe of the Grafton, the Cornwal, and the Lion, in Mr BYRON's action, where, with ſimilar gallantry, getting to leeward to cover their friends, they were conſtrained to ſuſtain the fire of the enemy's whole line, as they paſſed them to leeward.

Having now given five examples where the Britiſh, in diſplay of their innate deſire of making the attack, having always attain-

ed

---

* It has been ſaid, that the French Admiral, upon perceiving the approach of the Britiſh fleet, according to the firſt intention, broke out with an exclama-tion, That ſix or ſeven of his ſhips were gone !

† Vide Mode of Attack propoſed.

ed the windward pofition, and where they have made this attack in an extended line, where each fhip was fteered down upon her oppofite of the enemy, and where an idea has generally prevailed, of making the attack upon the enemy's headmôft fhips, in preference to an attack upon the fternmoft; the confequence of which has been, that the fhips making fuch attack could not be fupported but with difficulty: and likewife, where the French, on the other hand, as earneftly courting and attaining the leeward fituation, have always difabled the Britifh fleet: We now proceed to give other examples, where the French, by their anxiety in keeping to windward, have clearly fhown their diflike, as well of making the attack themfelves, as of fuffering the Britifh fleet to approach them, while in this windward fituation.

M.   SEC-

SECTION II.

OF ENGAGEMENTS WHERE THE FRENCH, BY KEEPING THEIR FLEETS TO WINDWARD, HAVE CLEARLY SHOWN THEIR DISLIKE, AS WELL OF MAKING THE ATTACK THEMSELVES, AS OF SUFFERING THE BRITISH FLEET TO APPROACH THEM WHILE IN THIS WINDWARD SITUATION.

1. That of SIR GEORGE BRIDGES-RODNEY, to windward of Martinico, May 15. 1780.

2. SIR GEORGE BRIDGES-RODNEY, near the same place, May 19. 1780.

3. SIR SAMUEL HOOD, off Fort-Royal, Martinico, April 29. 1781.

4. ADMIRAL KEPPEL, off Ushant, July 27. 1778.

SIR GEORGE BRIDGES RODNEY'S RENCOUNTER WITH THE FRENCH FLEET, TO WINDWARD OF MARTINICO, MAY 15. 1780.

EXTRACT OF A LETTER FROM ADMIRAL SIR GEORGE BRIDGES-RODNEY, MAY 31.1780, DATED CARLISLE BAY.

94. ' Since my letter of the 26th of April from Fort-Royal
' Bay, sent express by the Pegasus, I must desire you will please
                     ' to

' to acquaint their Lordſhips, that, after greatly alarming the
' iſland of Martinico, whoſe inhabitants had been made to be-
' lieve his Majeſty's fleet had been defeated, but were ſoon con-
' vinced to the contrary, by its appearance before their port,
' where it continued till the condition of many of the ſhips un-
' der my command, and the lee currents, rendered it neceſſary
' for the fleet to anchor in Chocque Bay, St Lucie, in order to
' put the wounded and ſick men on ſhore, and to water and re-
' fit the fleet; frigates having been detached both to windward
' and to leeward of every iſland, in order to gain intelligence of
' the motions of the enemy, and timely notice of their approach
' towards Martinico, the only place they could refit at in theſe
' ſeas.   Having landed the wounded and ſick men, watered and
' refitted the fleet; on the 6th of May, upon receiving intelli-
' gence of the enemy's approach to windward of Martinico, I
' put to ſea with nineteen ſail of the line, two fifty gun ſhips,
' and ſeveral frigates.

' From the 6th to the 10th of May, the fleet continued turn-
' ing to windward between Martinico and St Lucia, when we
' got ſight of the French fleet, about three leagues to windward
' of us, Point Saline on Martinico then bearing N. N. E. five
' leagues, Captain AFFLECK, in the Triumph, joining me the
' ſame day.

' The enemy's fleet conſiſted of twenty-three ſail of the line,
' ſeven frigates, two ſloops, a cutter, and a lugger.   Nothing could
' induce them to riſk a general action, though it was in their

M 2   ' power

‘ power daily : They made, at different times, motions which
‘ indicated a defire of engaging ; but their refolution failed them
‘ when they drew near ; and, as they failed far better than his
‘ Majefty's fleet, they, with eafe, could gain what diftance they
‘ pleafed to windward.

‘ As they were fenfible of their advantage in failing, it embol-
‘ dened them to run greater rifks, and approach nearer to his
‘ Majefty's fhips than they would otherwife have done ; and, for
‘ feveral days, about two in the afternoon, they bore down in a
‘ line of battle abreaft, and brought to the wind a little more
‘ than random-fhot diftance.

‘ As I watched every opportuniry of gaining the wind, and
‘ forcing them to battle, the enemy, on my ordering the fleet
‘ to make a great deal of fail, on the 15th, upon a wind, had the
‘ vanity to think we were retiring, and with a prefs of fail ap-
‘ proached us much nearer than ufual. I fuffered them to enjoy
‘ the deception, and their van fhip to approach abreaft of my
‘ centre, when, by a lucky change of wind, perceiving I could
‘ weather the enemy, I made the fignal for the third in com-
‘ mand, who then led the van, to tack with his fquadron, and
‘ gain the wind of the enemy. The enemy's fleet inftantly wore,
‘ and fled with a crowd of fail.

‘ His Majefty's fleet, by this manœuvre, had gained the
‘ wind, and would have forced the enemy to battle, had it not
‘ at once changed fix points, when near the enemy, and enabled
‘ them

Plate X. Part 1. p. 88.

Sir Geo. Brydges Rodney off the West
end of Martinico 17 April 1780.

Fig. 1.

B

F

Fig. 2.

B

F

Fig. 3.

B

F

Fig. 4.

B

A   C   D

F

A

B   D

F

G

' them to recover that advantage. However, it did not enable
' them to weather his Majefty's fleet fo much, but the van, led
' by that good and gallant officer, Captain BOWER, about feven
' in the evening, reached their centre, and was followed by
' Rear-Admiral ROWLEY's fquadron, who then led the van; the
' centre and rear of his Majefty's fleet following in order.

' As the enemy were under a prefs of fail, none but the van
' of his Majefty's fleet could come in for any part of the action,
' without wafting his Majefty's powder and fhot. The enemy
' wantonly expended a deal of theirs, at fuch a diftance as to have
' no effect.

' The Albion, Captain BOWER, and the Conqueror, Rear-Ad-
' miral ROWLEY, were the fhips that fuffered moft in this ren-
' counter. But I am fure, from the flacknefs of their fire, in
' comparifon to that of the van of his Majefty's fleet, the ene-
' my's rear muft have fuffered very confiderably.

' The enemy kept an awful diftance till the 19th inftant,
' when I was in hopes that I fhould have weathered them, but
' had the mortification to be difappointed in thefe hopes; how-
' ever, as they were convinced their rear could not efcape action,
' they feemed to have taken a refolution of rifking a general
' one; and, when their van had weathered us, they bore away
' along our line to windward, and began a heavy cannonade,
' but at fuch a diftance as to do little or no execution; however
' their rear could not efcape being clofely attacked by the fhips

' of

' of the van, then led by Commodore HOTHAM ; and with plea-
' sure I can say, that the fire of his Majesty's ships was far supe-
' rior to that of the enemy, who must have received great da-
' mage by the rencounter.

' The Albion and Conqueror suffered much in this last action,
' and several other ships received considerable damage ; a list of
' which, as likewise of the killed and wounded, I have the ho-
' nour to enclose.

' The pursuit of the enemy had led us forty leagues directly
' to windward of Martinico ; and, as the enemy had stood to
' the northward with all the sail they could possibly press, and
' were out of sight the 21st instant, the condition of his Majesty's
' ships being such as not to allow a longer pursuit, I sent the
' Conqueror, Cornwal, and Boyne, to St Lucia, and stood with
' the remainder of his Majesty's ships towards Barbadoes, in or-
' der to put the sick and wounded on shore, and repair the squa-
' dron. '

L. DESCRIPTION OF SIR GEORGE BRIDGES-RODNEY'S REN-
    COUNTER WITH THE FRENCH FLEET, TO WINDWARD
    OF MARTINICO, THE 15. MAY 1780, TAKEN FROM THE
    ABOVE LETTER OF 31. MAY 1780.

95. B, (Plate XI. fig. 1.) The British fleet extended in line
of battle to leeward, and endeavouring to get to windward.

F,

F, The French fleet, for feveral days, about the hour of two in the afternoon, bore down in a line of battle abreaft (as at F), and brought to the wind a little more than random-fhot diftance, (as at G).

(Fig. 2.)   The French, upon the 15th May, having imagined that the Britifh were retiring, came down with a prefs of fail, and approached nearer than ufual, (as at F, firft pofition).

B, The Britifh fleet in firft pofition.

Sir George fays, ' I fuffered them to enjoy the deception, ' and their van fhips to approach *abreaft* of my centre at B, ' when, by a lucky change of wind (*vide* I), perceiving I could ' weather the enemy, I made the fignal for the van to tack, as at ' C, and gain the wind of the enemy.   The enemy's fleet in- ' ftantly wore, as at GG; and fled with a crowd of fail on the ' contrary tack, (as at H.) '

B, (Fig. 3.)   The Britifh fleet having now gained the wind, (See I), would have forced the enemy to battle, had not the wind at once changed fix points to K, when near the enemy, which enabled them to recover the weather-gage, (as in Fig. 4.)

F, (Fig. 4.)   The French recovering the weather-gage, the wind having changed from I back to K.

G, The former line of courfe of the French fleet when the wind was at I.

B,

B, The Britifh van having now loft the weather-gage, by the wind changing from I to K, and endeavouring to reach the centre of the French line.

C, The line of the Britifh courfe before the wind changed.

Sir George fays, ' The van, led by Captain Bower, about fe-
' ven in the evening, reached the enemy's centre, and was follow-
' ed by Rear-Admiral Rowley's fquadron, who then led the van,
' the centre and rear of his Majefty's fleet following in order.   As
' the enemy were under a prefs of fail, none but the van of the
' Britifh fleet could come in for any part of the engagement, with-
' out wafting powder and fhot; the enemy wantonly expending
' a deal of theirs, at fuch a diftance as to have no effect. '

II.   DESCRIPTION OF SIR GEORGE BRIDGES-RODNEY'S REN-
COUNTER WITH THE FRENCH FLEET, TO WINDWARD OF
MARTINICO, MAY 19. 1780, TAKEN FROM HIS LETTER
OF MAY 31. 1780.

96.   B, (Plate XII. Fig. 1.)   The Britifh fleet, on the 19th May, again difappointed in gaining the wind.

F, The van of the French fleet weathering that of the Britifh.

' The * enemy kept an awful diftance till the 19th inft. (fays
' Sir George), when I was again in hopes that I fhould have wea-
' thered

---

* See Fig. 1. B, Britifh.   F, French.

Plate XI. Part I. *p. 92.*

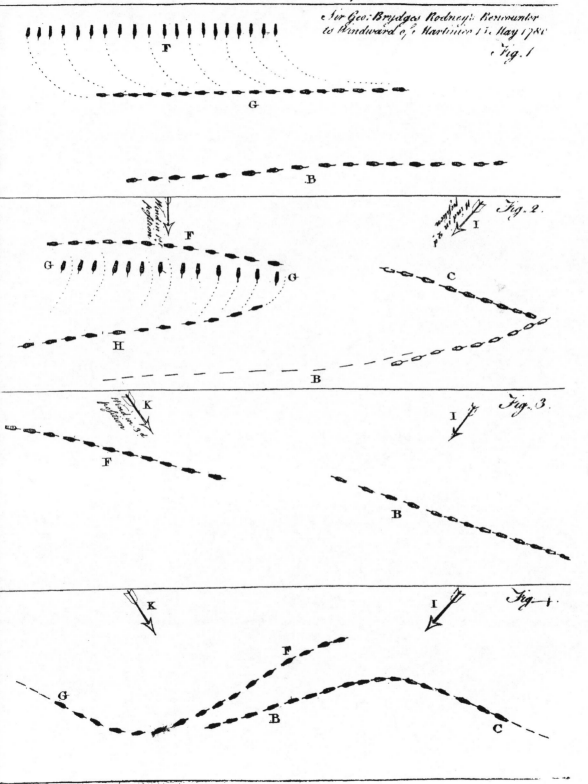

Sir Geo: Brydges Rodney's Rencounter
to Windward of Martinico 15 May 1780

Fig. 1

F

G

B

Fig. 2

Wind in 1st position

I

F

G

G

C

H

B

Fig. 3

Wind in 3d position

K

I

F

B

Fig. 4

K

I

F

G

B

C

' thered them ; but I had the mortification to be difappointed in
' thefe hopes. However, as they were convinced their rear could
' not efcape action, they feemed to have taken a refolution of rifk-
' ing a general one ; and, when their van had weathered us, they
' bore away, along our line, to windward,' (as in Fig. 2.)

F, (Fig. 2.) The French van having weathered the Britifh,
bore away, along the line, to windward, and began a heavy cannonade, but at fuch a diftance as to do little or no execution ;
however, their rear G could not efcape being clofely attacked by
the fhips of the Britifh van B, led by Commodore HOTHAM. Sir
GEORGE fays, ' It is with pleafure I can fay, that the fire from the
' Britifh fhips was far fuperior to that of the enemy, who muft
' have received great damage by the rencounter. '

97. Without farther obfervation at prefent on the nature of the
manœuvring which took place in either of thefe rencounters, it may
be proper to remark, that the French, in both, contrary to their u-
fual practice, have kept a windward fituation. However, it will be
evident, from Sir GEORGE's letter, that as it was their earneft defire to get back to Fort-Royal without being farther hurt, fo they
neglected to manœuvre to accomplifh their object ; and the feints
which they made of approaching the Britifh fleet for four or five
days in fucceffion, could be intended only as an attempt to throw
the Admiral off his guard : Therefore, as neither of thefe affairs
can be confidered as any thing more than accidental rencounters,
our general obfervations will remain with the fame force as before, and will confirm us in the belief, that the French will ne-

N. ver

ver be induced, in prejudice of their object in view, either to make or fuftain an attack, if it can poffibly be avoided, whether that object fhall be getting back to a port, an attack upon a particular place, the faving of their fleet in general, or the preferving of it entire to the conclufion of the war.

III. SIR SAMUEL HOOD'S ENGAGEMENT WITH THE FRENCH FLEET OFF FORT-ROYAL, MARTINICO, 29. APRIL 1781.

EXTRACT OF A LETTER FROM REAR-ADMIRAL SIR SAMUEL HOOD, MAY 4. 1781.

98. ' Saw nothing of the enemy or Amazon at day-light. A
' little before nine the Amazon joined me, the enemy then in
' fight, coming down between Point Salines and the Diamond
' Rock ; made the fignal for a clofe line, and to prepare for ac-
' tion. At nine the enemy appeared, forming the line of battle.
' Twenty minutes paft nine, the Prince William joined me from
' Grofs-Iflet Bay ; and, as I fent for her but the night before,
' Captain DOUGLAS's exertion muft have been great, and does
' him much credit, to be with me fo foon, having the greateft
' part of his crew to collect in the night. Twenty-feven minutes
' paft nine, hoifted our colours, as did the French Admiral and
' his fleet. At fifteen minutes paft ten, made the Shrewfbury's
' fignal to alter her courfe to windward, fhe being the leading
' fhip ; but foon perceived the wind had fhifted, and that fhe was

' as

' as clofe to the wind as fhe could lye. At thirty-five minutes
' paft ten, tacked the fquadron altogether, the van of the enemy
' being almoft abreaft of our centre, and at eleven began to fire,
' which I took no notice of. At this time the fhips in Fort-
' Royal Bay flipped their cables, and got under fail. At twenty
' minutes paft eleven, I tacked the fquadron altogether, and re-
' peated the fignal for a clofe order of battle. At twenty-five
' minutes paft eleven, finding the enemy's fhot to go over us,
' hoifted the fignal for engaging, and, in paffing our van and the
' enemy's rear, exchanged fome broadfides. At forty minutes
' after eleven, the enemy tacked. At forty-five minutes after ele-
' ven, made the fignal for the rear to clofe the centre. At fifty-
' five minutes paft eleven, finding it impoffible to get up to the
' enemy's fleet, I invited it to come to me, by bringing the
' fquadron to under their top-fails. At half paft twelve, the
' French Admiral, in the Bretagne, began to fire at the Barfleur,
' which was immediately returned, and the action became gene-
' ral, but at too great a diftance ; and, I believe, never was more
' powder and fhot thrown away in one day before : but it was
' with Monfieur de GRASSE the option of diftance lay : it was not
' poffible for me to go nearer. At one, I made the fignal for the
' van to fill, the French having filled, and drawn ahead. At fe-
' venteen minutes paft one, made the Shrewfbury's fignal, the
' leading fhip, to make more fail, and fet the top-gallant fails.
' At thirty-four minutes paft one, repeated the fignal for a clofe
' line of battle ; and finding not one of ten of the enemy's fhot
' reach us, I ceafed firing ; the enemy did the fame foon after ;
' but their van and ours being fomewhat nearer, continued to

N 2   ' engage ;

' engage ; and, though the French Admiral had ten fail aftern of
' him, and three others to windward, he did not make a nearer
' approach.   The merchant ships, at this time, were hauling in
' clofe under the land, attended by two ships of two decks, fup-
' pofed to be armed *en flute*, and two frigates.   At eighteen mi-
' nutes paft three, the firing ceafed between our van and that of the
' enemy ; made the Shrewfbury's fignal to make more fail, in or-
' der to get to windward of the enemy.   At forty-five minutes
' paft four, fent Captain FINCH to the Shrewfbury to order Cap-
' tain ROBERTSON to keep as near the wind, and carry all the fail
' he could, fo as to preferve the line of battle, and to return back
' along the line, to acquaint every Captain of the fame.   At fifty-
' feven minutes paft five, the packet going to Antigua, which
' had kept company with the fquadron, came within hail, to ac-
' quaint me, by order of Rear-Admiral DRAKE, that the Ruffel
' was in great diftrefs, having received feveral shot between wind
' and water ; that the water was over the platform of the maga-
' zine, and gaining upon the pumps ; and that three of their
' guns were difmounted.   At eighteen minutes paft fix, made the
' Ruffel's fignal to come within hail, which was anfwered ; the
' enemy's fleet, confifting of twenty-four fail of the line, at this
' time about four miles to windward.   At half paft feven, Captain
' SUTHERLAND of the Ruffel came on board, whom I ordered,
' if he could poffibly, by exertion, keep the ship above water, to
' proceed to St Euftatius, or any other port he could make, and
' acquaint Sir GEORGE RODNEY of all that paffed.   At forty-five
' minutes paft nine, the Lizard came within hail, to inform me,
' by the defire of Captain SUTHERLAND, that he had bore away.

' On

Plate XII. Part I. p. 96.

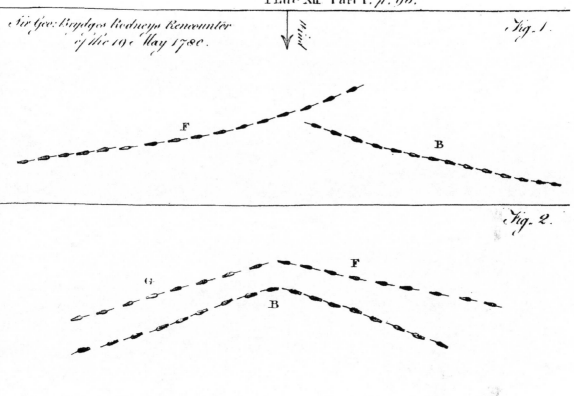

Sir Geo: Brydges Rodneys Rencounter
of the 19 May 1780.

Wind

Fig. 1.

F

B

Fig. 2.

G

F

B

' On Monday, April 30th, at day-light, found the van and
' centre of the fquadron feparated at fome diftance from the Bar-
' fleur and rear, owing to fluttering winds and calms in the
' night, which would not allow us to keep the Barfleur's head
' the right way, and fhe went round and round two or three
' times, while the other fhips had light airs; and, finding the
' enemy's advanced fhips fteering for our van, made all poffible
' fail towards them, and threw out the fignal for a clofe line of
' battle, the enemy's line being a good deal extended and fcat-
' tered.   At feven, the fquadron under my command being pret-
' ty well formed, the enemy's advanced fhips hauled off.   At
' fifty-fix minutes paft feven, made the fignal for the rear to clofe
' the centre, as the enemy feemed to fhow a difpofition to attack
' it.   At thirty-five minutes paft eight, having very light airs of
' wind, the fquadron was thrown nearly into a line abreaft;
' made the fignal for continuing in that form, left, by endea-
' vouring to regain the line ahead, it might become extended.
' At eleven, made the fignal for a line ahead, at two cables length
' afunder, the wind backing to the eaftward, favoured by form-
' ing in that order, the better to receive the enemy, then about
' three miles to windward.   At fourteen minutes paft eleven,
' made the fignal for the rear to clofe the centre.   At twelve,
' falling little wind again, and all the fhips being thrown into a
' line abreaft, made a fignal for a line abreaft, to keep the
' fquadron as clofe together as poffible.   At twenty-five minutes
' paft twelve, the wind blowing fteady at S. E., made the fignal
' for a general chafe to windward, with a defign of weathering
' the enemy, which I fhould certainly have fucceeded in, had the

' breeze

' breeze continued ; but the wind dying away at four, I found it
' impracticable to weather the enemy, and therefore made the
' fignal for a line ahead ; and having been informed that the In-
' trepid made fo much water they could fcarce keep her free, and
' that the Centaur was in the fame ftate, owing to the number of
' fhot between wind and water, and that her lower mafts were
' very badly wounded, I judged it improper to dare the enemy
' to battle any longer ; and therefore thought it my indifpenfa-
' ble duty to bear up, and made the fignal for it at eight o'clock.
' At ten, brought to for the fquadron to clofe ; at forty minutes
' paft ten made fail.   At five A. M. the 1ft inftant, faw the ene-
' my's fleet aftern, about eight or nine miles diftant.   At twenty-
' fix minutes paft five, brought to for the Torbay and Pocca-
' hunta to come up, which were then within reach of the ene-
' my's guns ; and the former received a good deal of damage in
' her mafts and rigging.   At forty-five minutes paft feven, the
' enemy ceafed firing upon the Torbay ; fent the Amazon to tow
' the Poccahunta up.   At eight, made the fignal for a clofe line,
' bearing north and fouth of each other.   At twenty minutes
' paft twelve, made the fignal, and brought to upon the larboard
' tack, and made the fignal for the ftate and condition of the
' fquadron, the enemy bearing eaft, ftanding to the northward.
' Thirty-three minutes paft three, made the fignal for a clofe line
' north and fouth.   At four, the enemy tacked to the fouth-
' ward, and were ftanding that way at fun-fet.   In the evening,
' though it was almoft calm, the main top-maft of the Intrepid
' fell to pieces over the fide.   At feven, made fail to the north-
' ward, it being the opinion of the officers of the fquadron ac-

' quainted

' quainted with this country, that it was the only way of getting
' to windward, as the currents run very strong to leeward, to the
' southward of St Vincents. '

The conduct of the French, in this affair with Sir Samuel
Hood, is much the same with the two last of Sir George
Rodney's. It is the third time where, contrary to their esta-
blished practice, *they have kept the wind*. But, aware of the
danger of this position, they approached so near the British only,
as to be able to amuse them with a distant cannonade, while their
merchant ships and transports might, with sufficient security, get
into port.

Besides the above object, and the usual unremitting attention
to the safety of their ships, they had to secure an easy access, by
keeping to windward of their port ; from which the armaments,
for carrying into execution the great schemes they had then in
contemplation, were to be fitted out. Of these, the first soon
after unfortunately took place in the Chesapeak.

From this battle, we may judge of the propriety of cannonading, even where there may be the smallest chance of reaching
an enemy. For, notwithstanding the great distance of the two
fleets, and though the French were to windward ; yet many of
their shot took place in the hulls of our ships, so far below the
water-line, that three of them could, with difficulty, be kept a-
float.

IV.

IV. ADMIRAL KEPPEL'S BATTLE OFF USHANT, JULY 27. 1778. *

99. B, (Plate XIII. Fig. 1.) The Britiſh fleet, at ſix o'clock in the morning, ſtanding upon the larboard tack, and lying up about W. by N. ; that is, with their heads northwards, and ranging between the fleet of the enemy and their port of Breſt.

F, The French fleet to windward, and nearly weſt, having kept that ſituation for four days before, as mentioned in Mr Keppel's letter ; they had their heads alſo to the north.

A, At ten o'clock, the whole Britiſh fleet tacked together, and ſtood for the enemy, after having run through the dotted lines, their ſuppoſed courſe, and now upon the ſtarboard tack, with their heads ſouthward.

C, The Britiſh fleet advancing in as regular a line as the purſuit would admit ; and the van having neared the enemy, a firing began between the headmoſt ſhips of both fleets about eleven o'clock.

While the Britiſh fleet was going through theſe movements, a ſquall of wind, attended with rain, aroſe, which prevented either fleet from ſeeing each other's motions ; during which time, that is, from ſix o'clock, till half an hour after ten, the French had firſt ſtretched away north, on the larboard tack, to G, where they tacked,

* Britiſh, 20 ſhips, 6 frigates.   French, 28 ſhips.

tacked, then returned on a ftarboard tack to the fouth, as far as
H ; here they attempted a fecond tack ; but fome fhips miffing
ftays, from the effect of the fquall, they wore altogether, and
were got again with their heads to the north, when the weather cleared up, and difcovered the Britifh fleet hard upon them,
but on contrary tacks : The wind veering a little about to the fouth
in this critical moment, favoured the fleet of the French, by enabling them to lye better up, while, of courfe, the Britifh fell off.

100. B, (Fig. 2.) The van of the Britifh, after having got as
near as they chofe, each fhip, as foon as it came within gun-fhot,
bore away, and run along the line of the enemy, firing at each
fhip in paffing ; the whole fleet following the fame example.

101. F, Shows the courfe of the French, wifhing to avoid the
battle, and taking the advantage of the wind, now more foutherly,
by which means the rear of the Britifh was able to fetch the centre
of their fleet only, while, at the fame time, the French van was
now far to windward, and preparing to wear and run to leeward of the Britifh fleet.

102. B, (Fig. 3.) The Britifh Admiral, in the Victory, together with other fhips of his divifion, after having paffed the rear
of the French, in the act of wearing, to return to the fupport of
their rear, or to give chafe to the enemy.

103. A, The Formidable, SIR HUGH PALLISER's fhip, after
having fetched, and given and received a broadfide with the
French Admiral, and other fhips, as fhe paffed along the line.
C, The van of the Britifh fomewhat farther to windward.

O 104.

104. F, The French fleet, after having wore, and running down before the wind, which, at that time, would give them the appearance of being in diforder, when feen from Sir Hugh Palliser's fhip, the Formidable.

105. G, The French forming in a new line of battle to leeward, upon the ftarboard tack, with their heads to the fouthward.

106. B, (Fig. 4.) Admiral Keppel, now to windward of the French fleet, between four and fix o'clock in the afternoon, on the ftarboard tack, with his fhips heads to the fouthward, and in hopes that the enemy would lye to, and try their fortune in battle with him next morning.

A, The fuppofed fituation of the Formidable.

107. F, The French fleet in order of battle, to leeward, alfo on the ftarboard tack, lying to, to receive the British Admiral, fhould he think fit to make an attack.

108. GGG, Three fwift failing frigates left with lights in their poops to amufe the British Admiral, while the reft of the fleet fhould flip into port before morning.

109. Mr Keppel, difcovering the French fleet to windward, ftruggled hard for four or five days to get up with them; at laft, the French, willing to give up the conteft, paffed to leeward, and formed their line of battle in their favourite pofition, as in the fore-mentioned cafe of Mr Arbuthnot off the Chefapeak; but, in accomplifhing this movement, it muft be evident, from former examples, that they could have no intention or inclina-

tion

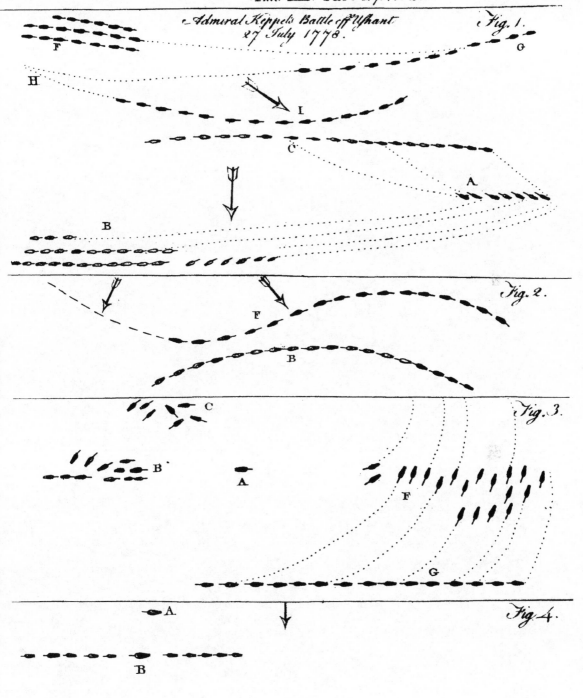

Plate XIII. Part I. p. 102.

Admiral Keppel's Battle off Ushant
27 July 1778.

Fig. 1.

Fig. 2.

Fig. 3.

Fig. 4.

tion to come within cannon-fhot of the Britifh fleet, when paffing on contrary tacks, as they were forced to do, by the effect of
a dark fquall of wind and rain, and which alfo prevented them
from feeing where they were, till clofe upon the Britifh fleet.

MR KEPPEL, in his letter to the Admiralty, having given his
reafons why he did not attack the French fleet in the afternoon,
it will be improper here to make any further remark upon it.

OTHER OBSERVATIONS. *

110. Let us fuppofe two adverfe fleets, A and F, (See Plate XIV.
Fig. 1.) with hoftile intention, contending to get to windward,

O 2   the

* With refpect to the above obfervations, it feems neceffary here to mention,
that they made part of a former defcription of this rencounter of the 27th of
July 1778, written foon after, and then put into the hands of a few friends:
That the author being in London in January 1780, many difcuffions were held,
at the defire, and in prefence of the fame friends, as well for improving upon,
as for the communicating of, thefe and other ideas on naval tactics, and particularly on one occafion, by appointment with an officer of moft diftinguifhed merit: That they were afterwards intended to be inferted in the firft edition of
this Effay, printed January 1. 1782, as being applicable to the two fimilar rencounters of Lord Rodney, of the 15th and 19th of May 1780, as well as to this
of the 27th of July, where the adverfe fleets had paffed each other on contrary
tacks. But it was afterwards thought proper then to omit them, as it was conceived it might be of prejudice to the other parts of the fubject to advance any
thing doubtful, no example of cutting an enemy's line, in an attack from the
leeward, before that time, having been given.

the one of the other, and, by dint of failing, or by change of
wind, that the leading fhips of the enemy F, fhall have gained
111. the wind of the fleet A ; it feems evident, if the van, or any part
of the leeward fleet A, was to continue the line of direction of
112. their firft courfe AB, and were not all, fhip after fhip, to bear
113. away, as per courfe CC (Fig. 2.), that, with great advantage, the
enemy's line of battle might be cut in twain, as at G (Fig. 3.),
and have thereby their rear H feparated from their van F,
114. (Fig. 3.) ; or otherwife, by fuch attempt, the courfe of all the
fhips aftern of this attack being thereby ftopped or retarded,
the enemy F (Fig. 4.), to fupport thefe fhips, will be compelled
to hazard an engagement, that fhall be clofe indeed, or he
muft altogether abandon the fhips fo ftopped in his rear at G,
(Fig. 4.)

Perhaps it will be faid, that the rifk or danger attending an attack of this kind might be greater than any advantage that can
115. be propofed.——To which it is anfwered, The very firft time ever
we fhall have the fpirit to make the experiment, the fuccefs will
be fufficient to juftify the attempt, by convincing us, that the rifk
or damage to fhipping in making the attempt, will be found to
be of lefs moment than in any one other mode of attack whatever.

116. But, fince the attempt of cutting the enemy's line had not
been thought an advifeable meafure upon this occafion, fhould not
fome other efficient plan of attack have been concerted, by which,
upon a fuppofition, if the two fleets fhould be brought to pafs
each other on contrary tacks, that the leading fhips of the Britifh
fquadron, after having ranged paft the line of the enemy, might
have

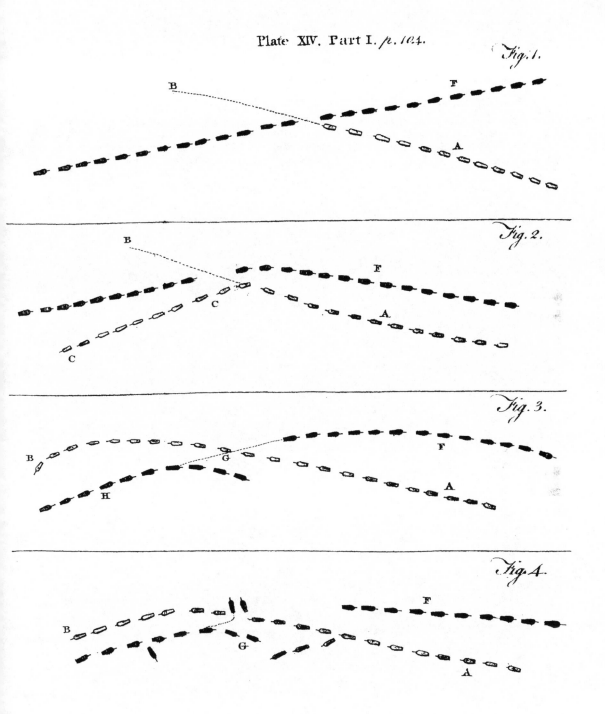

Plate XIV. Part I. p. 104.

Fig. 1.

Fig. 2.

Fig. 3.

Fig. 4.

have been appointed to tack, and, by doubling back, as per course B (Plate XV. Fig. 1.), have brought the ships in the rear of F between crofs fires?

117. A movement of this kind would likewife have brought on a clofer and more general engagement, or the enemy, of confequence, muft have abandoned their rear, as in the former cafe. Not having been able to forefee, provide for, or advife upon either the one or the other of the cafes, during the four days the Britifh fquadron was in purfuit of the enemy, is very extraordinary; becaufe, by being to leeward, the enemy, defirous of going off, and the wind not changing, it is without doubt demonftrable, that the rencounter of adverfe fleets in fuch pofition, and under fuch circumftances, will never be on the fame tack, but, of neceffity, will always be on contrary tacks.

118. The two fleets, upon this occafion, paffed each other in oppofite directions, at the rate of five miles per hour. That of the French confifted of 26 fhips; and, as the fpace occupied by each fhip, including the intervals between, may be about 294 yards, (fay 300 yards, No. 25.), their whole line (founded upon the fame proportion) may be fuppofed to be about five miles in length. From which it will be evident, that the *whole* extent of the refpective line of each fleet muft have paffed the complete line of the other in one hour; and each fhip in the Britifh line muft therefore have ranged paft the length of the whole French line (admitting nothing extraordinary to caufe a ftoppage) in the one half of that time.

119.

119. Again, let us make a fuppofition, that two, three, or more fhips, in line of battle, are paffing each other in oppofite tacks, at the rate of five miles per hour; then will the velocity of the tranfit be equal to ten miles per hour. Or, which is the fame thing, let us, for the fake of demonftration, fuppofe the one fleet at reft, that is, without any motion ahead whatever; but let the motion of the other ahead, and in an oppofite direction, be equal to ten miles per hour, then each fhip of the fquadron in motion will pafs through a fpace of 880 feet in one minute of time.

For the number of feet in one mile, being   -   5280
multiplied by 10, gives the velocity of the tran-⎤   10
fit ten miles, or 52,800 feet, performed in ⎪   ———
one hour; which fum being divided by 60, ⎪   60)52800(880
will give 880 feet, the velocity of one minute. ⎦

And as the length of each fhip will not much exceed 200 feet, then it is evident, that the duration of time in which one fhip will continue in direct oppofition to any one other fhip, of equal length, in the enemy's line, fo as mutually to annoy each other, cannot exceed one quarter of a minute of time.

120. Again, fuppofe any number of fhips, fix, feven, or eight, running upon a ftarboard tack, at the rate of five miles per hour, and an equal number of the enemy, paffing in oppofite direction, at the rate of five miles per hour likewife, (as in Plate XV. fig. 2.); then, according to what has been faid, each fhip of the

fquadron

fquadron B, will pafs each fhip of the enemy F, with the interval between fhips included, in one minute ; that is, (the motion
of both fhips comprehended), will amount to 880 feet in one
minute, fay 300 yards, that being the ufual allowance of fpace
for each fhip as extended in line of battle.

121. But, on fuch a fuppofition, the fhip F (Plate XV. Fig. 2.)
will be confined, in point of time, fo far, that fhe will be able to
give her fire to the fhip B, while fhe fhall be in direct oppofition to
her at the point A, becaufe fhe muft be in preparation to give a
fecond broadfide, when the fhip D fhall have come in direct oppofition alfo ; but, by the fuppofition, the tranfit of each fhip is
confined to one minute of time only.   Therefore, though it were
poffible that the guns of the whole of the fhip's broadfide could
be loaded, prepared, and repeated, in the fpace of one minute,
ftill it would be impracticable for the fhip F to give more than
one broadfide to the fhip B, even by following her in an angular
direction, as that reprefented by G firing upon C, and afterwards
to be in fufficient time prepared to give a proper reception to the
fhip D, now faft approaching.

122. Therefore, if the two fleets did pafs one another, each at
the rate of five miles per hour, and if it were poffible that the loading and firing of a fhip could be repeated once every minute of
time, each fhip ftill could be expofed to the fire of her antagonift
during the fpace of one quarter of minute only, that is, while
the two fhips in queftion were in direct oppofition, as at A from
F ; and, as the fleet of the enemy, on this occafion, confifted of
26 fhips, each Britifh fhip, in ranging along the whole of their
line,

line, could be expofed to a cannonade of fix minutes and an half
duration only : And, in place of five miles, if the two fleets had
paffed each other with a velocity equal to $2\frac{1}{2}$ miles per hour, (a
rate of motion required to make a fhip anfwer the helm, but
abfolutely neceffary to keep her under proper management in
line of battle, when working to windward, as on this occafion),
then, and in that cafe, each fhip would be expofed to a cannonade of not more than thirteen minutes duration.

123. Again, if it fhall be found impracticable to load and difcharge a complete broadfide in the fpace of one minute, and that
this operation fhall require fix, eight, or ten minutes, one time
with another, when it comes to be repeated, in an engagement of
any duration, how much then will the effect be different! It
muft be obferved, however, that thefe calculations are founded on
the average of motion and time, taken upon the whole number of the fhips comprehended in the French line of battle, and
that particular Britifh fhips, from accidents, might have made
their tranfit, by ranging paft the fire of the enemy, fome with
more motion, and fome with lefs.

124. Let any one imagine a rencounter of horfemen, where
the parties, on coming to the ground appointed, had pufhed their
horfes at full fpeed, exchanging a few piftol fhot as they paffed
one another in oppofite directions, at a diftance of forty or fifty
yards, and then fome idea may be formed of the effect of rencounters, where adverfe fleets are brought to pafs each other on
contrary tacks, having nothing further in view than exchanging
the few cannon fhot which can take place on all fuch occafions.

125.

Plate XV. Part I. p. 108.   Fig. 1.
N.º 116.

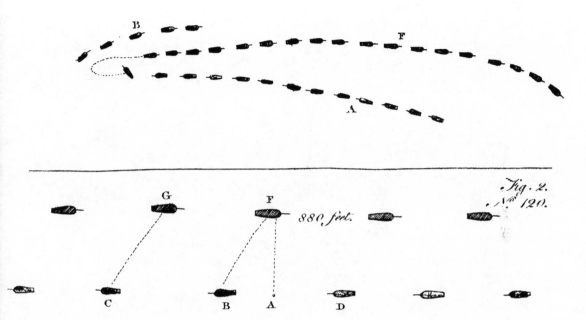

Fig. 2.
N.º 120.

880 feet.

125. From all which it muft be evident, that the moft artful management of fails, the clofeft approximation, or the moft fpirited cannonade, will avail nothing under fuch circumftances, and that it is vain to hope, that ever any thing material can be effected againft an enemy's fleet keeping to windward, paffing on contrary tacks, and defirous to go off, unlefs his line of battle *can be cut in twain*, or fome fuch other ftop can be devifed, as has already been defcribed.

P

SECTION III.

126. THE ENGAGEMENT OF THE BRITISH FLEET UNDER THE
COMMAND OF MR MATHEWS *, WITH THE COMBINED
FLEETS OF FRANCE AND SPAIN, IN THE MEDITER-
RANEAN, OFF TOULON, FEBRUARY 11. 1744 †.

127. B, (Plate XVI. fig. 1.) Admiral MATHEWS in the
Namur, commanding the centre of the Britifh fleet, at 10 o'clock,
when the fignal for battle was given, and three hours before the
engagement began.

A, The rear under Mr LESTOCK, at that time feveral miles
aftern.

C, The van, under Mr ROWLEY, fome miles ahead, and to
windward, faid by Mr LESTOCK to be in diforder.

F, The van and centre of the enemy clofed, and compofed of
fome Spanifh, but, the greateft part, of French fhips, then going
at the rate of three or four miles an hour.

G,

---

* Britifh, 21 fhips of the line, 2 of 50 guns, and 9 frigates.
French and Spaniards, 28 fhips, and 4 frigates.

† To this battle, diftinguifhed as it is by peculiar circumftances, and the better to exprefs a defire of doing juftice to the Admiral who commanded, it has
been thought proper to affign a place by itfelf. The account of it is taken from
plans, with defcriptions, prefented to the Houfe of Commons by Vice-Admiral
LESTOCK, who commanded the rear of the Britifh fleet, and who was the ac-
cufer before the Court-martial, by the fentence of which Mr MATHEWS was
condemned to be broke.

G, The Spanish Admiral, JUAN JOSEPHO NAVARRO, in the Royal Philip, with three ships of the rear division, a great way separated from the centre.

H, Five other Spanish ships, also belonging to the rear division, but far astern of the Admiral.

A, (Plate XVI. fig. 2.) The rear division of the British, under Mr LESTOCK, at one o'clock, still very far astern.

128. B, Mr MATHEWS, in the Namur, at one o'clock, three hours after the signal for battle, having broke the line, bore down, accompanied only by the Norfolk and Marlborough, his two seconds ahead and astern, and began the engagement with the Royal Philip and his seconds.

129. C, The van, under Mr ROWLEY, not yet engaged, but watching carefully to prevent the van of the enemy from getting the wind.

F, The centre and van of the enemy still far ahead of the rear.

G, The Royal Philip engaged with the British Admiral.

H, The five Spanish ships still far separated from the Admiral.

130. I, The Poder, a Spanish ship, cannonaded, but at a great distance, by five ships in the British line.

131. K, The Constant, the Spanish Admiral's second ahead, beat out of the line by the Norfolk, the Admiral's other second astern firing at her to make her to return.

A, (Plate XVI. fig. 3.) Mr LESTOCK still astern.

132.

132. B, Mr MATHEWS, affisted by his feconds, filences the fire from the Royal Philip, and fends the fire-fhip down the wind to fet him on fire; which fire-fhip, as fhe blew up fomewhere at L, in the intermediate fpace between the two fquadrons, did no hurt to either. The Lieutenant, Gunner, and four men, perifhed in the flames; the remainder of the crew efcaped in their boats.

C, The van of the Britifh cannonading the French, but at a great diftance.

D, Four fhips, which did not go down to fupport the Admiral and his feconds.

133. E, The Berwick, commanded by the gallant Mr HAWKE, though in the van divifion, broke the line, bore down *within half mufket fhot*, (while other fhips kept to windward), gave battle to the Poder, and, at the firft broadfide, killed twenty-feven of her men, and difmounted feven of her lower-deck guns *.

F, The French, ftill on the larboard tack, and far ahead.

134. G, The Royal Philip preferved from the flames, but a perfect wreck. Such a confternation took place on board, upon the approach of the fire-fhip, that many of her crew leaped overboard and were drowned.

135. H, The fternmoft fhips of the enemy firing at the fire-fhip as fhe was coming down, but did not feem to reach her.

A,

---

* In a little time afterwards, the Poder, lowering her colours, was boarded, at one and the fame time, by boats fent from feveral fhips of the Britifh fleet; but the commander, like a true Spaniard, declaring that he had ftruck to the Berwick only, delivered up his fword to the officer from that fhip.

A, (Plate XVI. fig. 4.)   Mr LESTOCK ſtill aſtern ; but it is ſaid had very little wind.

B, Mr MATHEWS, in the Namur, got to windward, Mr LESTOCK having ſaid, that, ſoon after the engagement began, he (MATHEWS) quitted his ſtation, and left the Marlborough M, in the heat of action.

C, The van of the Britiſh, now upon a contrary tack, and re-turning to join the centre.

E, The Berwick quitting the Poder.

F, The centre and van of the enemy now upon the ſtarboard tack, and doubling back to ſupport their rear, conceived to be in great danger.

G, The Royal Philip ; H, the five ſhips in his rear.

136. I, The Poder, which was retaken by the French, with a Lieutenant of the Berwick and twenty-three men on board.

N. B.—At this period (ſays Mr LESTOCK) Admiral MA-
THEWS thought proper to haul down both ſignals, that for engaging, and alſo that for line of battle.

A, (Plate XVI. fig. 5.)   Mr LESTOCK, with his diviſion, (as he has ſaid himſelf), falling into the line of battle ahead, ac-cording to the ſignal then abroad.

137. B, Mr MATHEWS, at half an hour after five, again made the ſignal of line of battle ahead, and put about ; but there be-ing little wind, ſome ſhips tacked, and others wore, as did the Admiral himſelf, and formed the line of battle ahead on the other tack, viz. the ſtarboard, leaving the Poder, as Mr LESTOCK ſays,

to

to be retaken by the French fquadron, with the Berwick's Lieutenant and twenty-three of her men. So precipitate was his
flight from the French (fays he) that there was not time to fave
his men.

> N. B.—Admitting all this fpeed and hurry, it might have been
> faid that Mr MATHEWS rejoined his rear,—not that his
> rear had advanced much to fupport and rejoin him, as Mr
> LESTOCK would have it believed, when pointing out his
> own fituation.

C, Mr ROWLEY, with the van, ftanding after the centre of
the fleet.

D, *The four fhips*, the Dorfetfhire, Effex, Rupert, and Royal
Oak, firing at the five fhips in the Spanifh rear, now within gun-
fhot, having fallen to leeward in wearing, when the Admiral did.

138. F, The French fquadron paffing the Britifh van, within piftol-fhot, (as has been faid), but without firing a fhot, being
intent only on difengaging the Spanifh fquadron in the rear,
which ought to have been taken or deftroyed long before this
time, even without Mr LESTOCK's affiftance, had every one
done their duty.

G, The Spanifh Admiral.

H, The five Spanifh fhips firing at the four fhips, now on
contrary tacks, and thought to be within reach.

I, The Poder, retaken by the French.

K, The Marlborough in tow, with frigates attending on her,
on her way to Mahon.

Night.

Night coming on, the combined fleets being to leeward, carried off their difabled fhips, by having them in tow, and taking with them the Lieutenant of the Berwick, with twenty-three of her men, who had been put cn board the Poder, and quitted her, where fhe was afterwards burned by the Effex.

Without entering into the merits of the difpute between Meffrs MATHEWS and LESTOCK, what might have been the moft proper time for giving the fignal for bearing down to clofe engagement, we have no doubt that the following obfervations will now be found juft :

139. That, if Mr MATHEWS and his feconds had been properly fupported, the greateft part of the Spanifh rear might have been cut off : Therefore, that the attack made by him upon the rear of the enemy, as it was fo far feparated from the centre and van, was both bold and well defigned at the time.

140. That, as Mr ROWLEY's pofition with the van did overawe the van of the enemy, it was a proper one.

141. That it is evident that the French, on this occafion, as as well as on all the others that have followed fince that time, had the fafety and prefervation of their fhips only as the principal thing in view.

142. Again, from this battle, we may be able to form fome judgment of the effect of cannon-fhot, with refpect to diftance.

The

The Royal Philip, the Spanifh Admiral *, in his combat with the Britifh Admiral and his feconds, had all his rigging deftroyed, not a top-maft left ftanding on end, his main-yard upon the deck, and two or three port-holes beat into one. He had 238 men killed, and 262 wounded.

The Conftant, the Spanifh Admiral's fecond ahead, during the fhort time fhe ftaid, had 25 men killed, and 43 wounded.

On the other hand, the Marlborough, oppofed to the Spanifh Admiral and his feconds, had her main and mizen-mafts beat overboard, and, though otherwife a wreck, had her enfign nailed to the ftump of the mizen-maft which remained. She had 43 men killed, and 128 wounded ;—amongft the firft was Captain CORNWALL, her brave commander, and Captain GODFREY of the marines.

143. Great and dreadful as thefe effects were, yet the diftance between the combatants muft have been very confiderable, that could have admitted of a fire-fhip being put in motion, fet on fire, time for her men to take to their boats, to quit her, and to get off, and, laftly, to blow up without injury to fo many fhips furrounding her. After fo many circumftances being allowed to take place, can the diftance be thought to be lefs than 400 or 500 yards at leaft ?

144.

*	Guns.	Men.	BRITISH FORCE.		
				Guns.	Men.
Royal Philip	114	1350	Norfolk	80	600
Ifabella	80	900	Namur	90	780
Conftant	70	750	Marlborough	90	750
	264	3000		260	2130

Plate XVI. Part I. p. 110.

Engagement of Admiral Mathews with the combined
Fleets of France & Spain 11. Feb.r 1744.

Fig. 1.

N.º 127.

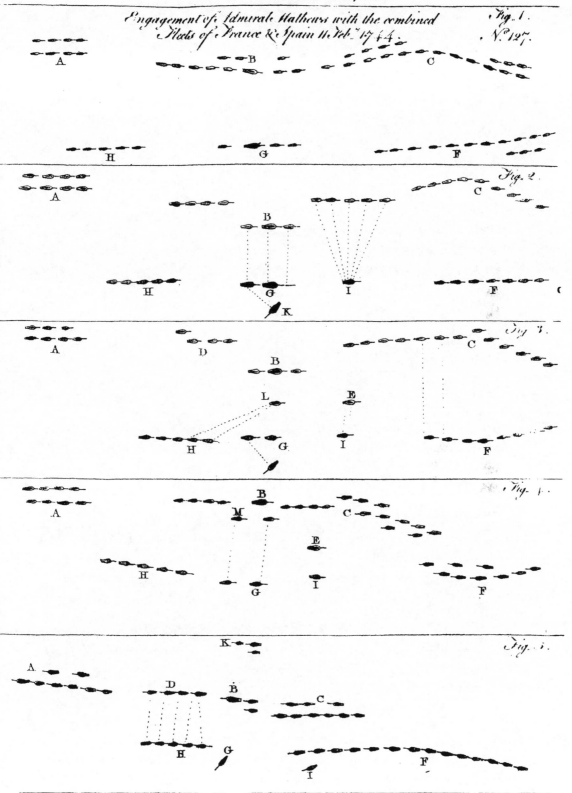

144. Again, the Poder of 64 guns, another Spanish ship, after having been exposed a long time to a cannonade from five ships in the British line, without having suffered material damage (vid. No. 14.); yet the first broadside from the Berwick (which had broke the foresaid line, and had approached within half musket-shot *) killed twenty-seven of her men, dismounted seven of her lower-deck guns; and, when she struck to the Berwick, had not a mast standing.

145. A General at the head of his troops, and leading them on to action, has long been considered as a sufficient signal; and Mr MATHEWS's ship, when going down to battle, as Admiral, in the centre, should have been the example for his whole fleet, whether the signal was given at ten or twelve o'clock. The brave commanders of the Norfolk and Marlborough, his seconds, were of this mind; as has also been Sir GEORGE RODNEY upon a later occasion: Therefore, every ship which kept her wind, and did not follow the Admiral, Mr MATHEWS, down to fight the enemy, ought only to be considered as breakers of the line. *And hence that Sentence of the Court-Martial which broke Mr* MATHEWS, *ought virtually to be considered as the source of all the many naval miscarriages since.*

Q   SEC-

---

* The distance between these two ships at this time may be supposed to be about 400 or 500 yards, not less than that between the two opponent flag ships. The boats from several ships of the British fleet getting on board the Poder when she struck, at one and the same time, is in some degree a confirmation of this opinion.

SECTION IV.

146. ADMIRAL PARKER'S ACCOUNT OF THE ENGAGEMENT
WITH THE DUTCH ON THE DOGGER BANK, 5TH AUGUST
1781. *

' Yefterday morning we fell in with the Dutch fquadron, with
' a large convoy, on the Dogger Bank. I was happy to find I
' had the wind of them, as the great number of their large fri-
' gates might otherwife have endangered my convoy. Having
' feparated the men of war from the merchant fhips, and made a
' fignal to the laft to keep their wind, I bore away, with a ge-
' neral fignal to chafe. The enemy formed their line, confifting
' of eight two-decked fhips, on the ftarboard tack. Ours, in-
' cluding the Dolphin of forty-four guns, confifted of feven.
' Not a gun was fired on either fide until within the diftance of
' half mufket-fhot. The Fortitude being then abreaft of the
' Dutch Admiral, the action began, and continued with an un-
' ceafing fire for three hours and forty minutes. By this time our
' fhips were unmanageable. I made an effort to form the line,
' in order to renew the action ; but found it impracticable. The
' Bienfaifant had loft her main top-maft, and the Buffalo her
' fore-yard ; the reft of the fhips were not lefs fhattered in their
' mafts, rigging, and fails ; the enemy appeared to be in as bad a
' condition. Both fquadrons *lay-to* a confiderable time near each
' other,

---

* Britifh, feven fhips, four frigates.   Dutch, eight fhips of two decks.

' other, when the Dutch, with their convoy, bore away for the
' Texel. We were not in a condition to follow them.'

147. This affair, though in itself greatly different from the
many we have had with another enemy, yet, with refpect to the
fubject before us, viz. the mode of attack, is perfectly fimilar.
The gallantry of the Dutch refufing to fire a gun until the Britifh Admiral fhould have made choice of his diftance, could have
no prior influence upon the determination of the Britifh Admiral
in his mode of attack; nor will it make any other difference in
the manner the French may afterwards receive us, than to re-
double their anxiety not to lofe the leaft poffible chance of annoying our fhips, let the diftance be what it will, whenever we
fhall be difpofed to attack them.

148. Though this battle has a greater refemblance to the old
Dutch than the prefent French manner of fighting, we cannot
help recalling to remembrance thofe glorious and obftinate conflicts of former times, which did fo much honour to both nations.

SECTION V.

GENERAL OBSERVATIONS.

149. From thefe examples, it appears, that the attack, in every
one of them, without variation, has been made by a long ex-

Q 2

tended.

tended line, generally from the windward quarter, by fteering or directing every individual fhip of that line upon her oppofite of the enemy, but more particularly the fhips in the van.

150. That the confequences of this mode of attack have proved fatal in every attempt; that is, our fhips have been fo difabled, and fo ill fupported, that the enemy have been permitted not to only to make fail and leave us, but, to complete the difgrace, have, in paffing, been permitted to pour in the fire of their whole line upon our van, without a poffibility of retaliation on our part *. The caufe, then, of thefe mifcarriages, can never be faid to have proceeded from a fault in our fhipping, and far lefs from a want of fpirit in our feamen.

151. And, though we have not yet been fo happy as to fee their innate naval fpirit exerted with advantage in the greater fights, we may yet have the confolation of being affured, even from thefe examples, that it does exift, if we take into confidera-tion the habitual defire they conftantly have fhewn of making the attack, in fpite of every difcouraging affront: On the other hand, that the enemy may juftly be faid to have it not in that degree, if we confider the habitual defire they have conftantly fhewn, as well in avoiding, as in refufing to make the attack.

152. From the mode of this attack, followed throughout moft of the examples we have given, it would feem that an idea had been formed, *by* ftopping the van, *of taking, deftroy-ing,*

* Section I. No. 38.

ing, or difabling the whole of the enemy's line*. The event has proved this attempt impracticable.   But will not this idea be alfo found contradictory to the general complaint of the deficiency of our fhips in point of failing?   For, if this deficiency is a truth, would it not have been more natural, upon a chafe of the enemy, to make fure of the floweft failing veffels to be found in the rear, than to attempt to get up with the fwifteft fhips to be found in the van?

153.   Another reflection will naturally occur :   That, by the great deftruction of rigging, the confequence of this mode of attack, the nation has been thrown into a moft enormous expence of repair, while our enemy, by their cautious conduct, preferving their fhips often unhurt, has been enabled not only to protract the war, but, if perfifted in, will, without doubt, enfure the poffeffion, perhaps, of a fuperior navy, complete and entire to the conclufion.

154.   Having now demonftrated, from evidence which fhould be fatisfactory, that the mode or inftructions hitherto followed for arranging great fleets in line, fo as to be able to force an enemy to give battle on equal terms, muft be fomewhere wrong, it will be required to fhow whether any other mode may be devifed, or put in practice, that will have a better effect.

But, as nothing can be devifed of worfe confequence than what has fo long and repeatedly been put in practice, an offer of

any

---

* Nos. 32. and 58.

any thing new, it is to be hoped, may be examined with that attention which the importance of the fubject demands.

By the phrafe *new*, is not here meant, that what follows was
never either fpoke of, or thought of before; but it is furely fo
far new, as never to have been put in demonftration by writing;
nor is there any examples of its having been put in practice in
actual combat.

155. But, if the method or practice of bringing fingle fhips
into action has been found, by long experience, to fucceed fo
well, why fhould not this practice, in fome degree, be applied
to numerous fleets? And if we have proved that the intrepidity
and perfeverance of our feamen muft be equal, if not fuperior, to
the enemy, ought we not at once to endeavour to bring this
fuperiority to avail us where it beft can, that is, in getting as clofe
alongfide of the enemy as poffible?   And that this may be done,
not only upon equal, but upon far fuperior terms, will be endeavoured to be proved by demonftration in the following mode
of attack.

MODE

MODE OF ATTACK PROPOSED.

SECTION I.

THE ATTACK FROM THE WINDWARD UPON THE REAR OF THE ENEMY.

156. Suppofe a fleet of ten, twenty, or more fhips, extended in line of battle at F, (Plate XVII. fig. 1.), endeavouring to avoid a clofe engagement, but, at the fame time, keeping under an eafy fail, with the intention of receiving the ufual attack from another fleet of equal number, three or four miles to windward, at B, failing in any form; but let it be in three lines or divifions: It is required, by what method fhall B make the attack on F with advantage?

The improbability, or rather impoffibility, of attacking and carrying the enemy's whole line of fhips having already been demonftrated (Vid. Nos. 32. 38.), the next confideration will be, How many fhips may be attacked and carried with advantage? Let it be fuppofed that the three fternmoft fhips only, and not exceeding the fourth, are poffible to be *carried*; let a fufficient ftrength, A, be fent down to force an attack upon thefe three fhips, difpofed

and

and fupported according to the judgement of the Admiral, while, in the mean time, he fhould keep to windward with the reft of his fleet, formed into fuch divifions as might beft enable him to attend to the motions of the enemy, and the effect of 'his attack; being himfelf fo far difengaged from action, as to be able to make his obfervations, and give his orders, with fome degree of tranquillity.

157. By placing the fleet B in the divifion (as in Plate XVII. fig. 2.), means only that the attacking fleet fhall be fo difpofed, and fo connected together, as to be able to give the fupport and attention that may be required to any fhip, or any part of the fleet, and in preference to a long extended line of fix or feven miles in length (No. 25.), where it muft be impracticable to give the neceffary fupport to fuch fhips as may be difabled *.

─────────

SECTION II.

ATTACK UPON THE ENEMY'S THREE STERNMOST SHIPS MORE PARTICULARLY.

158. Though the number of fhips contained in each fquadron may, by many, be thought a proper rule for determining the number of the fhips to be attacked, yet, as there will be next to a certainty of carrying three, we would choofe to keep

by

---

* Vid. Section IV. No. 15.

by that number. Wherefore, although it may afterwards be found proper to give other opinions, and to enter into a fuller difcuffion of the choice, and the beft arrangement of the particular fhips deftined for the approaching, and making this attack, it is neceffary here to carry on the following demonftration upon the fuppofition of three fhips being the number proper to be attempted.

159. It will be evident, however, that the headmoft, or fwifteft failing fhips of B may get clofe along-fide of the fternmoft of the enemy F, even though the fhips of F fhould, in general, be fafter failers than thofe of B; *an opinion which, for argument's fake alone, fhall be for once admitted.* But it will not, therefore, be admitted, that every individual fhip of a great fleet, or even of the number 15, as in the figure, will be able to outfail every individual fhip of a numerous Britifh fleet, or even of the number 15, as in the plan. Therefore, there will be a neceffity that the fwifteft fhips of B muft come up along-fide of the fternmoft and dulleft failing fhips of the enemy F; while, at the fame time, F (by an attempt of outfailing B) muft be thrown into the diforder of a downright flight: Therefore, of courfe, it muft be admitted, that, if the enemy F continues going off in line of battle, and endeavouring to avoid a clofe engagement, it will be impoffible to prevent the fleet making the attack from getting into the pofition of figure 2.

160. By this pofition, then, it is evident, that thefe three fhips at I, will be in the power of the Admiral of B. For, by keeping

R   fo

fo many fhips to windward, he will be enabled to fend down frefh fhips from time to time, either for the fupport, or to fupply the ftation of any of thofe that may be difabled in making the attack, while it may be imagined, that the three fhips in queftion, by being difabled, or being deprived of the wind, now taken out of their fails by the fhips to windward, will be prevented from following their friends.

161.   From hence the enemy ahead muft either abandon his three fternmoft fhips, or he muft double back to fupport them, which muft be done either by tacking or by wearing.   But let it be firft examined what is naturally to be done by tacking, and for the greater fatisfaction, let every poffible cafe that can happen be examined feparately.

―――――――

SECTION III.

THE ENEMY'S ATTEMPT TO SUPPORT HIS THREE STERN-MOST SHIPS BY TACKING HIS FLEET.

162.   (Plate XVII. fig. 3.)   Firft let us fuppofe, that the enemy at F has continued to protract his courfe in line of battle, upon the fame tack, and that the headmoft fhip H, with the three next aftern of her, have tacked to windward, and that the whole remaining fhips intend to tack the fame way, but in fucceffion (as in fig. 3.),

is

is it not evident, that F has then left his three sternmoft ships, at I, in the power of the ships at A; that he muft alfo leave expofed his fourth and fifth ship G to another attack from another divi-fion of the Britifh at C, which will alfo be on equal terms as with his three sternmoft at I; and, laftly, if he profecutes his inten-tion of fupporting his three ships, he will be obliged to begin a difadvantageous attack upon the Admiral, with the main body of the fleet lying ready to receive him.

163. (Plate XVII. fig. 4.) The confequence of all which will be, that he will not only lofe his three sternmoft ships, but, in all probability, the fourth and fifth alfo, as at G in fig. 4., and will be forced to begin an attack, and clofe, and mix, ship with ship, on equal terms; a fituation which he, at all times, with the greateft anxiety, hath avoided, and we, with equal anxiety, have always courted.

164. (Plate XVII. fig. 5.) Again, fuppofe that his three stern-moft ships have been attacked, and that he shall order his fleet to tack all at one time, as in fig. 5. The confequences will then be, that this movement having required fome time, and fome length of courfe, will have produced a confiderable diftance between his main body and his three ships; or, in other words, that they have been deferted; for it will not be in their power to tack with the reft of their friends.

165. He muft alfo, in bringing his ships heads round, expofe the ships neareft his enemy to be raked by a dreadful cannonade.

166.   (Plate XVIII. fig. 6.)   He muſt alſo run the riſk of having his fleet thrown into a general diſorder, by many of his ſhips miſſing ſtays, wearing, and running to leeward, as in fig. 6.   Laſtly, upon a ſuppoſition that his ſhips have all tacked, and none of them miſſed ſtays, ſtill he muſt, of neceſſity, begin the attack, mix ſhips, and come to a cloſe engagement, as in the former caſe.

SECTION IV.

THE ENEMY'S ATTEMPT TO SUPPORT HIS THREE STERN-MOST SHIPS, BY WEARING HIS FLEET.

167.   Having ſhewn the conſequences of an attempt to wind-ward, let us alſo examine what may be expected from an attempt to leeward.   Suppoſe the two fleets in the ſame poſition as in Plate XVII. fig. 2.; that is, the main body of the enemy ex-tended in line of battle to leeward, his three ſternmoſt ſhips en-tangled with the fleet B, whoſe Admiral, with the main body, keeps to windward, to obſerve, with a rigid attention, the motions of the enemy.

168.   (Plate XVIII. fig. 7.)   At the ſame time, ſuppoſe that the Admiral F has ordered his ſternmoſt ſhip G to wear, and

afterwards

afterwards the whole line, and that he is now running upon a contrary tack to leeward, as at H, wifhing to fupport or bring off his three fhips.

From infpection, it will be evident, that this attempt may be more dangerous than the attempt to windward; for it will expofe a number of his fhips to a raking fire while in the act of wearing, and the fquadron, by getting fo far to leeward, will be unable to give the proper fupport to the three fhips.

It will open a gap for the fleet of B (who will immediately wear alfo, and follow him) to break in, as at A, and cut off the three fhips, without hope of recovery.

And, if F fhall ftill perfift in the endeavour to recover his three fhips, he will be obliged to begin the attack, under all the ufual difadvantages.

169. (Plate XVIII. fig. 8.) Again, upon another fuppofi- tion, that the headmoft fhip of the enemy H, with the four or five next aftern, have wore, and are running upon a contrary tack, wifhing, as before, to fupport or bring off the three fhips, the reft of the fleet intending to wear alfo, and follow in fuccef- fion, is it not evident that this movement, being more unfeaman- like, will be worfe than the laft?

It will expofe an additional number of fhips, particularly the laft two, as at G, and will, at the fame time, make an opening for the main body of B's fleet to fall in and cut off the three fhips, as in the former cafe.

170.

170. (Plate XVIII. fig. 9.) Again, fhould the enemy F wear and bear away with his whole fhips at one and the fame time, as in fig. 9., it is evident that this movement muft have the confequence of a downright flight, with the certainty of lofing the three fhips.

171. Laftly, upon the fuppofition that fuch an attack has been made, and that the three fhips are entangled, it generally follows, that, though the wind may be blowing a frefh gale at the beginning of the battle, yet it often falls away fo much from the effect of a violent cannonade, that it may be impoffible for the headmoft fhips of F's fleet to give the leaft affiftance to his fhips diftreffed in his rear.

172. From what has been faid, it will appear, that a fleet B, keeping connected in a body to windward, *may* come up with, and entangle the three fternmoft fhips of an enemy F, extended in line of battle, and going off to leeward, and, at the fame time, be able to overawe the remaining main body of their fleet; and that, having forced the pofition, as in plan 2d, the whole confequences, as already defcribed, muft follow; that is, F muft fubmit to the lofs of three fhips.

What has been hitherto faid proceeds upon a fuppofition, that the fleet F has kept on his courfe till the fleet B has come up with his rear; let it then be examined what other attempts the enemy F can make to avoid coming to clofe engagement upon equal terms.

SEC-

Plate XVII. Part I. p. 30.

Mode of Attack proposed.

Fig. 1.
Nº 156.

B

F

Fig. 2.
Nº 157.

B

A

I

F

Fig. 3.
Nº 162.

B

H

A

C

I

G

F

Fig. 4.
Nº 163.

B

H

A

I

G

F

Fig. 5.
Nº 164.

B

A

F

SECTION V.

THE ENEMY ENDEAVOURING TO AVOID THE ATTACK UPON
HIS REAR, BY WEARING, AND PASSING ON CONTRARY
TACKS TO LEEWARD.

173.   (Plate XVIII. fig. 10.)   Suppofe a fleet of fhips of the
enemy ftanding on the larboard tack to leeward, and going off
as before at F, and a fleet of fhips in a collected ftate or pofition
to windward, as at B, fig. 10.

174.   (Plate XIX. fig. 11. and 12.)   And fuppofe that the
enemy F, perceiving the fleet B pointing an attack againft his
rear, as in fig. 11.; and that, in place of keeping on his courfe
upon the fame tack, he fhould wear, and endeavour to pafs on
contrary tacks to leeward, (for it will not be admitted that he
can get to windward, fee plan 12.), What will then be the
effect ?

175.   Is it not evident, that the headmoft fhips of F muft be
forced to leeward by the fleet B obftructing his line of direction,
or the line of his courfe ?   They muft be forced to begin an attack at any diftance B may choofe.

176.

176. (Plate XIX. fig. 13.) That they may receive such damage as will ſtop their way: That their way being ſtopped, will
of courſe be an obſtruction to the next aſtern; or, that theſe
ſubſequent ſhips, to prevent this ſtop, muſt bear away to leeward
of their crippled ſhips, as at G, which will not only prevent theſe
ſhips from damaging the headmoſt ſhips of B, but will give time
and opportunity to B to bring down his windward ſhips to fall in,
either ahead or aſtern, that is, to the right or left, of his headmoſt ſhips A, and oppoſe ſhip for ſhip of the enemy upon equal
terms. *Vide* fig. 13. plate 19.

177. But, ſhould none of the headmoſt ſhips of the ſquadron
F be crippled; that is, ſhould F paſs B without reach of cannon-
ſhot, which undoubtedly he will do, ſtill, while bearing away,
he may be forced to ſuffer a diſtant cannonade, ſhip with ſhip,
on equal terms.

178. (Plate XIX. fig. 14.) Whether he wears and gets
back upon his former tack, as at G, in fig. 14.

179. Or continues to run before the wind, as at P, in fig. 15.

180. (Plate XX. fig. 16.) But, if F perſiſts to paſs on a
contrary tack to leeward, and without reach of cannon-ſhot, is it
not evident, that B muſt ſome time or other come up with the
rear of F, whether B ſhall, at any time, be abreaſt of his centre,
as in fig. 16. ?

181.

Plate XVIII. Part 1. p. 132.

Mode of Attack proposed.

Fig. 6.
N. 166.

B

A

F

Fig. 7.
N.º 168.

B

A

G

F

H

Fig. 8.
N. 169.

G

H

Fig. 9.
N. 170.

B

F

Fig. 10.
N.º 173.

B

F

Plate XIX. Part I. p. 132.

Mode of Attack proposed.

Fig. 11.
Nº 174.

B

F

Fig. 12.
Nº 174.

B

F

Fig. 13.
Nº 176.

B

A

F

G

Fig. 14.
Nº 178.

F

B

G

Fig. 15.

B

F

181.   Or of his rear, (as in fig. 17. plate XX.)

182.   Or whether F puts right before the wind, (as in fig. 18. plate XX.)

Or runs off, fhip by fhip, as he beft can, (as in fig. 19. plate XX.)

=========

SECTION VI.

THE EFFECT AND CONSEQUENCES OF THE WIND SHIFT-
ING DURING THE ATTACK FROM THE WINDWARD,
CONSIDERED; IN WHICH SHALL BE ENDEAVOURED TO
BE COMPREHENDED EVERY CASE, AS WELL POSSIBLE,
AS WHAT MAY BE PROBABLE.

183.   So far the attack has proceeded with the wind fixed in one and the fame quarter.   To make the demonftration the more complete, it will be neceffary to inquire, What might be the effect produced by a change of wind, fhould that take place during the action? For this purpofe, let the opponent fleets be placed in fome one of the preceding pofitions, reprefenting the attack upon the three fternmoft fhips of the enemy (as in fig. 20. Plate XXI. *Vid.* No. 158. Plate XVII. fig. 2.)

S.

In

In which the fleet defirous of making the attack is reprefented in four divifions, as at B B B, A.

F, The fleet defirous of avoiding the attack, and abandoning his three fternmoft fhips at G.

<hr>

CASE I.

THE WIND SHIFTING BY DEGREES, AND COMING AFT.

184. In the commencement of the attack, let us fuppofe the wind, from being in the north at N, on the firft onfet, that it fhall come more and more after and by the weftern quarter to K. Then it is evident, by the difpofition of the two fleets, that the fleet F, by fuch change, will have acquired no advantage whatever; on the contrary, it will thereby be thrown juft fo much the farther to leeward.

<hr>

CASE II.

THE WIND SHIFTING AND COMING BY DEGREES ROUND AHEAD.

185. Again, if the wind, by taking an oppofite courfe, fhall fhift ahead, and fhall come round by the eaftern quarter to L (Plate XXI. fig. 21.), neither will F have it in his power to avail himfelf of this, providing the fleet B, in continuing carefully to

attend

Plate XX. Part I. p. 424.

Mode of Attack proposed.

Fig. 16.
N.º 180.

B

F

Fig. 17.

B

F

Fig. 18.

B

F

Fig. 19.

B

F

attend his motions, and, affected by the impulfe of the veering wind, fhall ftretch his fleet to leeward of him, but, at the fame time, to windward of the fhips as at O O, fhould F endeavour, by bearing round-up, to rejoin his own fhips that are engaged in the rear at G.

186. (Plate XXI. fig. 22.) Reprefenting both fleets on the ftarboard tack, fhows, at the fame time, that F has not thereby acquired any advantage.

CASE III.

OF THE EFFECT, SUPPOSING THE WIND TO VEER CONTINUEDLY ROUND AHEAD.

187. Again, upon the fuppofition that F, by this laft change, has now gained the wind (*Vide* Plate XXII. fig. 23.), it will not be denied that, in this cafe, he may maintain it, and that it may be poffible for him to make a circular courfe R R R to windward of B, keeping the wind, as it may be difpofed to veer round, by the eaftern quarter, from the north at N to the fouth at S, or to the weft at K, or even round to the north at N, from whence it fet out; but, as he can be attended all the while by the fleet B, who will cut him off to leeward, he never will be able to recover his three fhips at G.

CASE

━━━━━━━━

C A S E IV.

THE WIND, IN ONE INSTANT, SHIFTING IN DIRECT OPPOSITION.

188. Laftly, If the wind, in changing, fhall, in one inftant, fhift in direct oppofition to where it was when the attack began, that is, from the north at N to the fouth at S (*Vide* Plate XXII. fig. 24.), then, and in that cafe, before one can judge whether fuch change fhall be favourable for F or not, it will be neceffary that the relative fituation of the two fleets fhould be determined fuch as it was when the change took place. For example :

189. If the headmoft fhips of the fleet F, that is, if his van and centre fhall have feparated at any confiderable diftance from his rear, as per Plate XXIII. fig. 24.

190. Or if, in the farther profecution of this mode of attack, it fhall have advanced to the pofition reprefented in fig. 25. ; * it is evident, in both cafes, that F, though, by this change, he fhall have got to windward, yet, notwithftanding, he will not be able to avail himfelf of this feeming advantage, the fleet B having it ftill in their power to cut him off from his three fhips.

191. On the other hand, if this inftantaneous change of wind, in direct oppofition, fhall have taken place more early in the action,

━━━━━━━━
* *Vide* Plate XVIII. fig. 7. No. 168.

tion, that is, when the pofitions of the two fleets fhall be fuch as reprefented in fig. 26. Plate XXIII. viz.

The fleet B in the pofition of four divifions B B B and A, and the enemy in the pofitions F and G.

Then F, who before was to leeward, by this inftantaneous change of wind from the north (at N) to the fouth (at S), having now got to windward of every divifion of the fleet B, is it not evident, that it may be practicable for him to carry affiftance to his three fhips (at G) in the rear, and, perhaps, even to cut off fome one of B's fhips (at A), if they do not, with all convenient fpeed, bear away (as at C C), to put themfelves under the protection of their friends (B) to leeward?

192. But whether he (F) fhall attempt to effect this manœuvre, by wearing his fhips in the line (as at H H), or, what feems moft eligible, by making his fhips tack (as at I I), as it is to be prefumed that his three fhips, which have been fome time engaged, muft be confiderably crippled, and not able to make fufficient fail, while endeavouring to bring them off, it will be difficult for him to prevent being drawn into a general and clofe engagement, which, by the fuppofition, he has all along endeavoured to avoid.

193. A farther profecution of demonftrations, which are likely to lead us on to the *attack from the leeward*, we think proper to decline for the prefent. It is a new fubject, and, of itfelf, re-

quires

quires a feparate difcuffion. We will therefore proceed to bring into view thofe other accidents only which more immediately can
affect the *attack from the windward*; not that fuch can be attended with confequences much different from what have already been
treated of, but, the ideas once being ftarted, and having great apparent importance, it becomes neceffary to give them a full inveftigation.

SECTION VII.

OF PARTIAL BREEZES OF WIND.

194. *When the fleet in purfuit fhall be favoured with a breeze
of wind, while the fleet defirous of avoiding the attack fhall be becalmed;*

(Plate XXI. fig. 20.) Is it not felf-evident, how unfavourable this muft be for the enemy F? He will thereby be the more
eafily overtaken in the purfuit; and, fhould the attack be begun
upon his three fhips, they will with the greater certainty be
ruined.

195. *When the fleet defirous of avoiding the attack fhall be favoured with the breeze, while the fleet in purfuit fhall be becalmed.*

It being evident, that the enemy (F) will have it in his power to
make his efcape with his whole fleet, if this partial breeze in his fa-

vour

vour fhall take place before the attack has begun, we fhall pafs on to the oppofite cafe.

When the attack upon the three fhips fhall have commenced before this partial breeze in favour of F, the fleet purfued, has taken place.

196. (Plate XXI. fig. 20.) The variety of pofitions in which the two fleets may be affected is fo great, and the confequences which can be fuppofed attendant on this cafe fo numerous, it will not be attempted to give a feparate difcuffion of each. The reader, however, by applying his own ideas upon the fubject to the plans before him * will be able to fupply this for himfelf. In the mean time, as it is imagined nothing in fuch inveftigation will be found that can materially affect the general iffue, and fince no breeze whatever can favour the fleet F, fo as to enable it to fail round and round the fleet B, (the fleet B all the while fuppofed to be lying becalmed), it will not be too much to fay, that *this partial breeze in favour of the fleet F, taking place after the attack began,* although it may facilitate the efcape of his van and centre, will not avail him much in the recovery of the three fhips in his rear, perhaps not in any cafe as yet exhibited, excepting in this one, where the wind, in one inftant, had fhifted in direct oppofition, No. 191.

When the attack fhall have commenced before the partial breeze in favour of F, the fleet purfued, has taken place, fuppofing the wind in one inftant to have fhifted in direct oppofition.

197.

---

* Comprehended in Plates 17. 18. 19. 20. 21. 22. 23.

197.   That, even in this cafe, No. 191. (Plate XXIII. fig. 26.), the fame breeze which would favour F in the attempt to bring off his three fhips, would, at the fame time, favour the efcape of the fhips of B at A, as formerly defcribed.   That this partial breeze would require to be of confiderable duration, otherwife F, in thus attempting to bring off his three fhips, crippled as they will be, muft hazard a general engagement, in like manner as already defcribed, No. 192.

S E C T I O N   VIII.

OF WINDS BLOWING IN CONTRARY DIRECTIONS.

198.   In fuppofing, at any place, the exiftence of two diftinct ftreams of wind actually blowing in oppofite directions, the one from the north (for example), the other from the fouth, or from any two other oppofite points of the compafs; at that place alfo muft be fuppofed an intermediate fpace, a line of feparation between the two ftreams, parallel to both, and to be often diftinguifhed by a fort of calm upon the furface of the water, occafioned by the eddy winds partaking of the effect of the adjacent and contrary ftreams.

199.   That the requifite examples may the more eafily be exhibited, fuppofe Plate XXIV. to reprefent a fpace at fea, in which

two

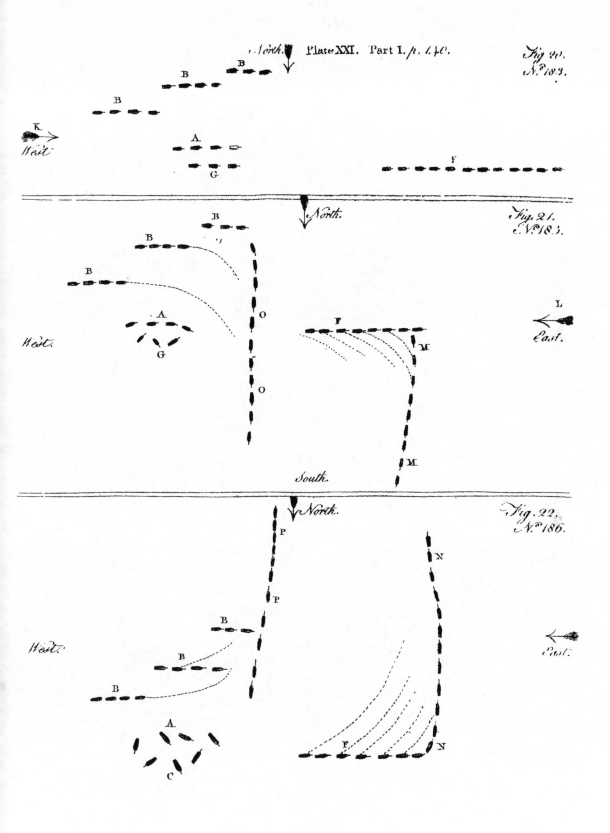

North. Plate XXI. Part I. p. 140. Fig. 20. N.° 183.

Fig. 21. N.° 185.

Fig. 22. N.° 186.

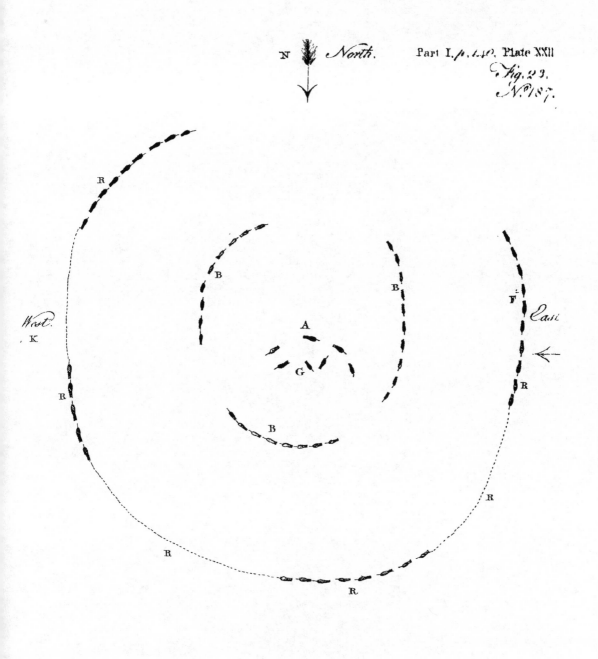

B

B

B

A

G

F

S South.

N North.

Fig. 25.
N.º 190.

B

A

G

B

B

F

S South.

N North.

Fig. 26.
N.º 191.

B

B

C C

B

A

G

H

H

F

I

I

S South.

two diftinct ftreams of wind are difcovered blowing from oppofite directions, the wind N N on the left fide of the plate blowing
down the page from the north, and the wind S S on the right
blowing up the page from the fouth, and let Y Y be the line of
feparation between the two ftreams ; under which defcription alfo,
let Plate XXV. be comprehended, and let the ufual characters
ferve to diftinguifh the different parts, viz.

B, the fleet in purfuit ;

F, the fleet purfued ;

G, the three fhips attacked ;

A, the four fhips making the attack.

200.   Now, whether fhips fhall be going large (as in fig. 1.),
or clofe haul'd. (as in fig. 2.), or running with the wind on the
beam (as in fig. 3.), ftill their encounter with the line of feparation Y Y will be fimilar, and to the fame effect ; and in no other
direction whatever can fleets encounter this accident of contrary
winds, than what can be comprehended under thefe three cafes.

The letters K L and M (fig. 1. 2. and 3.) reprefent the correfponding cafes, when fleets coming from an oppofite direction
fhall encounter, in like manner, fuch contrary ftreams of wind.

OF FLEETS ENCOUNTERING CONTRARY STREAMS OF WIND,
BEFORE THE ATTACK SHALL BE BEGUN.

201.   For example, after the two opponent fleets have been
manœuvring for fome time in the fame ftream of wind, and have

T

affumed

affumed pofitions as before defcribed, No. 156., or as B and F, (fig. 4. plate 24.) Let us fuppofe F the fartheft ahead, that he has perceived the wind as changing to a direct contrary direction, and, from having had his fhips on a larboard tack, as when at H, that he has got, or muft be getting, his ftarboard tacks aboard, as at F F ; or, in other words, that he has paffed from one ftream of wind, and has got into another, and contrary ftream—is it not evident, if the fleet B fhall ftand on and follow, and fhall get into this new ftream of wind, the fame with his enemy F, that he will be to leeward (as in fig. 5.), and, of courfe, that the mode of his attack muft be changed? (*Vid.* No. 192.)

202. Again, on the other hand, fuppofe B, in declining to ftand on, fhall continue in the northern ftream of wind, as in fig. 6.)—will it not be poffible for him, by putting before the wind, as at C, to recover a pofition A to windward of F, fo foon as ever he fhall choofe to pafs from the one ftream of wind to the other?

CASES AFTER THE ATTACK SHALL BE BEGUN.

203. Plate XXV. fig. 7. reprefents the attack already begun *, and continuing in the northern ftream, while F, abandoning his three fhips, has got into the fouthern ftream with his van and centre.

204.

* Plate XVII. fig. 2. and 3. Nos. 156. 157. 158. 159.

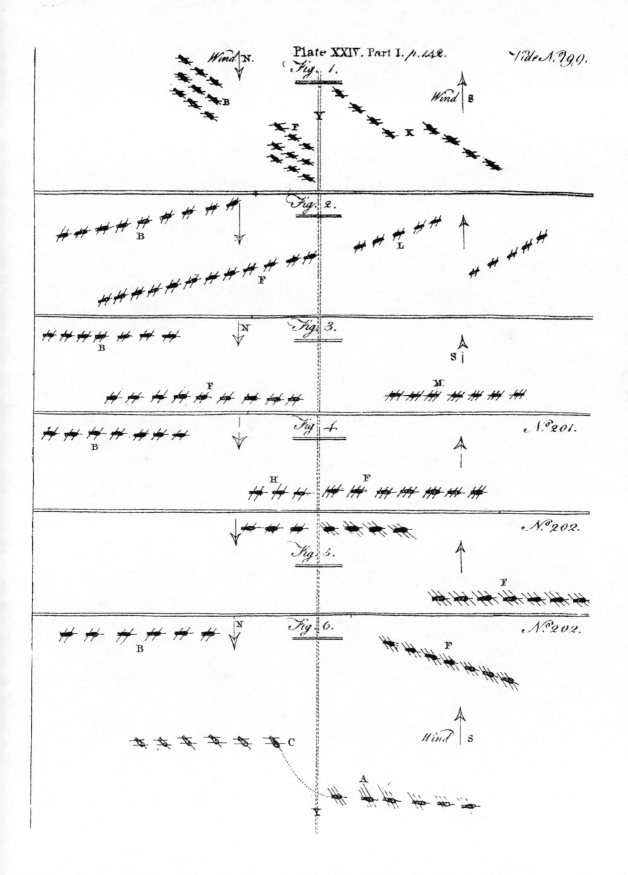

Plate XXIV. Part I. p.142.

Vide N.799.

Fig. 1.

Wind N.

Wind S

B

F

Y

K

Fig. 2.

B

L

F

Fig. 3.

N

S

B

F

M

Fig. 4.

N.°201.

B

H

F

N.°202.

Fig. 5.

F

Fig. 6.

N.°202.

N

B

F

Wind S

C

A

Y

204. (Fig. 8.)   The attack continued in the northern ftream,
and B, with his whole fleet, dropping down the wind together,
evidently will have the advantage of getting to the fouthward
equally with F, the enemy, notwithftanding the efforts of F to
get to windward in the oppofite ftream.

205.   The fleet B in another view (fig. 9.) is reprefented as
aware of the accident before him, and having pufhed ahead with
his van and centre, will be prepared to fupport his attack of the
three fhips, whether he fhall continue in the northern ftream, as
at C, or fhall pafs into the contrary ftream, as at D, (fig. 10.)

206.   (Fig. 11.)   Again, on the other hand, fhould the fleet
B, in continuing the attack, ftand on, as at B B B, and, without
precaution, fhall have followed, and got into the fame ftream
of wind with the enemy F; then F, of confequence, being to
windward, will immediately have it in his power to carry affiftance to his three fhips, but whether by wearing his other fhips
in the line, as at H H, or by tacking, as at I I, will ftill be expofed to the hazard of a general engagement, as before defcribed,
No. 192.

207.   From all which it follows, that a collected and connected fleet of fhips to windward will, on every occafion, be able to
make an advantageous attack upon a fleet of fhips to leeward, and
wifhing to avoid a clofe engagement; and that the attacked fleet,
lying at fuch difadvantage as no manœuvring whatever can com-
penfate, muft be worfted.

T 2.   S E C-

SECTION IX.

·OTHER OPINIONS HOW THIS ATTACK FROM THE WIND- WARD SHOULD BE CONDUCTED.

208. Many eminent feamen, however much they may be convinced that an attack made upon the rear of an enemy's fleet will have a much better chance of fuccefs than in the cafe of an attack upon the whole line, or even on the van, as hitherto practifed, have ftill different opinions how this attack fhould be conducted. Thefe, as given to me, it is proper fhould be laid before the reader, although they are not what I would approve of.

209. (Plate XXVI. fig. 1.) *Firft*, If it is fuppofed that the attack fhall be made by the greater part of the force of B's fleet, coming right before the wind, upon the fix fternmoft fhips of an enemy F, is it not evident, that the fhips of B, by making the attack in this manner, muft be expofed, without a poffibility of return, to as many broadfides from each of thefe fix fhips of F as can be got ready during a courfe of two miles?

Hence, as the faid fhips of B will affuredly be difabled, before they will have it in their power to hurt the enemy, this difadvantage fhould determine the impropriety of this mode.

210.

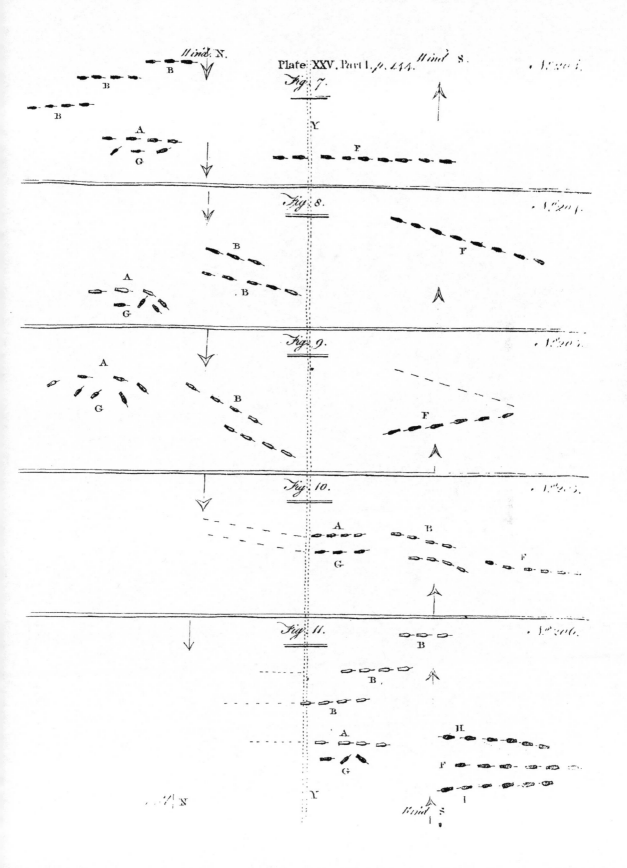

Plate XXV. Part I. p. 444.

Wind N.

Wind S.

N.º206.

Fig. 7.

Fig. 8.

N.º204.

Fig. 9.

N.º205.

Fig. 10.

N.º205.

Fig. 11.

N.º206.

N. N.

Wind S.

210.   (Plate XXVI. fig. 2.)   Suppofe again, that fome part of the force chofen to make the attack fhall be fent to leeward (as at A), as well as to windward of the three fhips determined to be attacked, (as at C.)

But the danger fuppofed, of fhot paffing over the enemy's fhips, and ftriking thofe of friends, may be an objection to this mode.

211.   (Plate XXVI. fig. 3.)   Others have been of opinion, that the headmoft fhip A, chofen to make the attack, fhall come clofe up along-fide of the fternmoft of the enemy, and, having delivered her fire, fhall pufh along the line as far as poffible, which may be fuppofed to be the fixth fhip of the enemy F ; and, as it is evident that this firft fhip A may have received fix broadfides, that is, a broadfide from every one of the fix enemy's fhips, during her courfe in paffing them, it has been thought poffible that the other five fhips C C G C C, by following clofe after her, may attain their ftations, each abreaft of her oppofite, without having received a greater number of broadfides than they have had it in their power to return ; and, therefore, that by this mode the number of fhips to be attacked will be determined : For as many fhips as the leading fhip fhall be able to reach, as many fhips will the attacking fleet be able to carry.

212.   (Plate XXVI. fig. 4.)   A fourth mode of attack, which feems to be compofed from a medium taken from the laft.   Let it be fuppofed, as in the former cafes, that the fleet B has been

brought

brought up to action in a collected manner, but fubdivided only fo far as the fervice may require (as formerly ftated in fig. 2.), and that the leeward divifion A fhall be more particularly deftined for the immediate attack, while, at the fame time, the body of the fleet, keeping to windward, fhall be fuppofed attentive to give the neceffary fupport where required.

Then let it be fuppofed, that the headmoft fhip C, making the attack, having been foon crippled, fhall not have been able to pufh farther than the third or fourth fhip of the enemy's line :

Is it not eafy to conceive, fay they, that fome one, or more, of the fhips to windward, attentive to fupport and fupply her place, may bear down on the fourth fhip of the enemy, under cover of the fmoke, throw in her fire, and pufh on to the fifth or fixth fhip, as at D, or, perhaps, farther ; and that fo far as this frefh fhip D, or a fecond frefh fhip E, may be able to pufh, fo many fhips of the enemy may be expected to be carried ?

For, whatever fhips of the enemy can be got abreaft of, at a proper diftance, *may be difabled, and therefore commanded*, by the numerous frefh fhips kept to windward for this purpofe.

213.   In all the different attacks upon the rear, it has, by fome, been thought a great object, if practicable, to throw a raking fire into the rear of an enemy's line of battle, by fhips detached for that purpofe, as at O.   For if fhot, as has been faid, can take effect at a diftance of two miles, from this pofition it will furely reach the fixth fhip, if the enemy's line fhall be formed at two cables length afunder ; and, if formed at one cable's length afunder, it will reach, and may cripple the twelfth fhip.

SECTION X.

CONCLUSION, WITH GENERAL OBSERVATIONS.

In the preceding Narrative and Demonſtrations, we think it is
ſhown,

214.   1. That Britiſh ſeamen, from the nature, as well as
the greater extent of the navigation upon our coaſts, muſt, of
neceſſity, be ſuperior, both in ſkill and intrepidity, as well as in
number, to thoſe of other nations.

215.   2. That deficiency in point of ſailing, upon many occaſions, evidently has not been the cauſe of theſe late miſcarriages; but, if it has *really* been the cauſe of miſcarriage in others,
is it not high time to ſet about ſuch reformation in our dock-yards
as may recover an equality in a point ſo important? Even ſup-
poſing this to be true, why ſhould we uniformly attempt
getting up with the enemy's van, with a view to carry their
whole fleet, inſtead of contenting ourſelves with a certainty of
cutting off a few of their dulleſt ſailing veſſels in the rear?

216.   3. That the mode of running down the wind in a line,
each ſhip directing her courſe upon her oppoſite, and pointing
the

the attack upon the van, with a view of ſtopping it, in preference to an attack upon the rear, has proceeded from an idea of carrying every ſhip in the enemy's fleet; but this mode has evidently given the enemy an opportunity of diſabling our ſhips, and preventing us from coming cloſe along-ſide of them.

A P P E N-

Plate XXVI. Part I. *p. 148.*

Mode of Attack proposed.

Fig. 1
N° 209

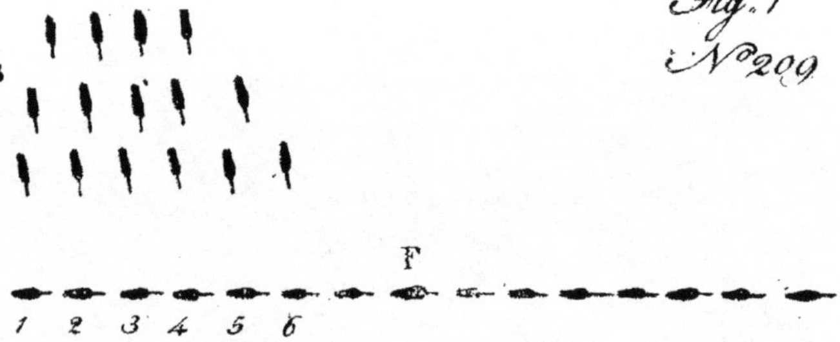

Fig. 2.
N° 210.

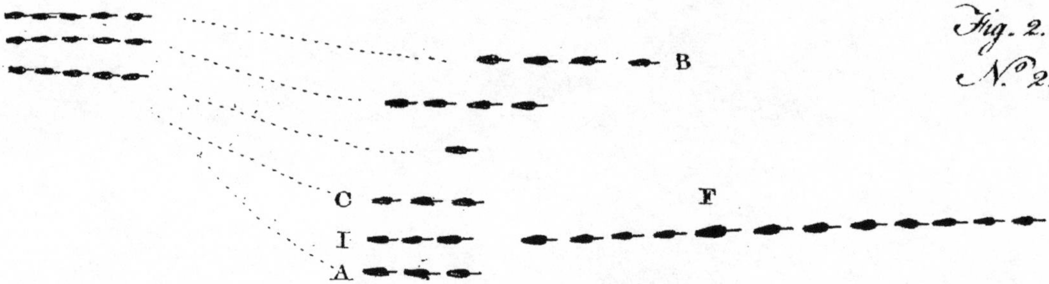

Fig. 3
N° 211.

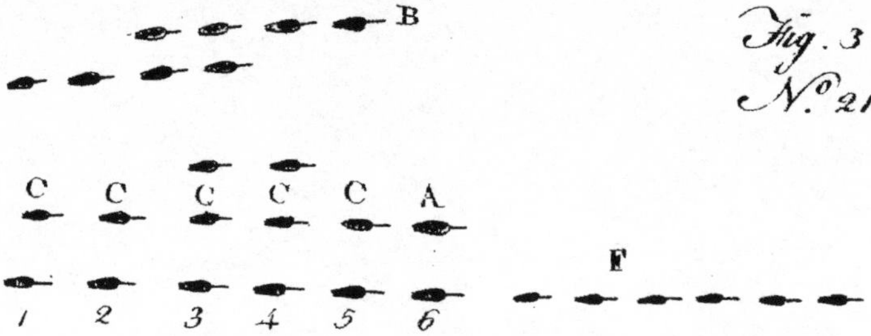

Fig. 4
N° 212.

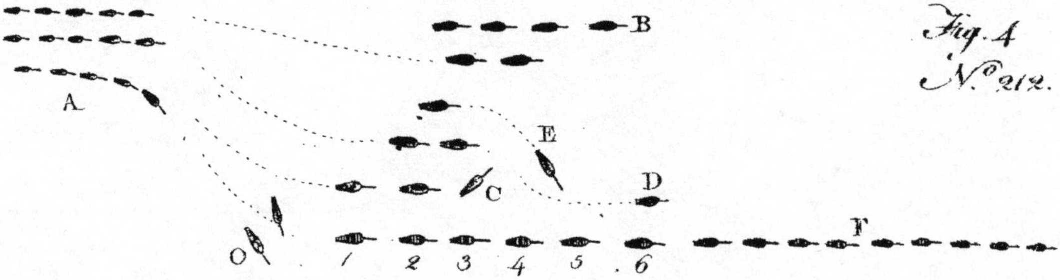

APPENDIX TO PART I.

_____

ADMIRAL SIR GEORGE POCOCK'S ENGAGEMENTS WITH THE
FRENCH FLEET, COMMANDED BY MONSIEUR D'ACHE, IN
THE EAST INDIES, *anno* 1758. *

_____

' *Admiralty-Office, October* 12*th* 1759.—Captain LATHAM, *late*
' *of the Tyger, arrived at Portsmouth on the* 9*th instant, in*
' *the East India Company's ship the Admiral Watson, with let-*
' *ters from* Vice-Admiral POCOCK, *giving the following ac-*
' *count.* '

' Admiral POCOCK being joined by Commodore STEVENS,
' in Madras road, with the reinforcements from England, and
' having put his ships in the best condition possible, April 17th
U
' 1758,

_____

* The printing had advanced thus far, before the Author thought of including these engagements. They were in the same war ; and about two years after
that of Admiral Byng. A description thereof, giving an opportunity of intro-
ducing new matter, will the more elucidate the subject, and will at the same time
complete the collection of those sea engagements, in which British Fleets, *being
to windward, by extending their line with the design to stop, take, destroy, or disable
the whole of the enemy's line to leeward, have been disabled before they could reach a
situation from whence they could annoy the enemy,* &c. &c. *Vide* p. 43. Sect. I.

' 1758, failed in order to get to windward of Fort St David's,
' to intercept the French fquadron, which by intelligence he
' was made to expect was on their approach from the weft-
' ward, from the Ifle of France : The 29th, in the morning, faw
' feven fhips in Fort St David's road, getting under fail; they
' joined two others in the offing; and, concluding them to be the
' enemy, immediately gave chafe : Thefe fhips, nine in all,
' ftanding off fhore under top-fails, formed the line of battle
' ahead : Admiral POCOCK formed his line of battle too ; and,
' as foon as his fhips had got into their ftation, being nearly
' within random fhot of the enemy, bore down upon the
' Zodiaque, on board which fhip Monfieur D'ACHE wore a
' cornette; but obferving the Newcaftle and Weymouth that
' they did not bear away at the fame time, he made their fig-
' nals. The enemy began to fire upon the Englifh as they were
' going down ; but the Admiral did not make the fignal to en-
' gage, till he was within half mufket-fhot of the Zodiaque,
' which was about three o'clock. A few minutes after, per-
' ceiving the fhips were not all got clofe enough to the enemy,
' he made the fignal for a clofer engagement; which was imme-
' diately complied with by the fhips in the van. At half paft
' four, obferving the rear of the French line had drawn up
' pretty clofe to the Zodiaque, the Admiral made the Cumber-
' land, Newcaftle, and Weymouth, fignals to make fail up and
' engage clofe. Soon after, Monfieur D'ACHE broke the line,
' and

Britifh Ships.

Elizabeth, 64	Yarmouth, the	Weymouth, 60	Queenborough,
Tyger, 60	Admiral, 64	Cumberland, 64	Protector ftore fhip.
Salifbury, 50		Newcaftle, 50	

' and put before the wind : his fecond aftern, who kept on the
' Yarmouth's quarter moft part of the action, then came up
' alongfide, gave his fire, and bore away.   The other two fhips
' in the rear came up in like manner, and then bore away ; and
' a few minutes after obferving the enemy's van to bear away
' alfo, the Admiral hauled down the fignal for the line, and
' made the fignal for the general chafe.   About fix, obferving
' the enemy join two fhips four miles to leeward, and at the
' fame time hauling their wind to the weftward, and feeming to
' form a line ahead, and the Yarmouth's mafts, yards, fails, and
' rigging, as well as the Elizabeth's, Tyger's, and Salifbury's,
' being fo much damaged as to prevent their keeping up with
' the fhips that were in the rear during action, who had receiv-
' ed but little damage, and night approaching, the Admiral
' followed the enemy as well as he could, ftanding to the
' fouth-weft, in order, if poffible, to keep to windward of them,
' in hopes of being able to engage them next morning.   But as
' they fhowed no lights, nor made any night-fignals, that could
' be obferved, he did not fee them through the night, nor
' next morning ; and therefore, concluding that they had wea-
' thered him in the night, by being able to carry more fail, he
' continued his endeavours to work up after them, until fix in
' the morning, May ift, when finding he loft ground confider-
' ably, he came to an anchor about three leagues to the north-
' ward of Sadras, where he was informed that the Bien Amie of

French Squadron.				Frigates.	
Le Bien Amie,	Le Zodiaque,	Le St Louis,		Le Sylphide,	
Le Compt de Provence,	Monf. d' Aché,	Le Duc de Orleans,		Le Diligent.	
Le Vengeance,		Le Duc de Bourgoyne,			

Le Conde,   —   Le Moras joined after the battle.

' 74 guns (a ſhip of the enemy) had received ſo much damage
' in the action, that they were obliged to run her aſhore a little
' to the ſouthward of Alemparve, where the French ſquadron
' was at an anchor.

' The French arrived in St David's Road at nine in the morn-
' ing, the day before the Britiſh Admiral fell in with them.
' They had not landed any troops before the engagement.   The
' action was about 7 leagues W. b. N. of Alemparve.   The Ad-
' miral obſerves, that Commodore STEVENS, Captain LATHAM,
' and Captain SOMERSET, who were in the van, and KEMPEN-
' FELT, the Commodore's Captain, behaved as became gallant
' officers; and that Captain HARRISON's behaviour, as well as
' all the officers and men belonging to the Yarmouth, gave him
' ſenſible ſatisfaction; and that, had the Captains in the rear
' done their duty as well, he ſhould have had a great pleaſure
' in commending them; but, their manner of acting in the en-
' gagement appeared ſo faulty, that, on his return to Madras, he
' ordered a court-martial to aſſemble, and inquire into their con-
' duct.   In conſequence of which, Captain NICHOLAS VINCENT
' was ſentenced to be diſmiſſed from the command of the Wey-
' mouth, Captain LEGG of the Newcaſtle to be caſhiered from his
' Majeſty's ſervice, and Captain BRERETON of the Cumberland
' to loſe one year's rank as a poſt-captain.

' Admiral POCOCK having repaired the moſt material damages
' of his ſhips, put to ſea May 10., with an intent to get up to
' Fort St David's, but was not able to effect it.   He got ſight of
' Pondicherry the 30th, and the next morning the French ſqua-
' dron, which had been there ever ſince the 5th, ſtood out of the
' road, and got away, notwithſtanding the Admiral's utmoſt en-
' deavours to come up with them.   On the 6th of June, upon

'   ' receiving

' receiving an account that Fort St David's had furrendered to
' the French, he judged it prudent to return immediately to Ma-
' dras, to refrefh his fquadron.

' The Admiral failed again, July 25th, in queft of the enemy;
' and on the 27th, in the evening, got within three leagues of
' Pondicherry road, where he perceived their fquadron at an-
' chor, confifting of 8 fail of the line, and a frigate. They got
' under fail the next morning, and ftood to the fouthward. The
' Admiral made the fignal to chafe, and endeavoured to weather
' them, as the likelieft means of bringing them to action;
' which, however, he was not able to accomplifh till Auguft 3d,
' when, taking advantage of the fea-breeze, he got the weather-
' gage, and brought on the engagement about one o'clock.
' Monfieur D' Ache fet his forefail, and bore away in about
' 10 minutes, his fquadron following his example, and continu-
' ing a running fight, in a very irregular line, till 3 o'clock.
' The Admiral then made the fignal for a general chafe; upon
' which the French cut away their boats, and made all the fail
' they could. He purfued them till it was dark, when they e-
' fcaped, by outfailing him, and got into Pondicherry road. The
' Admiral anchored the fame evening off Carrical, a French fet-
' tlement. '

Britifh lofs on this occafion 31 killed, 116 wounded. French
lofs, fays the Admiral's account, 540 killed and wounded.

DESCRIP-

———

DESCRIPTION OF ADMIRAL SIR GEORGE POCOCK'S ENGAGEMENT WITH THE FRENCH FLEET COMMANDED BY MONSIEUR D' ACHE, EAST INDIES, OFF FORT ST DAVID'S, 29TH APRIL 1758.

From the foregoing letters, although we have not been informed either of the particular direction of the wind at the time, or even upon what tack the two fleets were during this engagement, yet, from thefe letters, circumftances are fo far explained, that there can be no doubt of forming a defcription, which, in all other refpects, will be fufficiently fatisfactory.

(Plate XXVII. fig. 1.) F, The French fquadron formed in line of battle to leeward, upon the ftarboard tack, as it is fuppofed; for it was ftanding off from the land, with the wind in the weftern quarter.

B, Admiral Sir GEORGE POCOCK's fquadron; each fhip come to her ftation, and formed in line of battle, thought to be about random fhot diftance to windward.

(Plate XXVII. Fig. 2.) F, The Zodiaque, on board which fhip Monfieur D' ACHE, the French Admiral, wore a cornette.

A, The Britifh Admiral in the Yarmouth bearing down upon the Zodiaque, but making fignals to the fhips C C C aftern, the Cumberland, the Newcaftle, and the Weymouth; the captains of thefe veffels, as it appeared, not having bore away together and at the fame time with the Yarmouth, and the other

fhips

ships in the van B. The enemy all the while kept firing upon the British fleet during their courfe in coming down ; nor did Sir GEORGE POCOCK, the British Admiral, make the fignal to engage till he was within half mufket-shot of the Zodiaque, as at E, about three o'clock in the afternoon.

Neither the ships D in the rear, nor the ships in the van M, were yet come to their ftations, that is, at fighting diftance.

Fig. 3. B, The Admiral, in the Yarmouth, arrived at a ftation, within half mufket-shot of the Zodiaque F ; but, perceiving that all his other ships had not even yet got fufficiently close in with the enemy, he made fignal for a clofer engagement, which was immediately complied with by the ships of the van, as at C.

Plate XXVII. fig. 4. The Admiral, in the Yarmouth B, obferving that the ships in the rear of the French line had drawn close up, as at G, with a view to fupport their Admiral in the Zodiaque F, he made the fignals of the Cumberland, Newcaftle, and Weymouth, D, to make fail up and engage, that is, to fupport him in his ship the Yarmouth.

Plate XXVII. fig. 5. B, the Yarmouth. Sir GEORGE does not fay that the ships D in his rear complied with this laft fignal, but he fays that Monfieur D' ACHE, in the Zodiaque, immediately broke his line, and put before the wind, as at F F : That his fecond aftern, who had kept upon the Yarmouth's quarter the whole of the fore part of the engagement, afterwards came up alongfide,

gave

gave his fire, and then bore away in like manner, as at G. Immediately after this laft, the two remaining fhips H in the rear made fail, came up, and poured in their fire, referved for the purpofe (of difabling the Yarmouth), and in fucceffion bore away alfo. Laft of all, the fhips in the van I, taking example from the Zodiaque and the fhips in the rear, quitted the line alfo, and put before the wind; and leaving the Britifh van, which by this time were difabled from following them, they foon rejoined their centre and rear, when altogether forming a new line of battle four miles to leeward, as at K K, they were again prepared to give the Britifh fquadron a reception, fhould they have the leaft inclination to make a fecond attack.

OBSERVATIONS ON ADMIRAL SIR GEORGE POCOCK'S EN-GAGEMENT OF the 29TH APRIL 1758.

Sir GEORGE has not been particular in giving us the pofitive fituation of his fhip the Yarmouth when he bore away to attack the Zodiaque. Suppofing him to have been right to windward, and, in bearing down to attain a ftation at B, Plate XXVIII. fig. 6., abreaft, and at half mufket-fhot from the Zodiaque, had he affumed the lafking courfe, fo as to have formed the line of interfection A A, as in fig. 6., his fhips, in going down, by fuffering greatly, muft have been crippled. Confidering likewife, that the enemy, by running under topfails, muft have been getting much ahead, he therefore would have had the greater difficulty

in

Sir G.ʳ Pococks Engagement
East Indies 29 April 1758.

Plate XXVII. *Appen. p. 156.* Part I.

Fig. 1.

Fig. 2.

Fig. 3.

Fig. 4.

Fig. 5.

in getting the ships in his rear up into action, as has already been explained by former examples, of Admiral BYNG, Admiral BYRON, &c.

Plate XXVIII. Fig: 7. Again, had he been aftern of the enemy, as at A, Fig. 7., when he set out on this course, still the difficulty of getting the ships in the rear brought up would have been increased.

The attack, it seems, was not made according to this lasking form. Sir GEORGE has said, he bore down upon the Zodiaque, by which expression, and by what followed, it must be understood that it was his intention not only to steer his own ship with her head steadily directed upon the Zodiaque, but that his other ships, in the same manner, should be steered each with her head steadily directed upon her particular opponent.

In the prosecution of which intention, and while the enemy had way ahead, at the rate, perhaps, of two miles and a half, *per* hour, the Yarmouth and every other ship of the squadron, of necessity, must have assumed a course forming each of them a curve, as represented in Plate XXVIII. Fig. 8. ; which course, in mathematical disquisitions, has been termed the line or curve of pursuit.

The very specious and favourable aspect of this kind of attack, attempted so soon after that of the unfortunate Admiral BYNG, and considering also the case of the officers who commanded

X   manded

manded the fhips in the rear, who were difgraced on this occafion, will make the difcuffion thereof under a particular head by
itfelf the more neceffary.

―――――――――――

OF THE CURVE OF PURSUIT.

By the curve or line of purfuit is underftood that curve defcribed in the water by one fhip in purfuit of another, when the
fhip in purfuit from the windward, in bearing down, fhall fteer
her head continually directed upon the fhip purfued.

Plate XXVIII. Fig. 8. Let F reprefent the fhip purfued, to
leeward, having motion ahead in the line F G, as required for
good fteerage. Let B be the fhip in purfuit, two and a half miles
right to windward; which diftance being expreffed by the perpendicular B F, let it be called the line of diftance, or the line of
common departure. And F's motion through the line of courfe
F G, fuppofe it at the rate of two and a half miles *per* hour,
let it be expreffed by the Figures 4, 8, 12, in the line F G; and
the velocity of B required to overtake F, muft be greater than
the velocity of F.

―――――――――――

THEOREM.

To difcover what fpace the fhip F muft run through in the
line F G, before B, in defcribing the curve of purfuit, can overtake

take F; fay, as the difference of the fquares of the velocities affumed is to the product of the velocities, fo is B F, the line of common departure, to the fpace F G that the fhip purfued muft run through before fhe can be overtaken. Thus, when the velocities affumed fhall be as 5 to 3;—Say, as 16, the difference of the fquares of thefe numbers, is to 15, the product of thefe numbers, fo is 16 (of any quantity, furlongs, for example,) the diftance of B right to windward at the beginning of the courfe, to 15 furlongs, the fpace required for F to run before fhe can be overtaken.

THE CURVE OF PURSUIT CONSTRUCTED MECHANICALLY.

Plate XXVIII. Fig. 9. The line of common departure, F B, fuppofing it perpendicular to the line of courfe F G: Let any proportion, 5 to 3, be affumed: That while the fhip F moves in the line of courfe F G through the firft fpace No. 1., fuppofe it three yards, the fhip B from the windward, by fteering a courfe continually directed upon him, fhall in the fame time move through the fpace No. 1. in the curve of purfuit, at the rate of 5 yards; and, while F fhall move through the fpace 1 2, or fecond divifion in the line of courfe, that B in the fame time fhall have run through the correfponding fpace 1 2 in the curve, being other 5 yards, and fo on continually, protracting each their feparate courfes, in the proportion as 5 to 3, until they fhall come in contact, or clofe along-fide of each other, that is, until the lines of

X 2

their

their feveral courfes fhall meet in a point, as at G. Draw the lines 1 1, 2 2, and 3 3, &c. and they will nearly reprefent the curve of purfuit.

<hr />

OF THE APPLICATION OF THE CURVE OF PURSUIT IN SIR GEORGE POCOCK'S ENGAGEMENT.

That Sir GEORGE intended to make his attack in fome fuch fafhion, and that he attempted it with his own fhip, the Yarmouth, there can be no doubt; but not having communicated his intention, or given it out in orders, or by inftruction, to the commanders of his other fhips, it is not furprifing that this mode of attack, in the execution, did not come up to his expectation.

Plate XXIX. Fig. 10. After much previous practice of the manœuvre, had Sir GEORGE given inftruction that each fhip, in bearing down, fhould fteer with her head continually directed upon her particular opponent in the enemy's line, then each of his fhips, P, Q, R, with equal velocity affumed, would, along with B, the Yarmouth, have run down fpaces, each in their feveral fimilar curves, equal to the divifions 1, 2, 3, 4, marked as velocities at the rate of 5, in the particular curve defcribed by the Yarmouth, and in the fame time in which the Zodiaque, with her affociates, would have moved through the correfponding divifions 1, 2, 3, 4, marked as velocities at the rate of 3, in the line

of

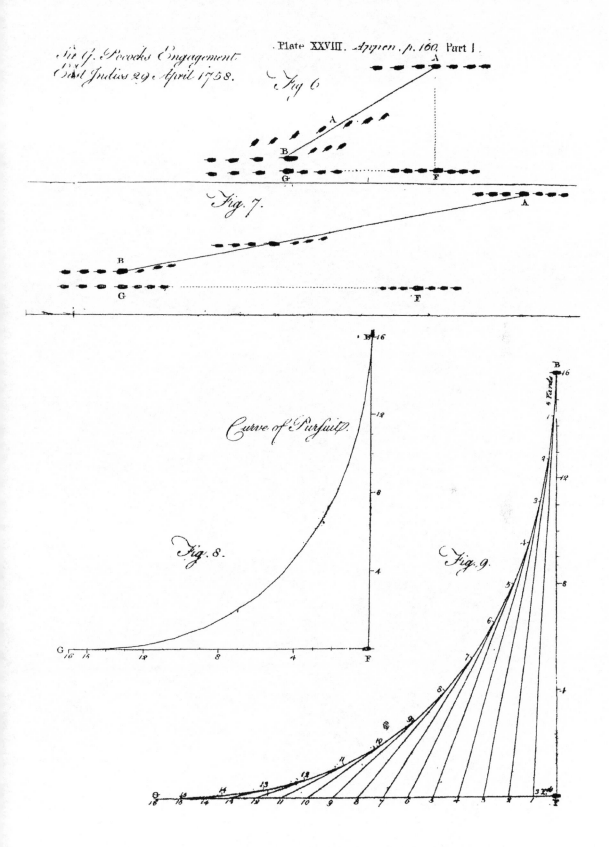

Sir G. Pococks Engagement East Indies 29 April 1758.

Plate XXVIII. Appen. p. 160. Part I.

Fig 6

Fig. 7.

Curve of Pursuit.

Fig. 8.

Fig. 9.

of courfe F G ; then B, the Britifh Admiral, with his three fhips
aftern, when arrived at the line C D, a ftation of fighting diftance · * which cuts the curve in the point numbered 10, (if
the enemy had not gone off), could alfo have continued his
courfe until his fhip the Yarmouth, as well as every other fhip of
his fquadron, might have come into contact, or clofe along-fide,
each of her particular opponent ; that is, the Yarmouth in contact with the Zodiaque at G, and the three fhips in the rear of
the Yarmouth, with the three correfponding fhips in the rear and
aftern of the Zodiaque.

It is to be obferved, however, that the Admiral, B, when arrived at the point marked 10 in the curve, as formerly remarked, within fighting diftance, far from having got abreaft of the
Zodiaque, by this time arrived at the correfpondent point 10 in
its line of courfe, has got little farther than abreaft of H, the
third fhip aftern of the Zodiaque ; and the three fhips D, in Sir
GEORGE's rear, at this time, are left aftern of the enemy's whole
fleet.

The Yarmouth never was in this particular fituation at any
time of the engagement.   For, however well Sir GEORGE's three
fhips aftern might have preferved their courfe, each in their
proper curve, according to inftructions, or according to the direction of their fteerage with which they might fet out in the
                                                          beginning

---

* Made parallel to F G, the enemy's line of courfe, about 400 yards diftance, termed fometimes piftol-fhot, or half mufket-fhot. By Mr BYNG's engagement it does not appear that his van was within this diftance ; as mufket-
fhot was not known, or thought, to have taken effect in any of the fhips even
in that divifion.

beginning of the purfuit, it is evident that Sir GEORGE had not kept his intended curve : For, had he preferved his courfe in his proper curve, he would infallibly have been at the point number 10 in the curve of purfuit, when the Zodiaque was got to her correfpondent point number 10 in the line of courfe F G.

From this fituation at the point 10 in the curve of purfuit, he muft have paffed along, and fuftained the fire of the whole fhips in the enemy's rear, before he could have attained a ftation at A, abreaft, and at half mufket-fhot diftance from the Zodiaque. That he never was in the fituation at the point 10 in the curve of purfuit, as defcribed, and did not pafs along the enemy's rear, and receive their fire, may be prefumed, fince he has not told us; but he has told us, that he did not give the fignal to engage (that is, to begin firing) till he was within half mufket-fhot of the Zodiaque, by which muft be underftood a ftation fomewhere at A nearly abreaft of the Zodiaque.

In which cafe, however much Sir GEORGE, in the beginning, might have wifhed to keep his courfe according to the curve of purfuit, yet, from farther confideration afterward, and while running down, forefeeing the confequences, he for certain made a change, and had given his courfe the lafking form, as M N, in order that he might attain this ftation at A, abreaft of the Zodiaque, at half mufket-fhot diftance, which he faid he did.

This change from the firft intention in the Yarmouth's courfe was not a thing of that kind which could, in one inftant, be comprehended by a fignal; and, if it was not in one inftant comprehended, and put in execution by the fhips in the rear, of neceffity they were to be left confiderably aftern.

But

But this reafoning, all the while, is founded upon the fuppofition, that each fhip of the fquadron, by her courfe and her velocity affumed, had or could, without previous practice, have
preferved her ftation in the curve of purfuit, fhould it even have
been allotted to her by the Admiral, which will not be admitted.
For in fuch cafe, each fhip in fucceffion, of neceffity taking the
rule for her velocity from the fhip immediately ahead, would
imperceptibly and unavoidably get into her wake as a leader, and
by that means the fhips in the rear, one after another, would fall
more and more aftern, from the very beginning of the courfe,
in form as at E.

Plate XXIX. fig. 11.   The curve of purfuit begun from a
diftance aftern, with the velocities 5 to 3 affumed as before;
and if this diftance F I fhall be equal to the diftance to windward I B, the Refolution will ftand thus—*As the difference of
the fquares of the velocities is to double the product of the velocities, fo is the diftance to windward I B,* 16 *furlongs to* 30 *furlongs, the fpace which the fhip purfued muft run through, before
fhe can be overtaken;* in which cafe, the fhips in the rear making the attack, when arrived at a ftation of fighting diftance, the
line L M, parallel to F G, the courfe of the enemy's line of
battle, will be left at a double diftance aftern, as appears from
the figure.

Plate XXX. fig. 12.   Again, fuppofe the courfe of B to be begun from right to windward, and that the velocities fhall be as 4
to 2 (a double proportion); fay, as the difference of the fquares of
the velocities 12, is to the product of the velocities 8, fo is the dif-

tance

tance to windward B F, 12-4ths of a mile to 8-4ths of a mile,
the space which the ship pursued has to run before she can be
overtaken ; and supposing L M, the parallel line of fighting-
distance, to be 440 yards as before, the ships in the rear, in approaching this station, will still be left astern about 400 or 500
yards.

From all which it may be concluded, that, whatever shall be
the proportion and rate of the velocities assumed, or how much
soever shall be the previous practice, the mode of attack, by this
curve of pursuit, will in no way be found preferable to the
mode in the lasking form ; but will be found so much the worst
of the two, as it will be more difficult in the execution, and the
ships in the rear will be left the farther astern ; and in general
it is evident, that the curve of pursuit, though a curve well adapted to bring one ship into the wake of another, is not at all suited
for bringing one ship abreast of another, and within a given
distance.

With respect to general observations, they are the same as have
formerly been introduced. By the nature of the attack, equally
as in the engagements of Mr Byng and Mr Byron, the headmost ships must have approached the enemy, before it was possible for the ships in the rear to get into fighting distance. By
the nature of this approach, the van and centre were disabled,
before they could get into a position from whence, by retaliation, they could annoy the enemy. By the address of the enemy, as in Admiral Byron's engagement, the rears of neither
squadron had got into action. Though the Admiral, like Sir
George Rodney, in his engagement off the Pearl Rock, had
the

the merit of great perfonal courage, yet the attack, as put in execution by his fhip the Yarmouth, being nearly the fame as that
of the Sandwich, of courfe was attended with the like want of
effect.

On the part of the enemy in this engagement, and fimilar to
every one of the other five of this clafs defcribed, the Admiral,
Monf. D' ACHE in the Zodiaque, fo foon as he felt himfelf expofed to the Britifh fire, quitted the line, and withdrew from
battle, leaving his fecond and other fhips aftern, not only as a
cover to keep up a good countenance, and to amufe Sir GEORGE
POCOCK, but, each fhip after another, throwing in their fire upon
the Yarmouth in paffing, by particular inftruction, bore away in
fucceffion, to form a new line to leeward.

Admiral Sir GEORGE POCOCK's fecond engagement, of the
3d of Auguft 1758, being fo much alike with that of the 29th of
April, no new defcription will be neceffary.

END OF PART I.

Y   NAVAL

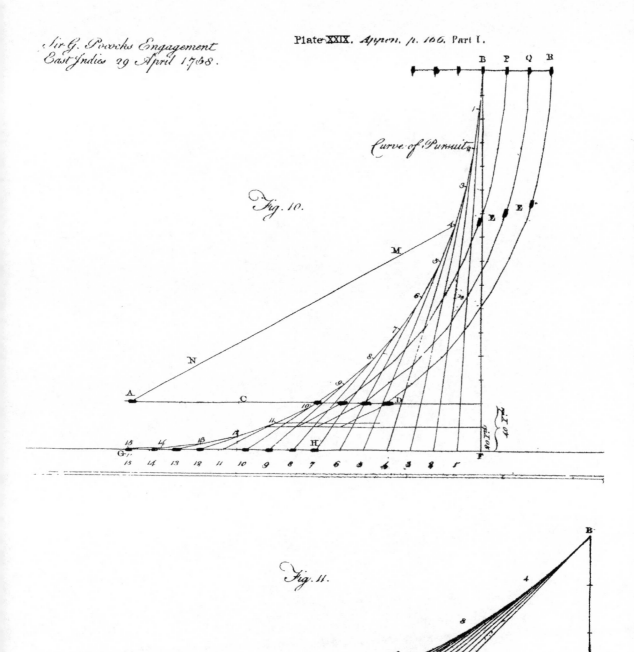

Plate XXIX. *Appen. p. 166.* Part I.

Sir G. Pococks Engagement
East Indies 29 April 1758.

Curve of Pursuit.

Fig. 10.

Fig. 11.

Plate XXX. *Appen. p.100. Part 1.*

Sir G. Pococks engagement
29 April 1758.

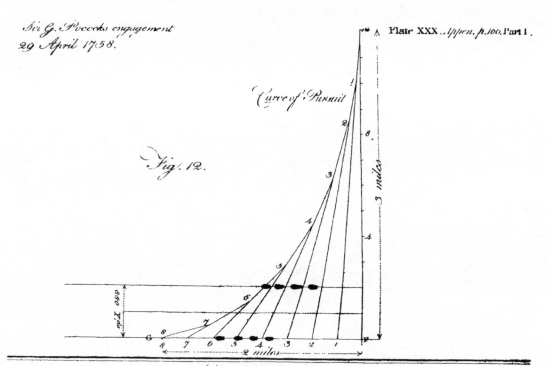

Fig. 12.

Curve of Pursuit

3 miles

2 miles

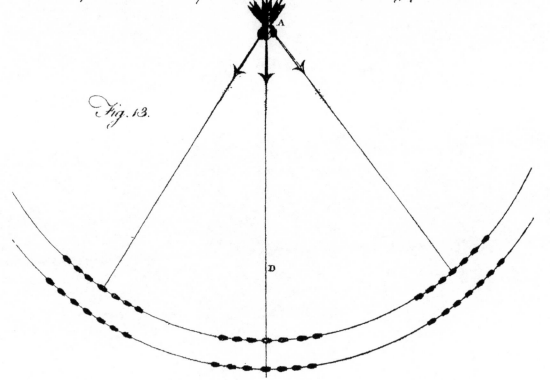

Historical Sketch.
Of the relative motion of 2 Fleets as dependant on the bearing of the Wind.

Fig. 13.

NAVAL TACTICS.

PART II.

INTRODUCTION.

IN the firſt part of this work, it has been eſtabliſhed, upon the cleareſt conviction, that the intention of our enemy, the French, in their mode of encountering our fleets, has conſtantly been to diſable the rigging, and, if poſſible, to avoid the bringing their ſhips to a cloſe engagement. It has been ſhown, no leſs clearly, that an Admiral, commanding an opponent fleet, and being in purſuit anywhere from the windward quarter, may have it in his power to bring the enemy either to give him battle on equal terms, and in a cloſe engagement, or otherwiſe to force him to abandon a number of his ſhips, let him be as ſhy, as artful, and cautious as he will. In this ſecond part, after the ſame manner, we ſhall endeavour to demonſtrate the practicability of forcing alſo an attack upon ſuch an enemy, and with equal ſucceſs, from the leeward quarter. And as in the firſt part it has been proved, that the fleet to windward, by mak-

ing

ing the attack, will, by this, have attained a fuperiority over the fleet endeavouring to avoid the attack; fo, there can be little doubt it will be found, that a fleet, by making the attack from the leeward, muft alfo attain an advantage over an enemy, who is defirous of avoiding the attack by making off to windward. *

* Great part of this fubject, the attack from the leeward, having been executed almoft twenty-fix years ago, and immediately after the 27th July 1778, already a part thereof has been introduced in illuftration of the action of that day. —*Vide* Part I. Obfervations, KEPPEL's Engagement, page 103.

THE

The ATTACK of FLEETS from the LEEWARD.

DEMONSTRATIONS.

SECTION I.

OF FLEETS WORKING TO WINDWARD.

THE following demonstrations, upon the working of fleets to windward, although perfectly known to all seamen, yet as they may afford some information to others not conversant on that subject, it is hoped they will not here be thought superfluous.

1. (Plate I. fig. 1.) Let us suppose a fleet of ten, twenty, or more ships to windward, as at F (Plate I. fig 1.), endeavouring to avoid being brought to an engagement; and another fleet of an equal number of ships some leagues to leeward, as at A, ardently desirous of getting up with F, and bringing him to an engagement :

ment : If every fhip of the fleet F, to windward, fhall be found
to fail equally well with every individual fhip of the fleet A to
leeward, then, unlefs fome change of the wind or fome accident
fhall take place, each fleet, in turning to windward, having uniformly kept their boards proportional, the diftance between the
two fleets will continually remain, the fame as at firft fetting
off; and the fleet A to leeward will never be able to get within
reach of his antagonift F : That is, the board A, to be made by
the fleet A, making the fame angle with the perpendicular line
W W (the line of the wind), as the board F G to be made by
the enemy F; and as it will be performed in the fame time and
with the fame fpeed, the diftance between the two fleets,
when they fhall have arrived at the points B and G, will be the
fame as when they were at the two points A and F, the places
where they fet off.

Again, fuppofing both fleets fhall tack at the fame time, and get
upon a ftarboard courfe, B C and G H, then the two fleets,
when they fhall have arrived refpectively at the points C and
H, the diftance between them will ftill remain proportionally the
fame as at firft fetting off; and the fleet A will never be able to
get up with, or reach, the fleet F, his antagonift.

But if the wind, during the courfe of a few days, fhould make
fome change, and if fome rigging fhould be carried away by an
overprefs of fail, which are accidents not to be prevented for
any confiderable time with fleets fuppofed to be engaged in a
ftruggle of this kind; it is evident that fuch accidents will be of
more

more dangerous confequence to the fleet endeavouring to get off to windward, than to the fleet in purfuit from the leeward. As, for example :

Let us fuppofe the enemy's fquadron in its progrefs to windward from H to F (Plate I. fig. 2.); that one of their fhips, from being crippled, had fallen to leeward, as at the point G ; is it not evident that fhe muft be cut off by the very next board, which part of the fquadron A fhall make, as at C; or otherwife, that the fquadron F, upon bearing away, or fhortening fail, as at H, to protect this crippled fhip, by falling within the reach of the fqua-dron A in purfuit, muft immediately be forced to come to action ? Whereas, *on the other hand*, fhould any fhip of the fquadron A come to be crippled, and fall to leeward, as at B, fhe will ftill con-tinue to be under the protection of the fquadron A, and will not thereby be expofed to the fleet of the enemy.

Again, upon a fuppofition that the wind may change in the courfe of a few days, the following demonftrations will fhow, that a wind from few other points of the compafs will make a change unfavourable for the fquadron to leeward.

Let us fuppofe two fhips, the one feveral miles to windward at F (Plate II. fig. 3.), endeavouring to get off, and the other in pur-fuit from the leeward at A ; and let the wind be at weft at W.

To fhow the effect of changes of wind upon thefe two fhips, let this change be from weft to north, at N N, in one inftant ; then

the

the ſhip A, which was ſeveral miles to leeward when the wind was at weſt apparently, will lye up with her courſe towards B, to windward of the ſhip F, now that the wind has got about to north, and evidently will have a courſe ſo much farther to windward (*vide* H G), though the diſtance between the two ſhips A and F may remain nearly the ſame.

Again, let A and F (Plate II. fig. 4.) be two fleets ; and let the wind, in paſſing from weſt to north, have changed ſo gradually, that each fleet has had ſufficient time to lye up and keep to the wind with the whole of their reſpective ſhips, extended in line of battle ahead, mutually as the wind ſhall ſhift : Yet, ſtill in this caſe, the fleet A, which was 7 miles to leeward when the wind was weſt, will now have got to windward, the wind having come fully ſhifted to the north, as may be ſeen by courſe laſt of F, at the line H I, and courſe laſt of A, at the line C D.

For, if the fleet A can lye up to the wind two points at the ſtation A, it will be able to lye two points up at the ſtation P, when the wind ſhall have changed two points, and will do the ſame at Q, and the ſame at the ſtation R, and alſo at S, when the wind has got full to the north.

In like manner, by the fleet F keeping the wind two points at the ſimilar ſtations, and at the ſame rate of motion on the different and equal boards ; the two fleets, when the wind ſhall have got to the north, will ſtill be at the ſame diſtance from one

another

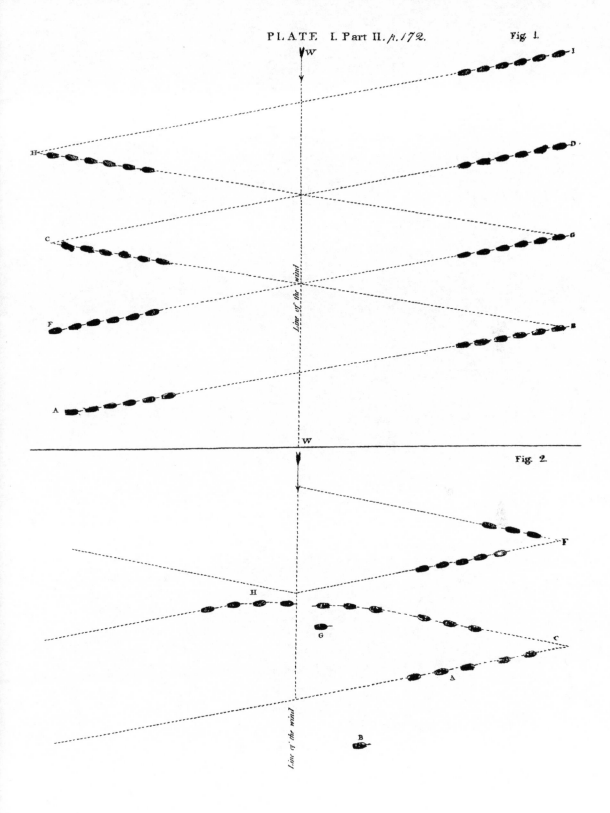

PLATE. I. Part II. *p. 172.*   Fig. 1.

Fig. 2.

another as before; but the fleet A, which was to leeward, will now have got far to the windward.

Fig. 4. Again, upon a fuppofition that the wind, in paffing from weft to fouth, has changed in like manner, fo gradually, that each fleet fhall have had time to lye up, as per lines L M and T U, then the fleet M, when the wind fhall have come to the fouth, and the fhip Z, will be found as far to the windward of the fhip U, as when the wind came round by the northern quarter.

From all which it may be conceived, that the leeward fleet in purfuit, by a fteady perfeverance, will fome way or other at laft get up with, and force an attack upon the enemy going off, either by getting to windward of him, or by fetching fome part of his fleet from the leeward; and as this muft be accomplifhed either while the opponent fleets fhall be running upon the fame tack, or when they fhall be brought to pafs each other on contrary tacks, the Attack of Fleets from the leeward quarter will naturally divide itfelf into two feparate cafes; and let the one be called, the Simple Attack, the other the Crofs Attack.

1ft, By the Simple Attack, let it be underftood to be that cafe, when the fleet A to leeward fhall be able to fetch fome part of the enemy to windward, and on the fame tack (as per Fig. 5. plate III.)

2d, By the Crofs Attack, let it be underftood to be that cafe, where the two opponent fleets fhall be brought to pafs one another on contrary tacks, as A and F (Fig. 6. plate III.)

Z

SIM—

S I M P L E   A T T A C K.

S E C T I O N   II.

W ITH refpect to the firft of thefe, the Simple Attack, few examples can be produced ; for the French commanders, upon
an apprehenfion of the fmalleft rifk of being overtaken from
the leeward, have hitherto found means to throw the fleets under their command on the oppofite tack to that of the fleet in
purfuit *.

But whether this fhall have arifen from the enemy's anxiety
of avoiding a fhock, or from a natural confequence attendant on
the neceffary movements of two fleets on fuch occafions, certain it is that the meeting, or rencounter of adverfe fleets, upon
oppofite tacks, have been more frequent than the rencounter of
fleets on the fame tack ; and of which meeting, on oppofite tacks,
there are four examples before us : That of the 27th July 1778,
two others of the 15th and 19th May 1780 ; and, laftly, that of
the 12th April 1782.

Which laft, the 12th of April, though perfectly decifive in the
end, was in the beginning of the battle fo far alike, and of the
fame

---

* Admiral Arbuthnot off the Chefapeak.

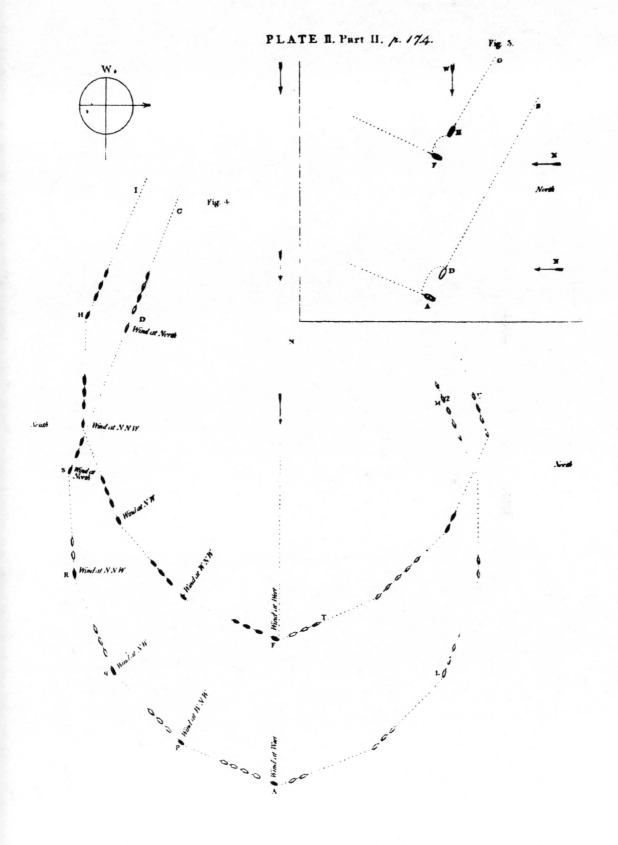

PLATE II. Part II. *p. 174.*

fame nature with the three firft, that the adverfe fleets having met, and the leading fhips of the enemy having gained the wind, (as in fig. 7. plate III.), the two fleets ranged paft each other in oppofite directions, each fhip giving and receiving their mutual fire until the line of battle of the one fleet was completely extended abreaft of the other, (as per fig. 8. plate III.); that is, when B, the van of the one, had got abreaft of G, the rear of the other mutually. Of thefe feveral actions, the three firft already have, in fame meafure, been defcribed. With refpect to the fourth, the 12th of April, the attention it requires is fuch, it would be improper to bring it into view until the whole fubject on the attack from the leeward fhall be completely difcuffed. In the mean while, by way of introduction to this defign, it will be neceffary to look back and recapitulate a few of the remarks formerly introdcced, (Part I. p. 103, beginning No. 10.)

Z 2

R E C .\-

RECAPITULATION OF A FEW OF THE REMARKS ON THE
BATTLE OFF USHANT, OF THE 27TH JULY 1778.

" LET us suppose two adverse fleets in contention to get to windward the one of the other ; and, by dint of sailing, or by a
change of wind, that the leading ships of the enemy F (fig. 9.
plate III.) shall have gained the wind of the fleet A ; it seems
evident, if the van, or any part of the leeward fleet A, was to continue the line of their first course A B, and were not all to bear
away, as per course C C (fig. 10, plate IV.), that, with great ad-
advantage, the enemy's line of battle might be cut in twain (as at
G, fig. 11. plate IV.), and have thereby their rear H separated
from their van F (as per said fig. 11.) Again, by such an attempt,
the course of all the enemy's ships, astern of this attack, would
thereby be so far stopped, or retarded, that a close engagement
with the enemy's whole line must be the consequence ; or otherwise their rear G, of necessity, must be abandoned by the van F,
(as per fig. 12. plate IV.)

" Perhaps it may be said, that the risk or danger of an attack
of this kind might be greater than the advantage proposed. To
which it is answered : As soon as ever we shall have the spirit
and steadiness to make the experiment, conviction will follow,
that the risk and damage to shipping making the attempt will be
found to be less than in any other mode of attack whatever.

" Again,

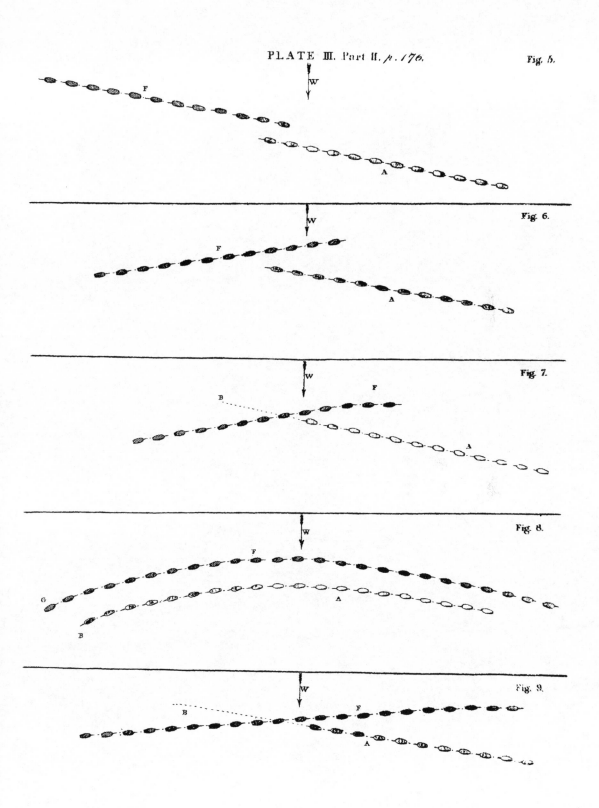

PLATE III. Part II. p. 176.

Fig. 5.

Fig. 6.

Fig. 7.

Fig. 8.

Fig. 9.

" Again, upon taking the fubject in another view, fuppofe, for example, that two, three, or more fhips (fig. 13. plate IV.) are paffing each other in oppofite tacks, at the rate of five miles per hour ; then will the velocity of the tranfit be equal to ten miles per hour ; or, which is the fame thing, let us fuppofe, for the fake of demonftration, the one fleet at reft, and the other in motion, at the rate of ten miles per hour; then each fhip of the fquadron in motion will pafs through 880 feet in one minute of time.

" According to which, then, each fhip of the fquadron A will pafs each fhip of the enemy F, with the interval between fhips included, in one minute ; that is, fhe will make a tranfit of 880 feet, or 300 yards (the general allowance of fpace for fhips drawn up in line of battle) *in one minute.*

" Therefore, if the two fleets did pafs one another on the 18th of July 1778, at the rate of 5 miles per hour, and if it were poffible that the loading of a fhip's guns could be repeated once every minute of time, ftill each Britifh fhip could be expofed to the fire of each French fhip during the fpace of one quarter of a minute only ; that is, while the two fhips were in direct oppofi- tion ; and as there were 26 fhips of the enemy, each fhip, on the whole, could be expofed to a cannonade of fix minutes only. And if the fleets had paffed each other at the rate of two miles and a half per hour (a motion abfolutely neceffary to make a fhip anfwer the rudder well), each fhip could then be expofed to a fire of 13 minutes duration. "

By

By fuch inveſtigation only can it be explained, how two ad-verſe fleets, amounting to 30 ſhips of the line each, carrying above 36,000 men, after having been brought in oppoſition of battle, and mutually ſuſtaining a furious cannonade from above 4000 guns, befides muſquetry ; how, I ſay, they have been brought to be ſeparated again without effect, without the ſmalleſt apparent deciſion ; that is, without the loſs of a ſhip on either ſide, and ſometimes with ſcarcely the loſs of a man, though the rencounter has often been ſaid to have been within piſtol-ſhot.

From all which it muſt be concluded, that the moſt artful ma-nagement of ſails, the cloſeſt approximation, or the moſt ſpirited cannonade, will avail nothing under ſuch circumſtances ; and that it is in vain to hope that ever any thing material can be effected againſt an enemy's fleet keeping to windward, paſſing on contrary tacks, and defirous to go off, unleſs his line of battle can be cut in twain, or ſome ſuch other ſtop can be deviſed, as has already been deſcribed.

CROSS

CROSS ATTACK.

SECTION III.

MODE OF ATTACK FROM THE LEEWARD ILLUSTRATED.

LET us fuppofe two fleets, the one to windward, endeavouring to make off as at F (fig. 14. plate IV.), and the other to leeward, having fufficient defire to get up with him as at A. We hope it will be granted, that A, the fleet in purfuit from the leeward, within the courfe of a few days, may be able to get up with, and bring the other, his enemy F, to fome rencounter. Or, otherwife, that F, the fleet to windward, may have the utmoft difficulty to make his efcape with his whole line entire. Alfo, that this rencounter, as it hitherto has been, may continue to be moft frequently on an oppofite tack.

Again, let us fuppofe that the enemy F (fig. 14. plate IV.), from the defire of getting off, will have exerted his whole art of feamanfhip to enable him to avoid the attack, it follows, that the fleet A in purfuit, though not able to fetch the van of the enemy now far got to windward, as at F, may ftill be able to fetch a part of his rear, as at G (fig. 15. plate V.); and as this may be conceived to take place with his headmoft fhips in the firft inftance, ſtance, we will, for that reaſon, begin with theſe examples, when this manœuvre, of cutting an enemy's line with the greateſt propriety, can be put in execution by the leading ſhips of the ſquadron in purſuit.

EXAMPLES OF CUTTING AN ENEMY'S LINE OF BATTLE BY THE HEADMOST SHIPS OF THE SQUADRON IN PURSUIT FROM THE LEEWARD.

1. WHEN the leading ſhips have fetched the rear of the enemy, ſuppoſe the three ſternmoſt ſhips.

2. When the leading ſhips have fetched the centre of the enemy's line.

3. When the leading ſhips ſhall have fetched the fourth or fifth ſhip, and ſhall cut off the van from the centre and rear of the enemy's line.

1. WHEN THE LEADING SHIPS SHALL HAVE FETCHED THE REAR OF THE ENEMY'S LINE, SUPPOSE THE THREE STERNMOST SHIPS.

LET it be ſuppoſed, in the courſe of ſome fortunate trip in working to windward, that any number (ſay three or four) of the headmoſt ſhips of A have had it in their power to fetch an equal number of ſhips of the enemy F (as at G, fig. 15. plate V.)

And

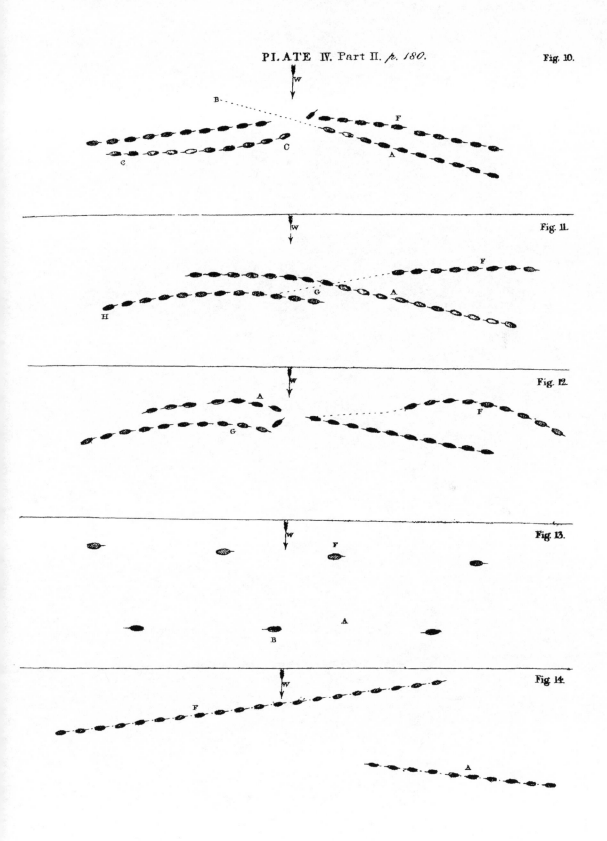

PLATE IV. Part II. *p. 180.*   Fig. 10.

And let it be fuppofed, that the headmoft, or any one of thefe fhips, by keeping her wind, fhall attempt to pierce between any one of the fternmoft of the enemy's fhips, between the third and fourth, for example, at G, (fig. 16. Plate V.); the confefequence will be, that the fhip making this attempt will force her way through the interval between thefe two fhips; or otherwife, by getting foul, or running aboard of the third fhip, (as in fig. 17. Plate V.), will not only ftop her courfe in the line, but will alfo throw the fhips aftern of her into diforder. In whichever cafe this fhall happen, here are three fternmoft fhips of the enemy which will be forced to leeward, as at G (fig. 18. Plate V.), where they muft be entangled with the remaining part of the fhips of A, which may now be pufhing up, as at B, to prevent their efcape.

If this manœuvre fhall be put in execution happily, and with fpirit, we have a right to think it will fucceed; and that the enemy, F, muft inevitably lofe thefe three fhips. For his van, by the fuppofition, having by this time got far to windward, as at F, the matter would be determined before affiftance could be given; and, in attempting to give this affiftance, he would be reduced to the neceffity of making the attack as at F, (fig. 19. Plate V.), which he before had endeavoured to avoid, and when in poffeffion of his whole force; therefore he will abandon thefe three fhips; as A, by this time, may be fuppofed to have environed them with fufficient force.

A a

Again,

Again, fuppofe the enemy, upon perceiving the danger his rear muft be expofed to, in place of holding his wind, (as in fig. 17. and 18.), fhall bear away along the line of A, (as in fig. 20. Plate VI), nothing can be gained by this; for it muft be done on equal terms, exchanging a few fhot only as he ranges paft to windward, and muft ftill be under the neceffity of giving up his three fhips at laft.

WHEN THE LEADING SHIPS SHALL HAVE FETCHED THE CENTRE OF THE ENEMY'S LINE OF BATTLE.

WHEN the leading fhips of the fleet A (fig. 21. Plate VI.), fhall have fetched the centre of the enemy F, the fhip B, which fhall attempt the paffage, as in the former cafe, will either make her way through the interval which will be given her, and the fhip G, with all the fhips aftern, will be forced to leeward, as in fig. 21.; or the fhip B, by running aboard of G, and both fhips coming to the wind (as per fig. 22.), the whole fhips aftern of fuch attack will be ftopped and retarded. But, in whichever of thefe ways it fhall take place, the line will be cut in twain (as in fig. 23.); the rear will be feparated from the van; and the whole fhips of the enemy aftern, will be forced to leeward (as in fig. 23.) Meanwhile, the van A (Plate VI. fig. 24.) ranging to windward, and B, the centre and rear of A, by this time come up, the rear of the enemy G prevented from getting ahead, and finding it impracticable to regain their van F, will prepare to put before the wind, as in fig. 24.

G,

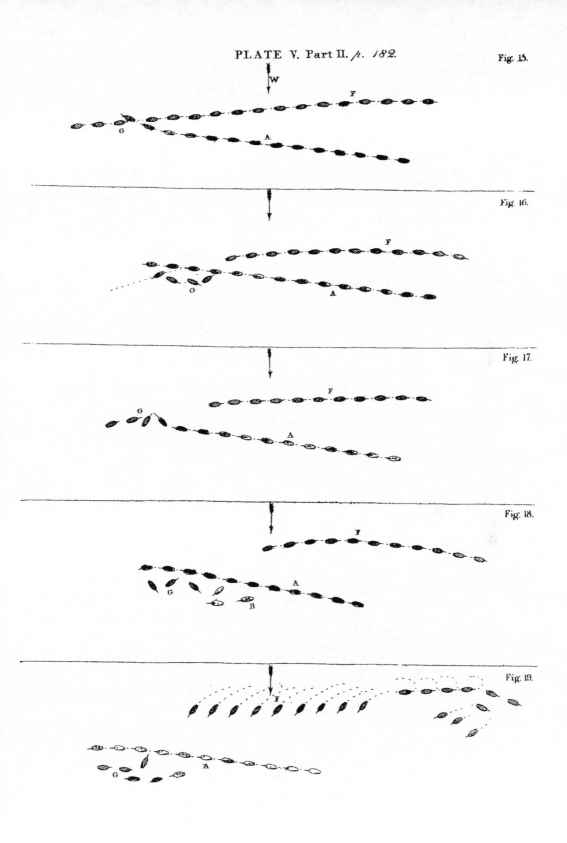

PLATE V. Part II. *p. 182.*

Fig. 15.

Fig. 16.

Fig. 17.

Fig. 18.

Fig. 19.

PLATE VI. Part II. *p. 182.*   Fig. 20.

W

Fig. 21.

Fig. 22.

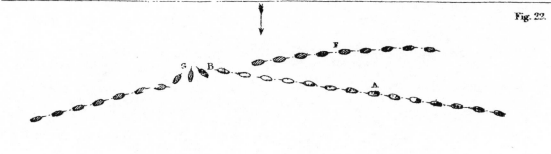

Fig. 23.

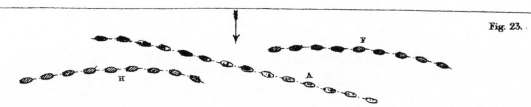

Fig. 24.

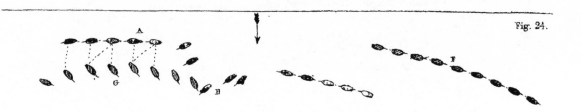

G, (Plate VII. fig. 25.) The rear of the enemy putting before the wind encompaffed by the whole force of A, van and rear.

A, The fhips in the van, after having forced the rear of the enemy to leeward, are now put before the wind in purfuit.

B, The centre and rear of A having prevented the enemy's rear from rejoining his van, are now in purfuit on his larboard quarter.

F, The van of the enemy (evidently) not having it in their power to prevent the effect of any part of thefe movements.

<hr>

WHEN THE LEADING SHIPS SHALL HAVE FETCHED THE FOURTH OR FIFTH SHIP, AND SHALL CUT THE VAN OFF FROM THE CENTRE AND REAR OF THE ENEMY'S LINE.

THE headmoft fhips of the van of A (fig. 26. Plate VII.), having fetched near the van of the enemy, and having cut his line between the fourth and fifth fhip, and having ranged along to windward, as at B, his fhips are now backing fail to give time for the remaining part of his fleet to get up, &c. That is, while D, the rear, having bore as per courfe C C, is preparing to intercept the enemy.

By which means the van A (fig. 27. Plate VII.) having got to windward, and the rear B having preffed forward, the remaining part of the enemy's fleet now diminifhed by four fhips, the

A a 2

number

number cut off, muſt be forced to leeward, where an action ſufficiently cloſe muſt enſue.

Fig. 27. A, The van in purſuit and endeavouring to get upon
the ſtarboard quarter of the enemy.

B, The rear diviſion ſticking cloſe upon his larboard quarter.

G, The enemy inferior by four ſhips.

F, The enemy's four ſhips now cut off.

OBSERVATIONS ON THE THREE FOREGOING CASES OF THE
ATTACK WHEN MADE BY THE HEADMOST SHIPS OF A
SQUADRON.

OF theſe three caſes, as it is eaſier to fetch the rear than any
other part of the line of a fleet going off, ſo the attack will be the
more aſſured of ſucceſs.

The ſecond, the attack on the centre, or anywhere near the
centre, as the object is greater and the ſucceſs equally probable,
ſo ought it always to be attempted, if poſſible, to be fetched by
the van of the fleet in purſuit.

The third, under which is comprehended the attack upon the
van, or anywhere a head of the centre, as it muſt be more upon
an equality with the enemy than any of the former two, ſo the
ſucceſs muſt therefore be more doubtful, and particularly where
an enemy ſhall be deſirous of fighting.

Fig.

Fig. 28. Again, let us ſuppoſe the leading ſhip of the ſquadron A, after a long ſtruggle, to have gained the weather gage of
the enemy, and are now ranging paſt him to windward, giving
and receiving a heavy fire, (as per fig. 28. Plate VII.)

This ſuppoſed advantage, which, notwithſtanding it has upon
every occaſion been the objeċt of our moſt earneſt efforts to obtain,
muſt evidently be of as little importance as the ranging to leeward
after having failed of gaining the wind (as per fig. 29. Plate VII.),
a movement which we have long been well acquainted with.

═══════════

OF CUTTING THE ENEMY'S LINE WITH THE FIFTH OR SIXTH
SHIP, OR ANY ONE NEXT ASTERN OF THESE, IN THE VAN
OF THE LINE, BUT LET IT BE THE FIFTH SHIP, FOR EX-
AMPLE; WHICH ALSO, LIKE THE FORMER, MAY BE DIVID-
ED INTO THREE SEVERAL CASES.

1.   THE attack on the rear of the enemy's line with the fifth
ſhip from the van.

2.   Of cutting the enemy's line, at the centre, with the fifth
ſhip.

3.   The attack on the van of the enemy's line, with the fifth
ſhip.

THE

THE ATTACK ON THE REAR OF THE ENEMY'S LINE, WITH THE FIFTH SHIP FROM THE VAN.

Fig. 31. Plate VIII.   In which, let it be fuppofed that it fhall be the lot of A, the fifth fhip from the van, to make the attack, and cut the line of the enemy; and let this be between the fourth and fifth fhip of his rear at G; while, in the mean time, the four headmoft fhips B, after having ftretched under the lee of the four fhips G, are preparing to put about and ftand after them, on the fame tack.

Fig. 32. Plate VIII.   The confequence of which will be, that thefe four fhips G, having already received the fire of eight fhips, A and B, will at laft be ftopped, and forced to leeward, by the weight of the centre and rear now coming up, as at D; while F, the van, not forefeeing, or perhaps not having it in his power to prevent this misfortune in his rear, may be much more defirous of making off to windward, than of ranging along the line of A, as at H.

A, The fifth fhip, with thofe aftern of him, which had cut the line and had gone to windward, now put about in purfuit of the four fhips G.

B, The four headmoft fhips of A, which ranged to leeward, now put about alfo in purfuit.

Fig. 33. Plate VIII. fhews the inevitable ruin of thefe four fhips G, driving along before the wind, and encompaffed with

eight

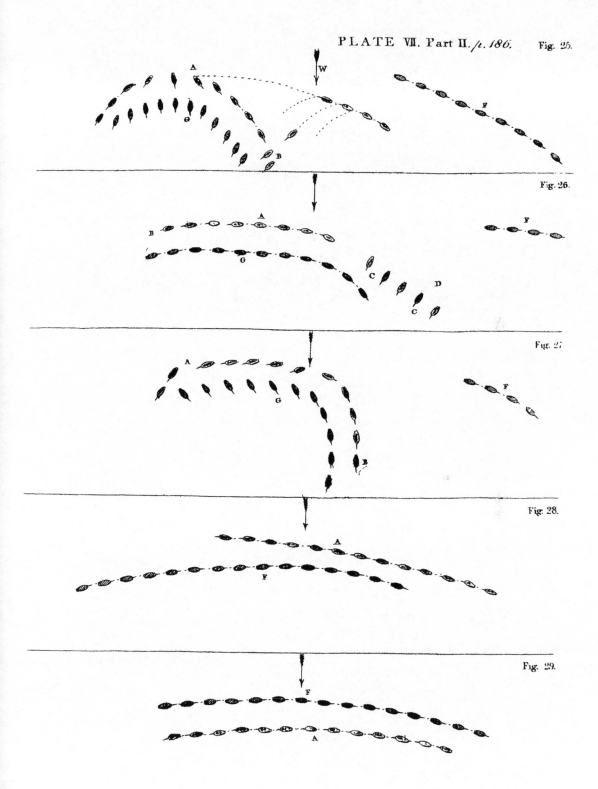

PLATE VII. Part II. *p. 186.* Fig. 25.

Fig. 26.

Fig. 27

Fig. 28.

Fig. 29.

eight ſhips, A and B, the centre and rear following after, as at D.

F, The van of the enemy going off.

OF THE CUTTING THE ENEMY'S LINE AT THE CENTRE WITH THE FIFTH SHIP.

Fig. 34. Let it be ſuppoſed that the fifth ſhip A has been appointed to cut the enemy's line at the centre, and that the four leading ſhips B, are in courſe ranged along under G, the enemy's rear.

Fig. 35. Plate IX. The conſequence will be, that all the ſhips of the enemy G H, which were aſtern of this attack, will not only be forced to leeward by A and the ſhips aſtern who followed him to windward, but will be ſtopped in their way ahead, and muſt be preſſed farther to leeward by the remaining part of the fleet coming up at D. By which time it may be ſuppoſed that the ſhips aſtern in their rear, ſeeing the ſtop ahead, will be preparing to put before the wind, as at H, when a complete rout of the whole of this diviſion of the enemy muſt follow.

B, The four headmoſt ſhips, having ranged paſt the enemy, are putting about to cut off their eſcape towards K.

F, The enemy's van going off.

THE ATTACK ON THE VAN OF THE ENEMY'S LINE WITH THE FIFTH SHIP.

In this attack, as well as that of the former caſe, the danger to which the four headmoſt ſhips may be expoſed is ſo great,

that

that it is not probable that either the one or the other will often
be attempted.

THE ATTACK WITH THE CENTRE.

FIG. 36. PLATE IX.

Let us fuppofe that the leading fhips of the fleet A, having
fetched fomewhere in the van of the enemy, and that they have
ranged along the whole of their line, and under their lee ; and
that B, the headmoft of thefe fhips, has advanced nearly abreaft,
or in immediate oppofition to the fternmoft of the enemy's fhips
G ; and, at the time that fome of the heavieft fhips D in the
centre, having kept their wind, fhall have cut the line fomewhere
near the enemy's centre, at F, in like manner as defcribed in the
former cafes.

Fig. 37. plate IX. The enemy's fleet having been cut in
twain in this manner, their van F from their rear G, the feparation will be fuch, it will be next to impoffible that thefe two divifions can ever be re-united together again. But the van F and
the rear G making two diftinct objects, the purfuit, with
propriety, ought to be confined to either the one or the other,
as the attempt to carry both evidently muft be inconfiftent.
And whereas, in the courfe of the preceding demonftrations,
the whole force of the fleet making the attack, has, of neceffity,

been.

PLATE VIII. Part II. *p. 188.*

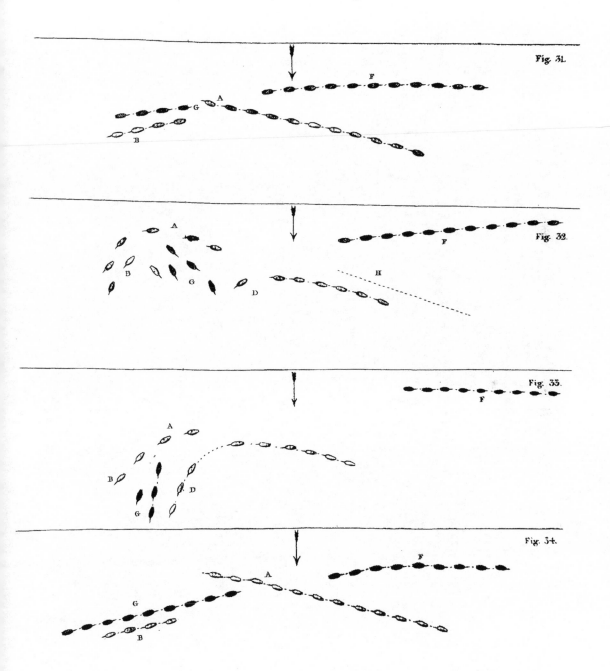

Fig. 31.

Fig. 32.

Fig. 33.

Fig. 34.

been more particularly directed againſt the rear diviſion, in preference to that of the van of the enemy ; and as the ſame cauſe
for this preference evidently ſubſiſts in this caſe, as well as in any
of the former, we will proceed, in the firſt place, with the de-
monſtration of the attack upon the rear G.

(Fig. 37. Plate IX.) The headmoſt ſhips of the rear diviſion
of the enemy having been forced to the leeward by A, the ſhip
which cut the line will ſtill be continued to be preſſed farther and
farther down the wind, by the additional weight of the ſhips a-
ſtern coming up in ſucceſſion as at B.

C, Some ſhips aſtern of the ſhips B, preparing to bear away
and ſtand after the enemy's rear diviſion G.

D, The headmoſt ſhips of the van having already ranged paſt
the enemy, and being aſſured of the improbability of any part of
his rear diviſion being ever able to get to windward, are preparing to put about, to be in readineſs to follow which way ſoever
it ſhall direct its courſe.

F, The van diviſion of the enemy thus ſeparated from his
rear, and ſeeing the danger it muſt be expoſed to, and that it
will never be able to get to windward, are putting before the wind,
as well to effect a retreat as to take all chances of effecting a junction with the ſhips of the rear, which may afterwards be ſo happy as to make an eſcape.

Fig. 38. plate IX. ſhows the attack with the centre a little farther advanced.

B b

A,

A, The ſhip which cut the line, and part of thoſe ſhips which followed up after him, ſtill ranging paſt to windward, and preparing to put about; in the mean while are keeping up a heavy raking fire upon the enemy going off.

G, The rear diviſion of the enemy, having the greateſt part of them diſengaged themſelves of the van of their adverſaries, are endeavouring to make off, by putting through the gap.

B, Theſe ſhips having ſtopped the headmoſt ſhips of the rear diviſion of the enemy, and having forced them to put before the wind, are preparing to follow him.

C, The rear of A, having now puſhed forward, will be in ſufficient time to get cloſe upon the larboard quarter of the enemy, and keep by him whereſoever he ſhall go.

F, The van of the enemy.

Plate 10. fig. 39. G, The rear diviſion of the enemy completely encompaſſed by the whole fleet, viz.

A, With the ſhips which cut the line and went to windward, now carrying every ſail in purſuit.

B, The ſhips in the rear having had ſufficient time to come up, and are now bearing upon the larboard ſide of G the enemy.

D, The ſhips of the van keeping cloſe upon his ſtarboard ſide.

F, The van of the enemy putting before the wind, and anxiouſly attending the iſſue of this unequal conteſt.

Notwithſtanding it muſt already have been ſelf-evident, why the proſecution of the attack on the rear of the enemy's line, and

not

PLATE IX. Part II. p. 190.

Fig. 35.

Fig. 36.

Fig. 37.

Fig. 38.

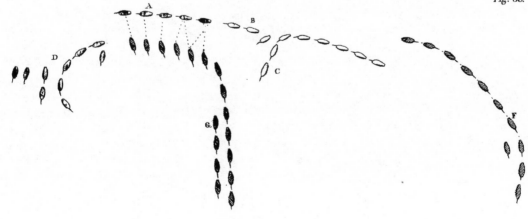

not on the van, has conftantly been confidered, in the preceding demonftrations, as the object of greater attention, it is ftill hoped that the following reafons will not prove unacceptable.

Becaufe a part of the force, by the fuppofition, having been detached, and already far advanced in the attack of the enemy's line *, it would be a manifeft impropriety not to follow the blow, and ftill more unpardonable not to give the neceffary fupport to the few advanced fhips, (B B, fig. 31. and 34.), which otherwife might be left at the mercy of the enemy's rear.

The purfuit of the rear is alfo more immediately practicable : For while the fhips in the van D, which have ranged paft the enemy's line (fig. 38.), are putting about to entangle his fternmoft fhips cut off, the centre fhips of A, together with his rear B, having now got almoft in contact with the fhips in the rear of F, are preparing to furround them.

Whereas, in the purfuit of the van, the headmoft fhips of the enemy having at the time in queftion got above three miles diftance even from the fternmoft and neareft fhips of A (fig. 40.), and above nine miles diftant from his headmoft fhips; to put about fhip, and get up with the van of the enemy at F, that is, to recover the time loft, would be a work of great difficulty.

B b 2

DEMON-

---

* *Vide* the four fhips at B (fig. 31.); the four fhips at B (fig. 34.); and more particularly the fhips in the van at B (fig. 36.)

DEMONSTRATION.

Plate X. fig. 40. Let A be the van divifion, confifting of 18 fhips, which have ranged paft to the northward ; and let B, which cut the enemy's line, be the fhip at the head of the rear divifion, confifting of eighteen fhips likewife. Then, as 300 yards is the fpace ufually allotted for each fhip, 6 fhips will require a fpace of one mile *; and 36 fhips, the number of the fleet A and B, will require a fpace of fix miles. But the van of the enemy F, fuppofed to confift of 18 fhips alfo, will likewife require a fpace of three miles. And as it is evident, that a fpace of fix miles muft be required for extending the whole line of the fleet A ; that is, from C to D, and a fpace of three miles muft be required for extending the van of the enemy F ; then the whole diftance between the headmoft fhip of the fleet A, and the headmoft of the fleet of the enemy, that is, the diftance between the points C and H, muft be a fpace of nine miles.

G, the rear of the enemy on the point of being furrounded.

Fig. 40. By the profecution of the attack upon the rear divifion, you will have your whole force, van and rear, undivided, fay 36 fhips combined againft 18 fhips, the number cut off from the van divifion of the enemy. Whereas, in the cafe of purfuing the van, it muft be evident, that your force being divided, the rear of your line only, after putting about fhip, can with advantage be employed in the chafe of the van of the enemy, now got to the diftance of three or four miles ; and if overtaken, to be

fought

---

* *Vide* Part I. No. 25.

fought with upon a perfect equality ; while at the fame time the fhips in your van are either rendered ufelefs, by having ftretched too far ahead, or, at the beft, will be obliged to follow the rear of the enemy, now got many miles to leeward, and equal in number, fhip for fhip, if ever they can be overtaken.

Fig. 41. Is fuppofed to fhow the van A, in the act of wearing to ftand after the rear of the enemy G ; while B, the rear of A, is fuppofed to get upon the larboard tack to ftand after the van F, and prevent his junction with his rear G.

Upon the whole of this inveftigation, Part I. and Part II. with refpect to the nature of both attacks, it may be concluded, that the attack from the leeward quarter can be executed with the greateft number of advantages, of which it is not one of the leaft, that when a fhip of the leeward fleet comes to be crippled, fhe will ftill continue to remain under the protection of her friends. Whereas, on the contrary, fhould a fhip of the fleet to windward come to be crippled, fhe will fall immediately into the power of her enemies, (as per fig. 2. plate 1.)

S E C-

―――――――

S E C T I O N　IV.

THE PERPENDICULAR ATTACK, OR THE ATTACK AT RIGHT ANGLES.

The following cafe, not very probable indeed, but as it fome time or other may happen, and as it has fome affinity to the attack from the leeward, is introduced in this place.

Plate XI. fig. 42. Let us fuppofe the wind at weft at W, and the numerous fleet F G in an irregular and diforderly line abreaft, extended to a great length from windward to leeward, that is, from the weftern to the eaftern quarter, and let them be proceeding on their way to the northward from F towards A. At A, let an opponent fleet be difcovered ahead at fome miles diftance, and fuppofe this fleet A fhall be greatly inferior in number, yet ftill the fleet F G muft be confidered as in a very dangerous fituation.

How the fleet F G has got into fuch a fituation, is not fo eafy a matter to be explained, unlefs we fhall be allowed to imagine, that its being found extended in a line abreaft from windward to leeward, might be accounted for in this manner; that having, for fome time before, been working to windward, with the wind either at fouth at S, or at north at N; and afterwards the wind coming

around

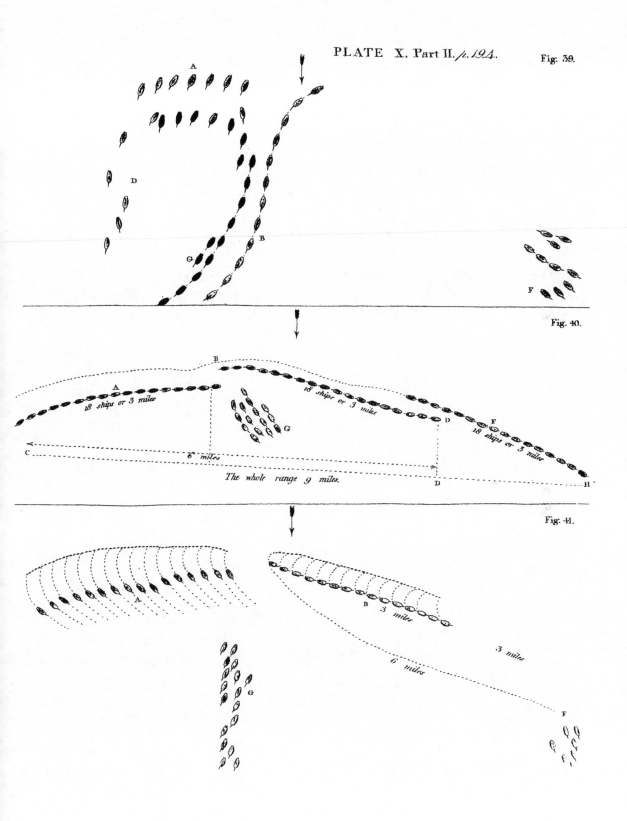

PLATE X. Part II. *p. 194.*   Fig. 39.

Fig. 40.

18 ships or 3 miles

18 ships or 3 miles

18 ships or 3 miles

6 miles

The whole range 9 miles.

Fig. 41.

3 miles

6 miles

3 miles

around all of a fudden to the weft at W, that there was not
time to arrange the fhips accordingly. Again, let us fuppofe this
to have taken place near day-break, that there was a fog fo thick
that the fituation of the fhips could not be difcerned, and that,
unfufpicious of the neighbourhood of an enemy, which could
be able to contend with them, they were carelefs, but that they
were firing guns as fignals for reftoring their intended order.

Again, let us fuppofe an opponent fleet A, in the courfe of a
cruife, and upon the look-out, that he fhall have heard the above
fignals, and, upon the clearing up of the fog, that he fhall difcover this enemy in the circumftances as defcribed, but extended
to fuch a length from windward to leeward, as to fatisfy him,
that, although their numbers were great, yet it might be poffible
to attack them with much advantage. It might be reafoned
thus : The right wing F, of this enemy, is at fo great a diftance, and fo far to leeward of the left wing G, that fhould an
attack be made upon this left wing, fo far to windward, and this
fhould be done with celerity, and before any material change
could be effected in the difpofition of their force, it will be next
to impoffible for this left wing G to receive the fmalleft affiftance
from F, the fhips fo far to leeward.

Plate XI. fig. 43. Accordingly, let us imagine that this opponent A, with his fleet, although inferior in number, as two to
one, fhall pufh on, with every fail fet, and at right angles, that
he fhall cut afunder this enemy's line abreaft at B, but in fuch
proportion that he fhall be fuperior in force to the fhips G to
windward, fo cut off and feparated.

Plate

Plate XI. fig. 44.   Again, fuppofe this fleet of A to have paffed on ahead towards the fouth at C, and that the whole of the
force, and in particular the rear, fhall have tacked and come
up again with G, is it not eafy to conceive, that this unfortunate
divifion being in this manner cut off and prevented from flying
to leeward, muft fubmit to fuperior force, while, in the mean time,
their friends, fo far to leeward at F, after attempting every thing
they can, will not have it in their power to give them the fmalleft
affiftance ? In this fingular cafe, it muft be obferved, that the feveral
fhips of the fleet A, in making this attack, muft be on equal
terms with thofe of the enemy, fhip for fhip, with their heads
in oppofition to each other.

END OF PART II.

NAVAL.

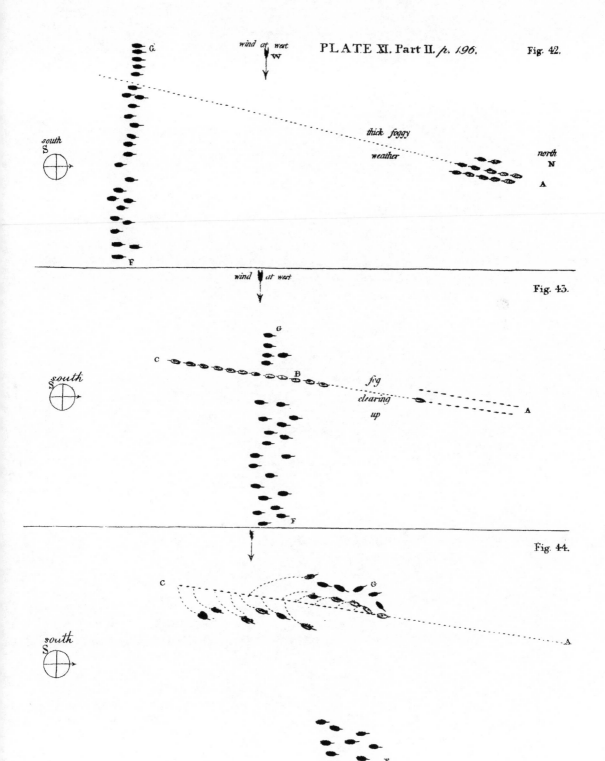

PLATE XI. Part II. p. 196.

Fig. 42.

wind at west
W

thick foggy

weather

south
S

north
N

A

G

F

Fig. 43.

wind at west

south

G

C

B

fog

clearing

up

A

F

Fig. 44.

C

G

south
S

A

F

NAVAL TACTICS.

PART III.

AN

HISTORICAL SKETCH

OF

NAVAL TACTICS.

SINCE the ftudy of NAVAL TACTICS is of the greateft importance to this Empire, and fince the abilities and fkill of
Britifh feamen, in the conduct and management of fingle fhips,
are fo manifeft, that nothing higher has exifted in any one profeffion or department of life; it is therefore the more worthy of
inquiry from what caufe or accident it fhould have proceeded,

that

that fo little progrefs has been made, in the moft important part
of the fubject; I mean, the mode of arranging and conducting
of fhips, when affembled in great fleets, for the purpofe of advancing to battle.

It is not, however, intended that the Naval Tactics of the an-
cients fhould be underftood to be affected by what has been faid;
on the contrary, from hiftory, we are made to believe that the
conduct of their commanders, in moft of their military operations at fea, was founded on principles equally applicable, and
equally underftood, with thofe which governed their military operations by land.   Of this, the battles of Salamis, of Actium, &c.
are examples.

That Naval Hiftory, in modern times, has not been fo perfect
in its information, may be admitted, if it is true, that, of all the
numerous engagements at fea, with the Spaniards, with the Dutch,
and with the French, fpirited and fuccefsful as they fometimes
were, not one fatisfactory plan or defcription has been obtained,
by which even the arrangement or movement of the different
fleets could be difcovered, more early than that of Admiral MAT-
THEWS, in 1744; nor one, from which an idea of any fyftem,
of either attack or defence, can be formed, more early than that
of Admiral BYNG in 1756.

From a diftinction fo remarkable as this, an idea has been fug-
gefted, of having Naval Hiftory divided into Periods, in which,
by comprehending and diftinguifhing the particular changes of

the

the weapons, in the fhipping, or in the modes of practice, fome caufe, fome effential error in principle, fome defect in conduct, will be difcovered, from whence fhould have originated this fingular difference of information, between the Naval Tactics of ancient and modern times; for it never can be imputed to the hiftorian alone.

The Hiftory of Naval Tactics may therefore be divided into the following Periods:

The FIRST PERIOD will comprehend the time in which the progreffive motion of fhips and fleets, advancing to battle, had continued to be dependent upon, and confined to, the propulfive power of the oar, and while the decifion of the conteft was entrufted to the fword, as in the fea battles of antiquity, Salamis, Actium, &c. as before mentioned; with which alfo may be included the battle of Lepanto in 1571.

The SECOND PERIOD includes the time that fails became the neceffary, and almoft the only means of the progreffion of fhips, now of greater dimenfions, more unwieldy, and no longer manageable by the exertion of the men within by oars. This Period begins with the Spanifh Armada, comprehends the engagements between the Englifh and the Dutch, together with the battles of Bantry Bay, Beachyhead, La Hogue in the feventeenth century, and of Malaga in 1719, of none of which have we been able to procure any particular plan or defcription, down to the year 1740.

The

The THIRD PERIOD, then, with propriety, will begin with thofe engagements of which we have been able to give a particular plan and defcription; that of Admiral MATTHEWS in 1744, including Admiral BYNG's engagement in 1756, Sir GEORGE POCOCK's in 1758, together with thofe of the AMERICAN WAR, from the year 1778 to 1782.

The year 1782, fo much diftinguifhed by extraordinary exertions of naval ability, at the fame time that it will form the commencement of a FOURTH PERIOD in the Hiftory of Naval Tactics, will alfo give occafion to add a Fourth Part to this Work.

PERIOD

PERIOD I.

As long as the progreffive motion of fhips and fleets, advancing to battle, was dependent upon, perhaps confined to, the propelling power of the oar, and the decifion of the conteft was entrufted to the fword, fo long the principles of arrangement and difpofition of force, whether at fea, or at land, fetting afide the more immediate influence of ftorms of wind, could not but be nearly alike. For, when it is confidered that the men engaged in both cafes, at fea and on land, were often the fame, actuated equally by courage or revenge, by fear or defpair; that the means of advancing and retreating, and advancing again, were equally in their power, and the weapons, offenfive and defenfive, nearly the fame; fhips of war, with their complements of men on board, under fuch circumftances, not unaptly might be faid to bear a near refemblance to cohorts, or battalions of infantry, or even to fquadrons of cavalry, in the fhock of battle.

Again, when we confider that fhips, in thofe ancient days, were of fmall fize, of little draught of water, and unembarraffed by the ebbing and flowing of tides, as in the Mediterranean; that, by keeping clofe by the fhore at all times, they could be concealed or covered behind headlands or iflands; fleets of

this

this defcription, compofed of numbers of fhips, in like manner might be confidered as refembling numerous corps of troops affembled and acting as armies at land, not only becaufe they could form ambufcades or ftratagems, but alfo could, on fimilar principles, attack, fecure, or defend a ftrength, or ftrait, choofing and occupying their ground at pleafure, as at Salamis, or Actium, and as in many other inftances exhibited between the Romans and Carthaginians, which it is needlefs to mention. And, to extend the bounds of this period, the battle of Lepanto, in 1571, may be included; which differs only in this refpect, that gunpowder was then known and ufed, but fimilar to, and even ftrictly connected with, ancient practice; in fo far, that the conteft, notwithftanding this knowledge of gunpowder, was decided by the fword alone. The veffels engaged, if not precifely of the fame conftruction, were ftill about the fame fize, and were, in like manner, propelled in their motions with oars, by the manual exertion of the men on board.

That a fleet of this defcription, in thefe circumftances, when to windward, had advantages over the fleet to leeward, will not be denied. When advancing to make an attack, the effect of their impetus or fhock muft have been the greater from their having the wind in their favour; and, when defirous of declining an engagement, it was more in their power to retire, and more difficult for the leeward fleet to get up with them. But, in advancing to battle, both fleets were upon an equal footing, propelled by their oars, each galley having her prow oppofed to that of her adverfary. Whatever, therefore, were the

weapons

weapons in ufe, catapultas, baliftas, or cannon fhot, as at Lepanto, placed, as they were, as a battery, in the fore part of the veffel, whether in making or fuftaining an attack, neither fleet, in this refpect, had any particular advantage over the other, whichever of them was to windward or leeward.

PERIOD

PERIOD II.

THE concurrence of many things uniting, would feem to mark out the bounds by which a fecond period in naval hiftory may be diftinguifhed. The extenfion of commerce and naval power to America and to the Eaft Indies, while it protracted the length of voyages, increafed alfo the hazard of the fea. The ufe of great guns being introduced, while at the fame time they were increafing in weight and dimenfions, were alfo multiplied in number, fometimes to the amount of an hundred on board. Ships, for thefe reafons, requiring to be of ftronger conftruction, large and unwieldy, and no longer manageable by the manual exertion of the oar, were obliged to have recourfe to the fail, as dependent on the wind alone, for carrying the requifite manœuvres into execution.

OF SAILS, CONSIDERING THEIR EFFECT ON THE MOTION OF A SHIP, COMPARED WITH OARS.

But fails, however neceffary for the managing of the motions of fhips of larger conftruction, compared with oars, were inadequate to the various operations and movements required in the ancient practice and mode of battle. In a calm, they were of

no

no ufe; and with the wind, could command, in the direction of the motion of the fhip, little more than one half of the plane of the horizon, and this only to leeward.

OF CANNON SHOT, CONSIDERING ITS EFFECT AS COMING FROM THE PROW OF A GALLEY, OR FROM A SHIP'S BROADSIDE.

When guns were planted as a battery in the forecaftle, as they generally at firft were in a galley, the application of their force, though inferior, at leaft with refpect to number, was ftill in the fame direction with the line of their courfe, and which courfe was perfectly under the command of the people within. But when planted on the fides of a fhip, their force and effect, from the greater number, though irrefiftible compared with a galley, yet being at right angles with the line of her courfe, and this courfe depending upon a foreign agent, the wind, and not under an equal command of the people within, the effect and confequences of courfe became fo completely changed and different, that every former idea of naval tactics was immediately overturned.

In the mean time, even during this extraordinary tranfition of circumftances, the naval exploits and enterprifes were, many of them, fpirited, and though not all of them decifive, were conftantly marked with ftrong effect. But when the fhip itfelf, the means of moving that fhip, and the weapons, were undergoing tranfitions fo very extraordinary, it is not eafy to conceive,

D d

that

that conduct adapted to such novelties could not at once be eftablithed.

In the Introduction *, many of thefe exploits have already been enumerated ; but how far the mode of conducting them was or was not the refult of any particular fyftem, remains yet a matter of inquiry.

OF THE SPANISH ARMADA.

PHILIP the Second, poffeffed of Spain, Portugal, and the riches of America, in planning the armament of the Spanifh Armada, confident, and trufting in his great fuperiority, thought only of gratifying his refentment againft ELIZABETH and her fubjects. His fhips being conftructed with lofty buildings at head and ftern, which, like caftles, might overtop and command the decks of the fmaller fhips of the Englifh, neither himfelf nor his admirals were aware how unfit fuch unwieldy, ill-conftructed, and, if poffible, worfe manned veffels, were for navigating feas that were narrow, and in a northern climate, and where, at the fame time, there was not one friendly port to leeward fufficient to receive or afford them fhelter in cafe of accidents. But this cumbrous fleet, (irrefiftible in his imagination), on approaching the Channel, while the fhips of the Englifh were every where to fkulk or fly before it, was to proceed to the eaftward to take on board the Prince of PARMA with his troops, collected in the Low Countries, and, without interruption or difficulty

---

* See the General Introduction prefixed to Part I.

ficulty of any kind whatever, was to enter the Thames, and at one blow to overwhelm ELIZABETH.

On the part of the Englifh, where can a more illuftrious example of naval fkill and forefight be met with, than in the conduct difplayed in accomplifhing the defeat and ruin of this Spanifh Armada, in which the prudence of fuftaining a defence, by fuffering that immenfe armament to wafte its force in an idle contention with the winds and waves, was no lefs confpicuous than the intrepidity and perfeverance with which the. repeated. attacks were made? *

OF THE BRITISH CHANNEL.

That an eftimate may be made of the probable fuccefs, or of the confequent hazard and rifk, to which a numerous armament of great fhips, engaged in an hoftile enterprife of this kind, may be expofed, the Britifh Channel fhould be carefully confidered :

In the firft place, as a barrier or boundary, defending and dividing us from all the reft of the world :

In the next place, as a fea, narrow, winding, and contracted by head-lands, in which the navigation, with all the fkill and attention that can be given, is both difficult and dangerous to mariners, even the moft familiar with it.

D d 2 As

---

* See Introduction, p. 8. Part 1.

As a barrier or boundary, it forms one continued canal, connecting the German and Northern Oceans with the Atlantic, and extends in length to above 1000 miles. The banks of this canal, on the Britifh fhore to the fouth, where wafhed by the Channel, and oppofite to France, far from being open and eafy of defcent to every invafion, as we have been made to believe, like this of the Spanifh Armada, or any other of them, with which, as bugbears, we have been fo often and long threatened, the coaft is bold and dangerous; and if it fhould be accefſible in any one particular and more interefting fpot, as at Portfmouth, the country behind and within is fo ftrong, that from the fouth, or acrofs the Channel, every attempt to approach the capital, or to overrun the kingdom, with common attention given, muft always be defeated.

Confidering the Channel as a fea, narrow, winding, contracted and broken by head-lands, it is affected by rapid tides, forming innumerable dangerous fhelves and banks. By the climate, and by its form, it is fubjected to tempeftuous and fudden changes of wind, fo that the boldeft and moft experienced mariners, from arriving in foundings in approaching the mouth of the Channel, even with a leading wind, and keeping in the fair way, till they get into port, feldom are at eafe. This is meant in the cafe of a fingle fhip. But let any one, ever fo converfant in this navigation, with every advantage of ports in his favour, fay what his feelings have been, when on board of a Britifh fleet cruifing in the Channel, and then we may judge with refpect to a numerous fleet of large fhips, ftrangers, with dark nights and

blowing

blowing weather, what the apprehenfions and feelings may be as well of the officers on board, as of the ftatefman on fhore, who wantonly commits and puts to hazard fo great a part of the marine of his nation in one enterprife, and in fuch perils.

By an eafterly wind (as often is the cafe with our own fhips) an hoftile fleet may be long detained from entering the mouth of the Channel; and by a wind at weft, when once embayed, fuppofe within the head-lands of Portland on the one fhore, and La Hogue on the other, it will not be eafy for them to return. * If the wind from the weft continues, and begins to blow with violence, which it often and fuddenly does, this fleet muft put before it (for there is not one port on the oppofite fhore fuffi- cient to receive and afford fhelter for large fhips for above 1500 miles from Breft, round to the entrance of the Baltic); and, paf- fing the ftraits between Dover and Calais, over fands and through fhelves, they muft get, without remedy, into great diforder. But all the while this fleet, by the fuppofition, has hitherto met with no interruption or annoyance of any kind from Britain, the greater part of her force being occupied at a diftance. What then ought to be the confequences, if followed by num- berlefs fhips, of every fize and denomination, which, in fuch a cafe, and for this occafion only, may be fitted out, and collected from the different ports, which, inceffantly hanging on the rear,

are

---

* No fleet of French men of war has been within thefe head-lands fince the battle of Cape La Hogue, May 19. 1692.

are enabled to take advantage of every accident, many of them at all times, from the fituation of the ports from whence they can be fitted out, being neceſſarily to windward, which way foever the wind ſhall blow? After confidering thefe circum-ſtances, is it to be imagined, that a fleet of ſhips from the fouthward, hoftile to Britain, fo large and fo numerous, will ever, without great lofs, be able to effeⅽt a return through the Channel? Will it not be expeⅽted, that they muft be forced into the North Seas, where, if late in the feafon, in the high latitude of 60 degrees, they will have to encounter all the horrors of winter, long nights, and continual ftorms, not lefs formidable than any thing experienced by Lord ANSON when doubling Cape Horn, as lately felt by the armament commanded by Monf. THUROT?

Of fuch a nature was the route planned for the Spaniſh Arma-da by PHILIP the Second, and by following which route was this mighty enterprife defeated.

OF THE BATTLES WITH THE DUTCH.

The engagements with the Dutch, ſtill later, by almoft one hundred years, than the Spaniſh Armada, glorious as they were to both nations, as exhibitions of courage and perfeverance, give little information with regard to a progrefs or improvement in Naval Taⅽtics. The only idea which I have been able to form of them, is that of numerous fquadrons affembled, to the a-mount of 250 or 300 ſhips, jambed together in narrow feas,

(the

(the Channel), where they have been confined by the shores on each side, and deprived, in a great measure, of every chance of manœuvring.——Here, in one place, ships in clusters entangled with one another, and, independent of all order, getting foul, each of their antagonists ; there, again, in another part of the scene, one ship, single and alone, unsupported, and beset with many enemies, left to make the most gallant resistance she could. Of course, on both sides, much bloodshed and loss of shipping must have been sustained. But, in these engagements, they differed in this from the case of the Spanish Armada, that each of the parties had their ports under their lee, to which they could retire, and from whence they could sally forth at pleasure, so soon as refitted.

OF SIGNALS, THE INVENTION OF WHICH, ABOUT THIS TIME, IS ASCRIBED TO THE DUKE OF YORK.

The invention of signals is generally ascribed to the Duke of York about this time. This, however, is absolutely incredible. He might, indeed, have improved them, but the invention must have been of older date. How could any military operation at sea or on land be conducted without signals ? It cannot be believed that, in reducing the subject of signals to any kind of *system*, he had made much progress, if it is necessary that Admirals, to this day, when entering upon the command of an expedition, have to compose a particular system for themselves ; an attempt which must be attended with much inconvenience ; for it is not conceivable of any new code of signals, however simplified it

may

may be, that it can be made familiar to every officer in a numerous fleet in the courfe of a few days, or even weeks; and therefore is the more abfurd if an enemy is to be encountered with
immediately, which has fometimes been the cafe after a few
hours departure from port.

OF NAVAL INSTRUCTIONS.

The Naval Inftructions about this time formed, for having
fhips extended in line of battle, and which were founded upon
the occafion of the above mentioned battles with the Dutch, in
order to ferve the immediate purpofe of fighting in narrow feas,
if ill qualified (as faid in another place *) for bringing on an
action with a fleet of fhips unwilling to come to a fhock, and
having fea-room to range in at pleafure, they have been no lefs
unfortunate in promoting the means of information; fince, of
all thofe numerous engagements, fo little of fyftem, fo little of
the difpofition or movement of fleets has been comprehended,
that the hiftorian Mr DAVID HUME, accurate and intelligent
as he was in every other fubject of inquiry, giving up the point,
as it would feem, has the following paffage: ‘ There is a natu-
‘ ral confufion attending fea-fights, even beyond other military
‘ tranfactions, derived from the precarious operations of winds
‘ and tides, as well as from the fmoke and darknefs in which
‘ every thing is there involved; no wonder, therefore, that re-
‘ lations of thefe battles are apt to contain uncertainties and con-
‘ tradictions, efpecially when compared by writers of the hoftile
‘ nations,

---

* See Introduction prefixed to Part I. p. 18.

‘ nations, who take a pleasure in exalting their own advantages,
‘ and suppressing those of the enemy *. ’

The part of Mr HUME's history from which this passage is
quoted, was not finished till almost an hundred years after the
battles in question, and not till after he might have consulted the
description of these others, Bantry Bay, Beachy-Head, and La
Hogue. He had likewise the assistance which might be procured
from the battles fought in his own time; that of Malaga in
1719, that of Admiral MATTHEWS in 1744, and that of Admiral BYNG in 1756; together with every degree of information
which could be acquired from the trials which took place in
consequence of the two last, both long and circumstantial †.
Mr HUME, at the same time, nothing at a loss when a battle at
land is to be described, but, like other historians, with infinite
pains, is sure to preface the same with a detail of every circumstance of situation, advantage or disadvantage of ground, by
which the reader is made to foresee whichever of the parties shall
obtain the victory.

Other writers, equally successful in their detail of military
transactions at land, but not a whit more fortunate in their con-
ceptions of operations at sea, talk of agility of shipping, of their

E e   heroes

---

* History of England, Vol. VII. p. 507. 8vo. edit. 1778.

† A later writer still, Mr M‘Pherson, when speaking of the battle of La
Hogue, has these words: ‘ The confusion and want of plan which prevails in
‘ all naval engagements, ought to have saved the victors from the censure which
‘ writers have thrown on their conduct. ’

heroes rushing furious through the squadrons of the enemy, of rushing to battle, of presenting themselves to every danger, of plunging into the middle of the foe, &c.; phrases applicable only to military operations at land, and confiftent, and perhaps in ufe, in fpeaking even of tranfactions at fea, when galleys, as in ancient times, were propelled in every direction with the oar, and actuated upon, and influenced by, the paffions of men within the veffel; but altogether inconfiftent with the motions of unwieldy fhipping, manageable only with the fails, confined, as they muft always be, to particular movements, as mere machines, dependent on the immediate effect of the wind alone, as they are in thefe days.

Is it to the hiftorian, then, that we are to impute this confufion of ideas, the continuation of the ufe of fuch phrafes, and this fo particular defect of information? No; for hiftorians muft have adhered to the fpirit of the defcriptions which have been put into their hands. Is it to the vanity of commanders, defirous of extolling and magnifying their own exploits? No; it can only be attributed to the particular ftate of things at the time, that the intellectuals of men, deranged by fo complete a tranfition of fo many circumftances combined, as before enumerated, have not as yet recovered any proper idea of fyftem, or principles of conduct, adapted to fuch novelties.

PERIOD

PERIOD III.

Supposing Period Third to commence about anno 1740, and to conclude with the end of the year 1781, it will be diftinguifh- ed by thofe fea engagements of which we have been able to pro- cure fuch an authentic and fubftantial information of circumftan- ces, as could authorife a particular plan and defcription. But, be- fore proceeding farther with this inveftigation, it will be neceffary to premife a few General Principles.

GENERAL PRINCIPLES.

Case I. A commander who fhall have fo difpofed of his force, that no one divifion or part can be attacked, without a poffibility of being immediately fupported by the whole, or at leaft by fome other part, has taken not only the firft precaution to prevent a defeat, but alfo has taken the firft ftep to obtain a victory.

Case II. The commander who, in leading on his force, fhall make his attack with great fuperiority, upon any one divifion or part of his enemy, and while this divifion fhall be pofted fo as it cannot be fupported, has, in like manner, not only taken the

E e 2

firft

firſt ſtep to obtain a victory, but alſo has laid hold of the firſt precaution to ſecure a retreat, ſhould it ever be neceſſary.

CASE III. Hence, on the other hand, and in oppoſition to Caſe I. ſhould ever a commander have ſo diſpoſed of his force, that any one diviſion or part may be attacked, by a great ſuperiority, without a poſſibility of having it ſupported by the whole, or by any one part of his remaining force, that commander muſt be defeated.

CASE IV. Hence alſo, in reverſe of Caſe II., a commander who, by the mode of his attack, ſhall ſo diſpoſe of his force, that any one diviſion or part, difficult to be ſupported, ſhall be expoſed to his enemy when greatly ſuperior, ſuppoſe it a cannonade greater, by many degrees, than he can bring up to oppoſe it, ſuch commander undoubtedly will be worſted.

That rules, ſuch as theſe, are applicable to, and ſhould have influence upon, military operations at ſea as well as at land, every one will allow. By them, the following ſtrictures upon modern naval practice, and the mode of attack which have been propoſed, muſt be judged ; and to ſome error or neglect of them it is, that the defect of information, which has diſtinguiſhed the former period, muſt be imputed.

OF

OF THE MOVEMENTS OF SHIPS AND FLEETS IN RELATION
TO EACH OTHER.

Ships, or fleets, managed as they are in thefe days with fails
only, though not, as animals, felf-moving bodies, that is, under
the perfect command of the men within, to be carried with oars
againft wind and tide, at pleafure, in every direction, yet, confidered as machines, governed by, and confined to, the laws of
mechanics; their paths in the fea, and their military evolutions,
may be traced and delineated upon proper principles. Now, the
moving power or agent being the wind, and this affecting any
number of them mutually, at one and the fame time, and in the
fame direction, as in the cafe of fleets when in oppofition, the
movement of the feveral fhips or fleets, in relation to each other,
will be reciprocal, confonant, and regular.

Not only fhips, but whole fleets, in hoftile oppofition, when
in the fame ftream of wind, muft equally, and, at the fame time,
both of them in their motions relatively, be fo affected, that,
fuppofing the face of the fea to be conceived as a plane, on paper, and the wind as a point A (Plate XII. fig. 13.), from which
both fleets B and F are operated upon; we alfo may carry the
fuppofition fo far as to conceive that both might be affected in
fome way, as fufpended from the fame point, as at the pendu-
lum D, D, D.

Hence, when confidering the connexion between two fleets,
fuppofing the one to be to windward of the other, whatever way
the

the wind fhall veer about, both being dependent on the fame
wind, the motion and manœuvring of each, in relation to each
other, can ftill be of the fame nature.

———————

OF THE FACE OF THE OCEAN, CONSIDERING IT AS A FIELD
FOR THE MILITARY OPERATIONS OF HOSTILE FLEETS.

That the face of the ocean, confidering it as a field for military operations, but more particularly as a field for immediate
engagement, the hoftile fleets oppofed, having neither rivers, ra-
vines, banks, woods, or mountains, to ftop progrefs, or interrupt
the fight, fo that ambufcades or ftratagems can be formed, and
while each are extended in line of battle, where every individual
fhip, and the line into which fhe belongs, is operated upon by
the fame wind, at the fame time, and, by the laws of mechanifm,
confined to movements in every refpeft confonant in relation to
each other; Should not every occurrence, every tranfaction, for
thefe reafons, and in fuch circumftances, be the more eafily conceived, underftood, and explained, than even in military operations on land ?

A fleet on the face of the ocean, on the defenfive, extended in
line of battle, and prepared to receive an enemy coming down to
make an attack, as has been the late practice, from the windward, may be compared to an army pofted to great advantage,
and provided with numerous batteries of cannon, impenetrable if
attacked in front; and fhould any fuch attack be made, that each

fhip,

Historical Sketch
Of the relative motion of Fleets as dependant on the bearing of the Wind.

PLATE XII Part III. *p.218.*

fhip, comparing it with a fingle battalion, or party of cavalry, may retire, fuppofe to leeward, under cover of feconds on either fide (ahead and aftern), and choofing a new pofition, from whence the enemy could be annoyed again and again, this may be repeated with equal advantage as at firft, while the fleet, and each fhip that makes fuch an attack muft be ruined, crippled, and rendered incapable of purfuing, or following.

OF THE APPLICATION OF THE FOREGOING PRINCIPLES AND IDEAS, WITH SOME OF THE SEA ENGAGEMENTS OF THIS PERIOD OF NAVAL HISTORY.

Admiral MATTHEWS's engagement in 1744 is the firft of this Third Period of Naval Hiftory; it is alfo the firft in the lift of thofe of which we have been able to procure authentic and fub-ftantial information of circumftances; it is alfo the firft to be confidered, with refpect to the application of the foregoing prin-ciples, &c.

APPLICATION OF THESE PRINCIPLES TO THE CONDUCT OF ADMIRAL MATTHEWS, AS MAKING THE ATTACK.

According to Cafe II., for example, the commander who, in leading on his force, fhall make his attack with great fuperiority, upon any one divifion or part of his enemy, and this divifion fo pofted that it cannot be fupported, has taken the firft ftep to ob-tain a victory.

By

By the pofition of Admiral MATTHEWS's fleet before the engagement, his force was fo difpofed, that, had that force been
led on, or had the force which was led on been fupported as
it fhould have been, the attack might have been made with fuch
a fuperiority, that the Spanifh Admiral, with the fhips in his
rear aftern of him, feparated as they were from the van and centre of the combined fleet, there is not a doubt that the whole
might have been cut off.

But, confidering this attack in another view, and according to
principles, Cafe IV., that Mr MATTHEWS, by carrying down his
fhip, the Namur, and her feconds, the Norfolk and Marlborough,
in the manner he did, had them expofed to a cannonade, unfortunately greater, by many degrees, than he could at the time
bring to oppofe againft it, and by which thefe fhips were fo difabled, that, had the Spaniards thought fit to retire, (a manœuvre
which the French, their allies, have many times fince, on the like
occafion, put in practice), Mr MATTHEWS neither could have
ftopped them, nor could he have followed them *.

APPLICATION OF THE SAME PRINCIPLES TO THE CONDUCT OF THE SPANISH ADMIRAL.

Confidering that the fleet of the Spanifh Admiral was extended to a great length, that he was feparated at a great diftance
from

---

* *Vide* Admiral MATTHEWS's Engagement, Part I. p. 110., and Plate XVI.
fig. 2.

from both his van and centre, and that his own divifion was left unfupported; according to principles, Cafe III., he fhould have been defeated.

Again, in another view, had the principles, as laid down, been thought applicable by the Spanifh commander, or had he been inftructed, or aware of what has fince been the practice of French commanders; neither would he have neglected to avail himfelf of difabling Mr MATTHEWS, while coming down to attack him, that is, while he had the fuperiority of fire in his favour; nor would he, by patiently lying ftill, have given time fufficient for Mr MATTHEWS to retaliate, by difabling him in his turn, but, unhurt, would have withdrawn his fhips from battle for the prefent; and, by bearing away, would have attained a new fituation, where he might be out of the reach of cannon-fhot, and where he might be in preparation to form a new line of battle to leeward, No. 17.

OF ADMIRAL BYNG'S ENGAGEMENT, CONSIDERING HOW IT MAY BE AFFECTED BY THE APPLICATION OF THE FOREGOING PRINCIPLES.

In Admiral BYNG's engagement, twelve years after that of Mr MATTHEWS, the French *now* themfelves alone the opponents, their mode of defence adopted *, though defective with refpect to the difpofition of their force, according to principles, Cafe II., and

F f which

---

* *Vide* No. 48. Part I. BYNG's Engagement.

which has been proved in another place; * yet, confidering the mode in which the attack was made upon them, feems to be the beft which could be imagined in their fituation and circumftances. In great ftrength, arranged in line of battle themfelves, they not only difabled their enemy while coming on to attack them, but, unhurt, they retreated, and accomplifhed, in the moft complete manner, the full purpofe of their deftination, by making prize of the caftle and ifland of Minorca.

That the French were in noways beholden to chance for fuch defence, but that it was ftudied and intended, muft be evident from this, that, in every one of the many engagements which they have had with our fleets fince that time, when to leeward, as on this occafion, it has been the mode they have put in practice, and it has been juftified by an equal degree of fuccefs, in every inftance.

If, then, this ftate of the fubject fhall be admitted to be juft, Admiral BYNG's engagement off Minorca, May 20. 1756, will be the firft in modern times from which any degree of fyftem can be formed.

Again, with refpect to the mode of attack, the part which Mr BYNG had in the action, how applicable foever it is with principles Cafe IV., his van, by this mode of attack, was fo difpofed, that it could not be fupported. It was expofed, while coming down, to a cannonade greater by many degrees than could be brought

at

---

* The mode of attack propofed, p. 123. Part I.

at the time againſt it; and being thereby diſabled, and rendered incapable of following or purſuing his enemy, and the purpoſe of his deſtination left unaccompliſhed, Mr BYNG muſt be allowed to have been worſted. This attack appears to have been founded upon an idea of taking, deſtroying, or diſabling, the whole of an enemy's fleet, and, upon this idea, to have aſſumed a line of approach improper, as having given the enemy the greateſt poſſible advantage.

In the mode of attack according to this idea, of taking, deſtroying, or diſabling the whole of an enemy's fleet, extended in line of battle, two lines of approach have been diſtinguiſhed; the firſt, the line of interſection, the line of neareſt approach, or laſking line, as put in practice, and ſo named by Mr BYNG; the other, that line put in practice by Sir GEORGE POCOCK in his engagement, April 29. 1758, two years after, in the Eaſt Indies, and which, for diſtinction ſake, has been termed the line of purſuit, or curve of purſuit.

Of the firſt of theſe lines, (the laſking line), five examples have been collected; and, upon theſe examples, as claſſed in Section 1. p. 43. Part I. the obſervations and demonſtrations, pointing out the defects in the accuſtomed mode of attack from the windward, are founded.

Of the ſecond of theſe lines, the line of purſuit, it has *alſo* been defined in the deſcription given of Sir GEORGE POCOCK's engagement in the Eaſt Indies. It is not, however, wiſhed to be underſtood that ſome one, or all of theſe five examples given, do not, in ſome degree, partake of the properties of both of theſe

F f 2

lines.

lines, or that Sir George Pocock's engagement, becaufe of this diftinction, fhould not be included in the fame clafs with thefe five examples, but becaufe, on no other occafion, has any thing been faid that could give rife to have this line of purfuit defined fo accurately as in this engagement of Sir George Pocock.

OTHER OBSERVATIONS, BUT APPLICABLE TO PERIOD THIRD ONLY.

1. That, in the many engagements with which this third period has been diftinguifhed, the enemy, whether they were to windward or to leeward, have never once attempted to make or begin the attack.

2. That not only through the whole, has this period been dif‑tinguifhed by a fafhion of exalting the character of the fhips of the enemy, in point of failing, compared with our own; but, for the greater part, it has been diftinguifhed by a fafhion, as perni‑cious as unjuft, viz. that of depreciating the character of Britifh feamen.

A gentleman *, but not of the profeffion, after reading the foregoing naval inquiry as it was firft printed, communicated to me the following obfervation: ' The only thing which tempts ' one to entertain a doubt with refpect to your fyftem is, that the ' beneficial effects are fo manifeft, that one wonders they fhould ' not have occurred to profeffional men.

To

---

* Dr Adam Smith, author of the Wealth of Nations.

To which obfervation, after what has been faid, it is fufficient to reply, that fome defect has exifted fomewhere; for if the many examples given during this laft period fhall be confidered, the uniformity of effect, fhewn by them to have taken place, authorifes us to conclude, that chance of war had not been concerned; for otherwife fome one unlucky fhip might have been taken or funk, or might have been blown up in the air, accidents frequent, nay infallibly attendant on fuch other occafions, during the courfe of the former period of naval hiftory.

END OF PART III.

NAVAL

NAVAL TACTICS.

PART IV.

INTRODUCTION.

WITH the year 1782, the laſt of the American war, re-markable for a ſeries of intereſting events, and of new and ſingular exertions of naval ability, we will begin the Fourth part of this work. The fortunate turn which then was given to naval affairs, and the ſplendid achievements then performed, render that important year the proper commencement of a Fourth period in the hiſtory of Naval Tactics. But, although victories, equally ſplendid with thoſe of the year 1782, have been recent-ly obtained *, and merit particular examination in a treatiſe on Naval Tactics, yet this part of the preſent work does not profeſs to embrace any account of theſe late glorious tranſactions, and will extend no farther than what was originally propoſed.

That

* Earl HOWE's, 1ſt of June 1796.—Earl of ST VINCENT's, 14th of Fe-bruary 1797.

That the whole of this Fourth part was written while the author was under the immediate impreſſion of the enthuſiaſm excited by the merit of the actions at the time, he cannot deny: nor will he diſſemble, that the event, with the conſideration of which this part is to commence, viz. the plan and enterprize to relieve the iſland of St Chriſtophers, is, of all naval exhibitions, the firſt, which had given him any real pleaſure in making the deſcription. With reſpect to the other obſervations, they expreſs what were the feelings of moſt people at the time; and now, after a lapſe of more than twenty years, he has not yet ſeen reaſon ſufficient to induce him to make any alterations.

SIR

SIR SAMUEL HOOD'S ENGAGEMENT.

DESCRIPTION OF THE SEVERAL ACTIONS BETWEEN THE
BRITISH FLEET, COMMANDED BY SIR SAMUEL HOOD, AND
THE FRENCH FLEET, COMMANDED BY COUNT DE GRASSE,
OFF ST CHRISTOPHERS, THE 24TH, 25TH, AND 26TH OF
FEBRUARY 1782.

A few months after the unfortunate cataſtrophe of Lord
CORNWALLIS's army at York-Town in the Cheſapeak river, Sir
SAMUEL HOOD being at Barbadoes, and hearing that an attack
had been made upon the iſland of St Chriſtophers, by a powerful
armament under the command of Count de GRASSE, ſet ſail for
its relief with twenty-two ſhips of the line, five frigates, and
two ſchooners.   He arrived off the ſouth-eaſt end of the iſland of
Nevis, at day-break of the 24th February 1782 ; when, directing
the ſquadron to be formed in line of battle, he determined to
attack the fleet of the enemy, conſiſting of thirty-three ſhips, and
then lying at anchor in Baſſa Terra Road, iſland of St Chriſtophers.

Plate XIII. fig. 1. A, The Britiſh fleet ſuppoſed on their courſe
round the iſland of Nevis, on the morning of the 24th.   F, The
fleet of the enemy at anchor in Baſſa Terra Road, having their
van far to windward of the rear.

SIR SAMUEL's inſtructions to each ſhip, given in St. John's
Road,

Road, Antigua, were, ' To ſtand on till abreaſt of the van of the
' enemy, as per courſe B B ; and after having delivered each ſhip
' her whole fire upon the two headmoſt ſhips of the enemy, to
' haul off in ſucceſſion, as per courſe C C C ; and then, by tacking,
' to return in the ſame ſucceſſion, and again, and again, to repeat
' each ſhip her whole fire. ' By which ingenious method it was
intended, firſt, to cut off or deſtroy theſe two headmoſt ſhips,
which being effected, to repeat, in the ſame manner, the attack
upon the next two ſhips aſtern.

The misfortune of the ſhip Alfred running aboard of the
Nymph in the morning, ſoon after the ſignal was thrown out,
occaſioning much delay, the enemy had intelligence of SIR SA-
MUEL's approach ; and, dreading the conſequences of an attack,
in the ſituation they were then in, quitted their anchorage and
put to ſea, as per courſe G G ; and in the afternoon, and during
the whole night of the 24th, kept three or four miles to leeward
of the Britiſh fleet, which was ſtill under the weſt end of the
iſland of Nevis.

────────

EXTRACT OF SIR SAMUEL HOOD'S LETTER.

' At day-light of the 25th, we plainly diſcovered 33 ſail of the
' enemy's ſhips, 29 of which of two decks formed in a line a-
' head. I made every appearance of an attack, which threw
' the COUNT DE GRASSE a little from the ſhore : And as I
' thought I had a fair proſpect of gaining the anchorage he left,
' and

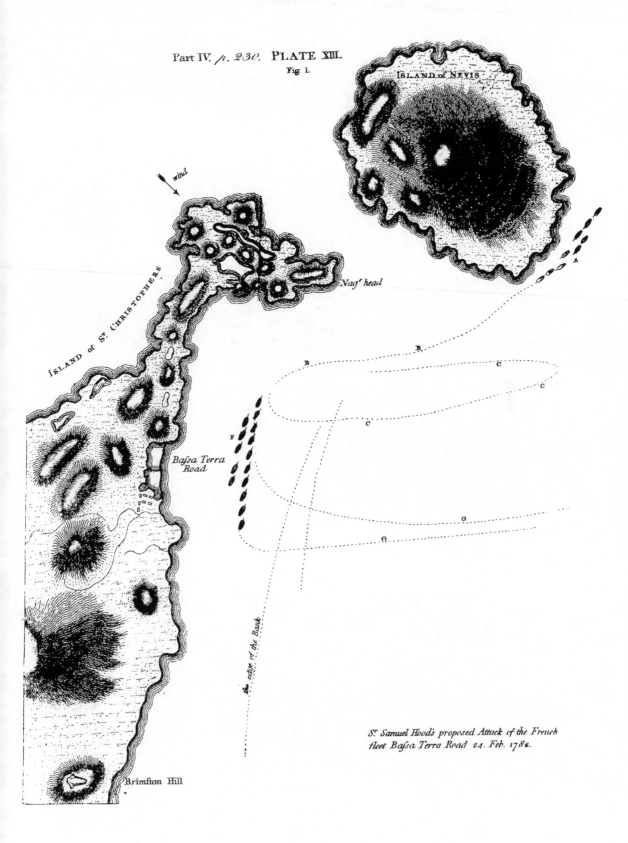

ISLAND of NEVIS

wind

Nag's head

ISLAND of St CHRISTOPHERS

Bassa Terra Road

the edge of the Bank.

Brimston Hill

Sr Samuel Hood's proposed Attack of the French fleet Bassa Terra Road 24. Feb. 1782.

' and well knowing it was the only chance I had of faving the
' ifland, if it was to be faved, I pufhed for it, and fucceeded, by
' having my rear and part of my centre engaged.

' The enemy gave a preference to COMMODORE AFFLECK ;
' but he kept up fo noble a fire, and was fo fupported by his fe-
' conds, CAPTAIN CORNWALLIS and LORD ROBERT MAN-
' NERS, that the lofs and damages fuftained in thofe fhips were
' but trifling, and they very much preferved the other fhips in
' the rear,' &c.   (*And afterwards he fays*), ' Would the event of
' a battle have determined the fate of the ifland, I would without
' hefitation have attacked the enemy, from a knowledge how
' much was to be expected from an Englifh fquadron, command-
' ed by men amongft whom is no other contention than who
' fhould be moft forward in rendering fervices to his King and
' Country : herein I placed the utmoft confidence, and fhould
' not, I truft, have been difappointed.

' I anchored his Majefty's fquadron in a clofe line ahead.
' Next morning about eight o'clock, I was attacked from van to
' rear with the whole force of the enemy (29 fail), for nearly
' two hours, without having the leaft vifible impreffion made
' upon my line.   The French fhips then wore and ftood off
' again, and in the afternoon began a fecond attack upon my
' centre and rear, with no better fuccefs than before ; fince which
' the COUNT DE GRASSE has kept a fafe diftance.——Many of
' the French fhips have fuffered confiderably.'

DESCRIP-

DESCRIPTION.

Plate XIV. fig. 2. A, Sir Samuel Hood with the British fleet lying off the north-weft end of the Ifland of Nevis in the morning of the 25th February at day-light, and intending to bring his fleet to an anchor in the ground Count De Grasse had left; but, at the fame time, endeavouring to amufe the Count with the appearance of a defign of making an attack upon him.

B, The van of the British fquadron now come to an anchor under Green-point in a clofe line ahead, and with fprings to bring the broadfide of each fhip to bear upon an enemy, who might attempt to come down and attack them.

C, The rear of the British fleet under Commodore Affleck, with part of the centre fuftaining, while coming to an anchor, an attack from the enemy.

F, The French cannonading; but at fuch a diftance, as nowife obftructed the British fquadron from coming to an anchor.

The French fleet then wore and ftood off to fea again, as per courfe G G.

Plate XIV. fig. 3. A, The Alfred, Canada, and Refolution, in the morning of the 26th at 6 o'clock, having been ordered to fhift their ground, as the evening before they had anchored too far to leeward, and too near to the edge of the bank *,——and being under way, thefe fhips, from this pofition, had it more in their power to overawe the enemy, and prevent them from doubling back upon the British fquadron, when they came to make the attack fome hours after.

B,

---

* Without the bank, from the immediate depth of water, there is no an-chorage.

B, The Britifh fquadron in the morning, confifting of other 19 fhips, at an anchor with fprings, fo that each fhip in the line might, at one and the fame time, be brought to bear upon an enemy coming down to make an attack.

F, The French fleet, about 8 o'clock in the morning, advancing to the attack with 29 fhips; and, having begun the attack upon the van, as at H, they ranged along the whole Britifh line, as per dotted line of courfe I I; then hauling up aftern, as at K K, they evidently meant to rake the fhips in our rear, or might have intended to have doubled back towards A; but, overawed by the three forefaid fhips, the Alfred, Canada, and Refolution, under way at A, they wore in fucceffion, and hauled off to fea, as per courfe L L L.

M M, The enemy now on the ftarboard tack, and on the return to the fecond attack, which they made upon the centre and rear, in the afternoon of the fame day, after having taken fuch an offing as enabled them to fetch our fleet.

N, Guana Hill, from which the Britifh fquadron was threatened to be bombarded.

O, Mooring's Hills, where GENERAL PRESCOT had the fkirmifh with the Irifh brigade; and where MONSIEUR DE BOUILLE declined attacking him.

The enemy afterwards kept in the offing, not choofing to make another attack upon SIR SAMUEL, who, not having it in his power to give farther affiftance to the ifland, after 10 or 12 days, cut his cables, laying hold of the opportunity, while the enemy had come to an anchor off the ifland of Nevis; and taking his courfe by the north end of the ifland of St Chriftophers, and by Sambriro, ftood to the northward.

OBSER-

OBSERVATIONS.

The fingularity, or rather novelty, of this affair, fo very important in all its confequences, cannot be paffed over without endeavouring to give it a full confideration; and that this may be done with the greater impartiality, it will be neceffary to ftate the facts fimply as they are.

Hearing that a fleet of 33 fhips of the enemy were lying at anchor, Baffa Terra Road, in fupport of the powerful attack which they were then making upon the ifland of St Chriftophers, Sir SAMUEL HOOD, with a much inferior force, confifting of 22 fhips only, refolves to attack them in this fituation.

The French, difcovering his intentions before his approach, and feeling, it feems, the fituation which they were in difadvantageous, quitted it, and put to fea.

Sir SAMUEL, thus difappointed in his intended attack, but confident that the obtaining a communication with, and fupporting the fame, was the only chance left him of faving the ifland, by a daring ftroke in feamanfhip, feldom before this time attempted, in the face of this enemy, and even while in the act of fuftaining a furious attack from the enemy, brings his fleet to an anchor in the felf-fame pofition, or ftation, which they but a little before, and with a fleet fo very much fuperior, had quitted, as thinking it untenable.

The enemy firft having fuffered themfelves to be diflodged, and afterwards having fuffered this inferior fleet to come to an anchor, determined, if poffible, to wipe off the double affront, by attempting an attack in their turn.

But

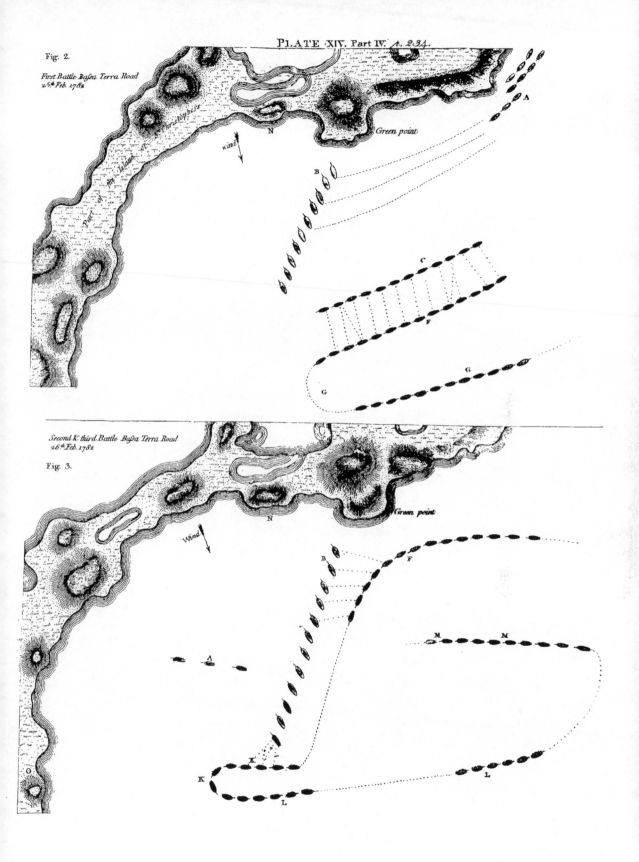

PLATE XIV. Part IV. *t. 234.*

Fig. 2.

First Battle Baſſa Terra Road
25ᵗʰ Feb. 1782

Part of the Island St. Christophers

wind

N

Green point

A

B

C

F

G

G

G

Second & third Battle Baſſa Terra Road
26ᵗʰ Feb. 1782

Fig. 3.

N

Green point

Wind

B

F

A

M

M

A

K

K

L

O

K

L

But this attack was either so ill conducted, or so feebly supported, that, though it was twice attempted, they, as unequal to the task, patiently permitted the British Admiral to keep his post for 12 days, without ever afterwards attempting to disturb him.

On the part of the enemy there were here no accidents, which, as in all other former cases, might be laid hold of, and held up as an excuse for want of success; nothing from winds, tides, or blowing up of particular ships, not the loss of a single mast or yard to furnish the shadow of an excuse, either for quitting their anchorage, or, after they had, for not overpowering with their numbers so inferior a fleet, occupying, and even fixed to, an anchorage, and affording an equal opportunity of being attacked for 12 successive days.

On the part of the British will be found a plan, gallantly, but prudently formed, to attack a force superior, as three to two, which if it was not put into execution, it was because the enemy had prudently declined.   Again, in consequence of a still more daring plan having been formed immediately upon the above disappointment, we find them, in defiance of all former rules (in the face of this superior fleet, who had taken every means of obstruction, and even while they were maintaining a combat with this fleet), bringing their ships to an anchor without a possibility of being prevented.   Afterwards, we find them disposed at anchor in so masterly a manner, that little loss was sustained, though two several attacks were made in the same day, by an enemy who had it in their choice to take every advantage.

Lastly, that there might be nothing wanting to establish a complete proof of British superiority, we find them keeping,
without

without difficulty, that poſt which had been thought untenable, ſending relief on ſhore, and maintaining a communication with the iſland for 12 days, without interruption.

During the more ancient and even more heroic days of naval prowefs, one fleet, at one time, might have had the good fortune to ſhew their valour in the attack, as thoſe at Cadiz, at Vigo, &c. ; and another fleet, at another time, might have been ſo happy as to have an opportunity of exhibiting their ſteadineſs in ſuſtaining an attack, ſuch as that under BLAKE in the Downs ; but on no occaſion whatever has one and the ſame fleet been ſo fortunate, as in this of Sir SAMUEL HOOD forcing their opponents to ſo complete and unequivocal an acknowledgment of their ſuperiority in both caſes, whether we ſhall conſider their courage and perſeverance, or their ſkill in ſeamanſhip.

As there can be no doubt that this contraſt drawn between the two fleets is a juſt one, what ought then to be the feelings of our countrymen upon this occaſion, compared to that ſtate of univerſal deſpondence into which the whole nation was plunged but a few months before ?

Perhaps it may be ſaid, by thoſe who wiſh to lower or depreciate the importance of this event, that the enemy, being conſcious of their great ſuperiority in the Weſt Indies, had, without thinking it neceſſary to take the proper precautions, come to an anchor in diſorder ; but, not thinking it proper for them to ſuſtain, or permit an attack in this ſtate from a fleet even much inferior, had prudently quitted their anchorage ; or, being adviſed of the approach of the Britiſh fleet, inferior in ſtrength, they had put to ſea, with the intention to cut off all hopes of their making a retreat ; or, being ſatisfied of the importance of poſ
ſeſſing

feffing a fuperior fleet to the end of the war, and knowing, at the fame time, that nothing could be done effectually to retard their operations in taking the ifland, they were determined to rifk nothing.

All this, however, if it proves any thing, proves their inferiority in feamanfhip, or that they were determined to fight fhy, as they have done on every former occafion, and fhould as effectually exalt the fpirits and courage of Britifh feamen, as it fhould deprefs thofe of the enemy.

It has been afked, it is true, Why fhould not this fleet have put to fea? Twenty-two well coppered fhips, of which it confifted, might be faid to have been a match fufficient for the fleet of COUNT DE GRASSE, although fuperior in number. No opinion will be given on this point; but, from the whole of the conduct, and, by keeping this ftation fo long in the face of fuch a fuperior force, it fhould fhew what might have been the fortunate iffue, had the Britifh fleet at once been carried into the Chefapeak in fupport of LORD CORNWALLIS, in place of the vain and fruitlefs attempt of bringing the enemy to action, but a few months before, on the 5th of September 1781, which was afterwards attended with fuch dreadful confequences. *

---

* About two or three years after thefe engagements off St Chriftophers, being in converfation with a gentleman, an officer who commanded a fhip there at the time, and who, rather offended with the obfervations expreffed as above (for he, it feems, had been of a different opinion from the Admiral, about the plan of the fervice projected), upon being afked, what truly had paffed in his mind on feeing his gallant friend Commodore AFFLECK bringing to an anchor the rear of the fleet, while yet warmly engaged with the enemy? (for the fhip commanded by this officer had been among the firft in the van to be brought to an anchor),

H h   'Why,

' Why, ay, ' fays he, with an enthufiaſtic agitation, ' why, ay, that was a mag-
nificent fight, a fight the moſt intereſting that ever was feen ! '   And how was it
the next day, while the enemy made their attack, and twice run down along your
line from van to rear, without being able to make impreſſion upon a fingle ſhip ?
' Why, ay, ' returned he again, ' that was ſtill more glorious indeed ; and there
' was not a boy on board the whole fleet, who did not feel he was a feaman. '
And a Britiſh feaman, thought I, a charaĉter the like of which never did in the
world exiſt before.   This is all I have to require, was my reply ; for it was the
ſpirit and gallantry difplayed in the execution of the enterprife itfelf, which was
the objeĉt of importance with me.

SIR

SIR GEORGE BRYDGES RODNEY's ENGAGEMENT,
ON THE 12TH APRIL 1782.

INTRODUCTION.

IT is with great pleafure that we ftill are able to bring forward an accurate defcription, and in all its great extent, of Sir GEORGE BRYDGES RODNEY's moft celebrated battle of the 12th of April; and that the accuracy of this defcription may be properly fupported, we have only to mention, that, befides Lord RODNEY's letters to the Admiralty, we have the teftimony of the late Lord CRANSTOUN, one of the Captains of the Admiral's fhip the Formidable. This very able and intelligent officer, who firft took poffeffion of the Ville de Paris, Admiral COUNT DE GRASSE's fhip, and was fent home with the difpatches, did me the honour to feek me out, and was fo kind as to furnifh a number of fketches, and even to affift with a great part of the defcription. Lord RODNEY too himfelf, in a private letter, of a date fo late as 14th June 1789, has given an account, by way of narrative, of his tranfactions, campaign 1782, in which is included this battle of the 12th April *.

H h 2

FROM

---

* This letter was tranfmitted to me by a common friend, the late General ROBERT CLERK, together with a copy of Naval Tactics, as printed January 1. 1782 : which copy contains a number of valuable marginal notes in his Lordfhip's own handwriting; but, coming too late, they could not be introduced, though particularly relating to part firft of this work, when reprinted and publifhed 1790.

FROM THE LONDON GAZETTE.

Admiralty-Office, 18*th May* 1782.

Lord CRANSTOUN, *one of the Captains of his Majesty's ship the Formidable, and Captain* BYRON *of the Andromache, in which ship his Lordship came a passenger, arrived early this morning with dispatches from Admiral Sir* GEORGE BRYDGES RODNEY, *Bart., Knight of the Bath, and Commander in Chief of his Majesty's ships at the Leeward Islands, to Mr* STEPHENS, *of which the following are copies.*

Formidable, at Sea, April 14. 1782.

IT has pleased God, out of his divine providence, to grant to his Majesty's arms a most complete victory over the fleet of his enemy, commanded by the COUNT DE GRASSE, who is himself captured with the Ville de Paris, and four other ships of his fleet, besides one sunk in the action. This important victory was obtained the 12th instant, after a battle which lasted, with unremitting fury, from seven in the morning till half past six in the evening, when the setting sun put an end to the contest. Both fleets have greatly suffered ; but it is with the highest satisfaction I can assure their Lordships, that though the masts, sails, rigging, and hulls of the British fleet are damaged, yet the loss of men has been but small, considering the length of the battle, and the close action they so long sustained, and in which

both

both fleets looked upon the honour of their King and country to be moft effentially concerned.   The great fupply of naval ftores lately arrived in the Weft Indies, will, I flatter myfelf, foon repair all the damages his Majefty's fleet has fuftained.

The gallant behaviour of the officers and men of the fleet I have the honour to command, has been fuch as muft for ever endear them to all lovers of their King and country.   The noble behaviour of my fecond in command, Sir SAMUEL HOOD, who, in both actions, moft confpicuoufly exerted himfelf, demands my warmeft encomiums.   My third in command, Rear-Admiral DRAKE, who, with his divifion, led the battle on the 12th inftant, deferves the higheft praife ; nor can lefs be given to Commodore AFFLECK for his gallant behaviour in leading the centre divifion.   My own Captain, Sir CHARLES DOUGLAS, merits every thing I can poffibly fay ; his unremitted diligence and activity greatly eafed me in the unavoidable fatigue of the day.   In fhort, I want words to exprefs how fenfible I am of the meritorious conduct of all the captains, officers, and men, who had a fhare in this glorious victory, obtained by their gallant exertions.   The enemy's whole army, confifting of 5500 men, were on board their fhips of war.   The deftruction among them muft be prodigious, as, for the greateft part of the action, every gun told ; and their Lordfhips may judge what havock muft have been made, when the Formidable fired near eighty broadfides.

Enclofed, I have the honour to fend, for their infpection, the Britifh and French lines of battle, with the account of the killed

led and wounded, and the damages fuftained by his Majefty's fleet. Lord CRANSTOUN, who acted as one of the Captains of the Formidable during both actions, and to whofe gallant behaviour I am much indebted, will have the honour of delivering thefe difpatches. To him I muft refer their Lordfhips for every minute particular they may wifh to know, he being perfectly mafter of the whole tranfaction. That the Britifh flag may for ever flourifh in every quarter of the globe, is the moft ardent wifh of him who has the honour of being, with great regard,

SIR, &c.

G. B. RODNEY.

EXTRACT OF A LETTER FROM SIR G. B. RODNEY TO MR STEPHENS.

Formidable, at Sea, April 14. 1782.

ON the 5th of April, I received intelligence that the enemy were embarking their troops on board the fhips of war, and concluded they intended to fail in a very few days. Captain BYRON of the Andromache, an active, brifk, and diligent officer, watched their motions with fuch attention, that, on the 8th inftant, at day-light, he made the fignal of the enemy's coming out, and ftanding to the north-weft. I inftantly made the fignal to weigh; and having looked into the bays of Fort Royal and St Pierre, where no enemy's fhips remained, I made the fignal for a general chafe; and, before day-light, came up with the enemy under Dominique, where both fleets were becalmed, and continued
nued

nued fo for fome time.   The enemy firft got the wind, and ftood
towards Guadaloupe.   My van divifion, under that gallant officer Rear-Admiral Sir SAMUEL HOOD, received it next, and
ftood after them.   At nine the enemy began to cannonade my
van, which was returned with the greateft brifknefs.   The baffling
winds, under Dominique, did not permit part of the centre divifion to get into action with the enemy's rear till half paft eleven,
and then only the fhip next to me in the line of battle.

Their Lordfhips may eafily imagine the mortification it muft
have been to the fixteen gallant officers commanding the fhips
of the rear, who could only be fpectators of an action in which
it was not in their power to join, being detained by the calms
under Dominique.   The enemy's cannonade ceafed upon my
rear's approach, but not before they had done confiderable damage to the fhips of the van, and difabled the Royal Oak and
Montague, and his Majefty had loft a gallant officer, viz. Captain
BAYNE of the Alfred, and a number of officers and feamen, as
mentioned in the account tranfmitted to their Lordfhips; but fuch
was the fteady behaviour of Sir SAMUEL HOOD, and the fhips
of the van, that the enemy received more damage than they occafioned.   The night of the 9th inftant the fleet lay to, to repair
their damages.   The 10th, they continued to turn to windward
under an eafy fail, the enemy's fleet continuing to do the fame,
and always had it in their power to come to action, which they
cautioufly avoided, and rendered it impoffible for me to force
them in the fituation they were in, between the Saints and
the ifland of Dominique.   On the 11th of April, the enemy having gained confiderably to windward, and the wind blowing a

frefh

freſh and ſteady gale, I made the ſignal for a general chaſe to windward, which continued the whole day. Towards ſun-ſet, ſome of the headmoſt ſhips of the fleet had approached near to one of the enemy's ſhips that had received damage in the late action, and had certainly taken her, if COUNT DE GRASSE had not bore down with his whole fleet for her protection, which brought him ſo near, that I flattered myſelf he would give me an opportunity of engaging him the next day. With that view I threw out the ſignal for the form of ſailing, and ſtood with the whole fleet to the ſouthward till two o'clock in the morning; then tacked, and had the happineſs, at day-light, to find my moſt ſanguine deſire was near being accompliſhed, by my having it in my power to force the enemy to battle. Not one moment was loſt in putting it into execution: The conſequence has been ſuch as I have had the honour to repreſent in my former letter of this day; and can ſay no more, than that too much praiſe cannot be given to the gallant officers and men of the fleet I had the honour to command.

G. B. RODNEY.

THE

THE DESCRIPTION OF THE BATTLES OF THE 9TH AND 12TH
OF APRIL 1782, FOUGHT BETWEEN THE BRITISH SQUA-
DRON, COMMANDED BY SIR GEORGE BRYDGES RODNEY,
AND THE FRENCH SQUADRON BY COUNT DE GRASSE.

ON Monday, the 8th of April 1782, fignal was made from
the Britifh cruifers off Fort Royal Bay, Martinico, that the
French fleet, attended by a number of tranfports, were then got
under way. Our fleet immediately weighed from Groffe Iflet
Bay, St Lucia, and ftood after them to the northward, under
the weft end of Martinico, and foon got fight of part of their
men of war. The purfuit was continued, during the night, with
all the fail that could be made, directed by the enemy's night fignals. The wind a frefh gale at N. E. by E. At two in the morning, the Valiant, being to windward, difcovered the enemy under
the north end of the ifland of Dominica. At three o'clock the
fleet brought to by fignal; the enemy at that time nearly bearing
north, &c.

Plate XV. fig. 1. A, The Britifh fleet, at two in the morning of the 9th of April, difcovering part of the French fleet under
the north end of Dominica at F; at three o'clock brought to by
fignal; at half paft five the fignal was thrown out to prepare for
battle. The line to be formed at two cables length afunder, and
the fleet to fill and ftand on.

G, The French fleet afterwards, at five in the morning, on the ftarboard tack, working to windward in the Channel, between the iflands of Dominica and Guadaloupe, where they had a fteady breeze.

H, One of the enemy's fhips, at this time fo far to leeward, that fhe muft have been taken, had not the wind failed us, while fhe had it fo frefh as ferved her foon to recover her ftation.

Plate XV. fig. 2.   A, The van of the Britifh having at laft got the breeze, fetched up with the centre of the enemy, ftill up-on the ftarboard tack, when they were fired upon about nine o'-clock, where, for the fpace of an hour, they fuftained a diftant cannonade from as many of the enemy's fhips as could be brought to bear upon them.   The centre and rear, in the mean time, ly-ing ftill becalmed under the ifland of Dominica, at B.

F, The French not all in order of battle, as fome of their fhips were endeavouring to work to windward.

Plate XV. fig. 3.   A, The centre of the Britifh having after-wards got the breeze, joined the van about noon, when the ac-tion, after an interval of two hours, was renewed ; but the Duke, the Formidable's fecond aftern, was the fternmoft fhip engaged upon this occafion ; the 16 fhips in the rear divifion, and aftern of her, not being able to get up.

B, The van of the Britifh.

The centre now having joined the van, the cannonade was continued an hour and three quarters, until the rear, which had, in the mean while, been becalmed at C, began to join and clofe the line alfo, as at D.

F,

F, The enemy, (who, during all this time, kept, as ufual, at fuch a diftance as fhewed that they meant to difable), as foon as they faw the junction of the whole Britifh fleet, hauled off to windward, tacking from the van, as per line of courfe H H.

G, The enemy's fleet of tranfports ftretching away to windward of the Saints.

The enemy did not at firft appear to have fuffered much; but foon after, however, one of them feemed to be crippled; and, afterwards, we found two had received fo much hurt, that they were obliged to bear away to Baffe Terre, Guadaloupe, to refit; fo that they were not in the fecond action, which was afterwards fought on the 12th *.

The 10th of April was fpent in refitting and keeping our wind, and fhifting the van and rear divifions, as the van had fuffered in the action of the ninth.

I i 2   Plate

---

* *From* LORD RODNEY'S NARRATIVE, *contained in his private letter above mentioned.*

' About two o'clock in the morning of the 9th of April, the Britifh fleet came
' up with the enemy's under Dominique; both were becalmed. The enemy firft
' got the wind, and ftood towards Guadaloupe; the Britifh van followed, as did
' the centre, when the breeze reached them. The enemy attacked the van, and
' a cannonade enfued; but it ceafed when the Admiral and his two feconds
' joined his van. In vain; when the Admiral got abreaft of the Ville de Paris,
' he laid his main-top fail aback for the French Admiral to bear down and en-
' gage: He kept his diftance; and plainly indicated it was not his bufinefs to
' bring on a battle, as the enemy's whole fleet had got the wind, and could have
' brought them to engage half of the Englifh. Admiral RODNEY had his fignal
' ready to wear and ftand to his rear, feven fail of which were becalmed at a
' very confiderable diftance. However, the enemy would not rifk the attack;
' and the breeze foon reaching the rear, it foon joined the centre. '

Plate XVI. fig. 4. A, The Britiſh fleet, in the morning of the 11th, perceiving two diſabled ſhips under the iſlands of Saints, at G, chaſed them into Baſſe Terre, Guadaloupe ; but, ſoon after, diſcovering two others far to windward, and diſabled, at H, near the north end of Dominica, a general chaſe was ordered, only three or four of the French fleet being at this time viſible, at I, from the Formidable's maſt-head. But, upon the Agamemnon and others, at B, coming near the ſhips, at H, COUNT DE GRASSE, though far to windward, bore down, as at F, to proteĉt his two diſabled ſhips. Upon this the Agamemnon, and the other ſhips, advanced in the purſuit. Upon the ſignal to call in all cruiſers, they returned to their reſpective ſtations in the line.

Plate XVI. fig. 5. A, the Britiſh fleet, at two o'clock in the morning of the 12th, after having run to the ſouthward from B, their poſition the evening before, having taken advantage of the wind, as at W, which generally hauls to the northward in the Weſt Indies in the evening. At which time, (viz. two o'clock), having tacked to the northward, the French were diſcovered broad under their lee-bow, in ſome confuſion, at F ; and one of their ſhips was directly to leeward, at G, with her bow-ſprit gone, and her fore-maſt acroſs her fore-caſtle, towed by a frigate, and the wind at E. S. E., as at Z.

C, The Valiant and Monarch were ordered down from the rear to engage this diſabled ſhip with her conſort, which obliged COUNT DE GRASSE to edge down, as at H, to their protection.

D, The van of the Britiſh, about 4 or 5 o'clock, leading on the
ſtarboard

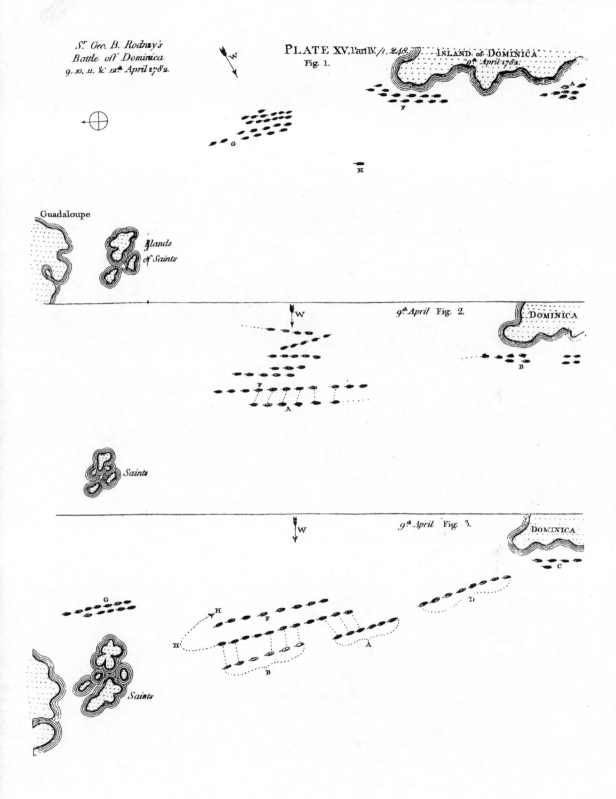

St. Geo. B. Rodney's
Battle off Dominica
9. 10. 11. & 12th April 1782.

PLATE XV. Part IV. p. 248. ISLAND of DOMINICA
Fig. 1.   9th April 1782.

Guadaloupe

Islands
of Saints

9th April   Fig. 2.   DOMINICA

Saints

9th April   Fig. 3.   DOMINICA

Saints

ſtarboard tack; and the Admiral judging the COUNT DE GRASSE might now have got ſo far to leeward, by the laſt mentioned movement, that it would not be poſſible for him to avoid an action, the Valiant and Monarch, the ſhips in chaſe, were ordered into their ſtations. *

I, The French, aware of their ſituation, forming on a larboard tack; and the wind afterwards coming about from E. S. E. to nearly eaſt, as at Y, they conceived hopes of regaining their uſual fighting diſtance, more eſpecially as their van, at this time, began to point to windward of the Britiſh.

Plate XVII. fig. 6.   A, The Britiſh fleet.

F, The French fleet; their leading ſhips having gained the wind.

At half paſt ſeven in the morning, the Marlborough, the leading ſhip of the van of the Britiſh, having fetched the fifth ſhip

of

---

* LORD RODNEY'S NARRATIVE *continued.*

' The 10th and 11th April were employed in endeavouring to bring the enemy
' to battle; and on the 11th, late in the afternoon, the enemy bore down to pro-
' tect two of their ſhips, who were in danger of being cut off. This brought
' them to the poſition the Admiral wiſhed. He inſtantly iſſued orders to ſail dur-
' ing the night, according to the order of ſailing; to put all lights out; to ſtand
' to the ſouthward till two o'clock in the morning; and then the whole fleet to
' tack without ſignal. This deceived the enemy, who had no conception that
' the Britiſh fleet ſhould be ſo near them at day-light, and inſtantly formed the
' line of battle upon the ſtarboard tack; the enemy formed theirs upon the lar-
' board tack, and had made the ſignal to wear; but the nearneſs of the Britiſh
' fleet prevented its being put in execution; and the Britiſh fleet taking the lee-
' gage, the Admiral made the ſignal to engage and cloſe. '

of the line of the enemy, was fired upon; * when the fignals for clofe action, and to clofe the line, were thrown out.

Plate XVII. fig. 7. A, The van of the Britifh ranging flowly and clofely (but on oppofite tacks) along the enemy's line, each fhip giving and receiving a heavy fire.

F, The enemy's fleet having gained the wind, ranging in like manner in oppofite directions.

B, The Formidable, the Admiral's fhip, not bearing away, but keeping the wind, &c. at the time when the two fleets might be fuppofed to be completely abreaft of each other.

Plate XVII. fig. 8. A, The Formidable, the Britifh Admiral's fhip, after having given her firft fire to the enemy's fifth fhip, and having paffed the Ville de Paris, F, and her feconds almoft in contact, kept her wind, and piercing the enemy's line between the fourth and fifth fhip aftern of COUNT DE GRASSE's own fhip, the Ville de Paris, was followed by the Namur and Duke, the two next fhips aftern. † By which fpirited, bold, and

---

* N. B.—This fhip, the Marlborough, having fetched the fifth fhip, as mentioned; and after fuffering a cannonade from thirty-one fhips, the remaining part of the enemy's line, along the whole of which fhe had run, and clofe under their lee; in performing this and other fervice, from the ninth to this day the twelfth, had three men killed only, and fixteen wounded.

† LORD RODNEY's NARRATIVE continued.

' The Britifh Admiral's fhip, the Formidable, reached the enemy's fourth fhip
' from their van, and began a very clofe action within half mufket-fhot, and conti-
' nued fuch action clofe along the enemy's line, under an eafy fail, till an opening
' appeared

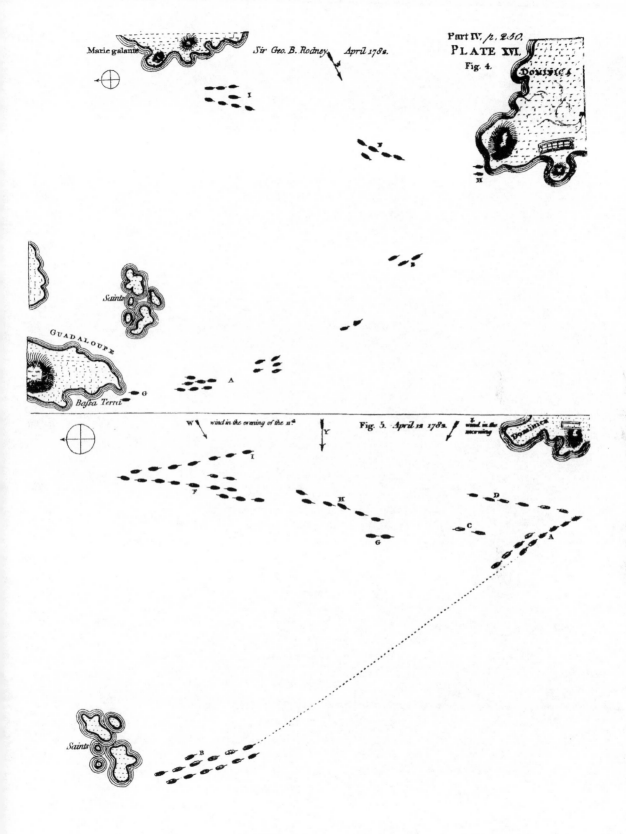

Marie galante

Sir Geo. B. Rodney   April 1782.

DOMINICA

Saints

GUADALOUPE

Bassa Terra

W   wind in the evening of the 11th   Y   L wind in the morning

Fig. 5. April 12 1782.

DOMINICA

Saints

and new mode of attack, the enemy's line was not only cut in twain, their van from their rear, but the headmoft fhips of their rear divifion, then coming up, were forced away to leeward, as at G.

B, The van of the Britifh ftill ranging along the remaining part of the enemy's rear.

C, The rear of the Britifh line following up after the Admiral.

H, The Glorieufe, the laft fhip of the van of the French, ftretching paft the rear of the Britifh line. *

Plate

' appeared at the third fhip aftern of the enemy's Admiral, which gave an op-
' portunity of breaking their line, and putting their rear in the utmoft confufion;
' when fix of their fhips falling on board each other, in that condition the Ad-
' miral and divifion attacked them, tore them to pieces, and the moment they
' had difengaged themfelves, they bore away right before the wind. '

* Whether it was between the third and fourth fhip that the line was cut, or between the fourth and fifth fhip, as the text has it, is of little moment. But we cannot well omit the following anecdote, as related to me by the late Admiral C. INGLIS. He commanded the St Albans, one of the next fhips aftern of the Formidable, in cutting the French line. When he got along-fide of this fhip H, fuppofed to be the Glorieufe, the laft of the van divifion of the enemy, where it was cut afunder from the rear, he remarked that fhe did not return a fingle gun, nor was any body to be feen on board, but one man upon the poop; and fome accidental mufket-fhot being fired by the marines, this poor fellow dropped, and was no more to be feen. After Captain INGLIS had paffed on a-head, directing his attention ftill to this fhip H, as well as to the Canada, the Britifh fhip which followed him next aftern, he obferved that neither did the Glorieufe return a gun to this fhip: But the Canada, pouring in a whole broad-fide into the Glorieufe, fo dreadful was the appearance to Captain INGLIS, who faw the duft, the pieces of timber, and fmoke, which flew to a great diftance from the fide oppofite to that where fhe had received the blow, it feemed as if the fhip (literally fpeaking) had been blown out of the water, and as if the whole in a mafs had been driven to windward.

Plate XVII. fig. 9. A, B, C, The Formidable, Namur, and Duke, after having cut the line, kept up a powerful raking fire upon thefe fhips of the rear divifion of the enemy, which they before had forced to leeward, and which are now going off before the wind, as at G.

D, The rear of the Britifh, under Sir S. Hood, following up after the Admiral.

E, The van of the Britifh, under the command of Admiral Drake.

G, The headmoft fhips of the rear divifion of the enemy, which were forced to leeward by the Formidable, &c. having got into a huddle, or group, were, for fome time, expofed to a cannonade from three fhips, the Formidable, the Namur, and the Duke; when the whole of this rear divifion of the French line, confifting of the rear and part of the centre, now under the conduct of M. Bougainville, as foon as the Britifh van had ftretched paft, put before the wind with all the fail that could be carried, efcaping through the gap, evidently made in the Britifh line, between the van and the attack made by the Formidable; which part of the enemy's fleet, for diftinction's fake, fhall be called the northern divifion of flight, which was not purfued.

F, The van of the enemy, ftretched paft the rear of the Britifh line, preparing to break into two divifions.

H, The middle divifion which made to the weft.

Plate XVIII. fig. 10. So foon as the van divifion of the enemy had ftretched paft the rear of the Britifh line, in bearing away, it broke into two divifions; one, confifting of feven fhips, fteering weft, as at H, and which may be called the middle divifion;

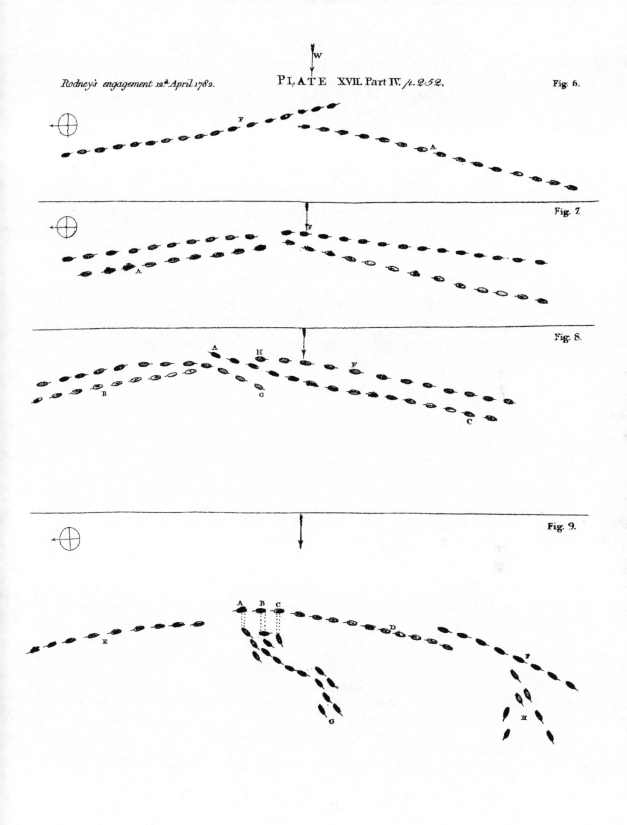

vifion; the other, taking a S. S. W. courfe, confifting of about 12 or 13 fhips, and where COUNT DE GRASSE was himfelf, making the fouthern divifion of flight, as at F.

A, The Formidable, with part of the centre, putting about in purfuit of the enemy's van.

B, The rear of the Britifh line putting about for the purfuit alfo. The fignal for the rear to clofe the centre being foon after made, both thefe divifions, in purfuit of the fouthern divifion F, where COUNT DE GRASSE was himfelf, paffed to windward of the middle divifion of the enemy H, without annoying it.

C, The Britifh van.

F, The COUNT DE GRASSE, with the fouthern divifion, flying under every fail he could fet, purfued by the rear and part of the centre of the Britifh, and fteering a S. S. W. courfe. It was from this divifion of the enemy from which all the captures were afterwards made.

H, The middle divifion of the enemy fteering a more wefterly courfe; and, as they were not purfued, they did not carry a prefs of fail; but, repairing the damage they had received, waited for, and the fame evening, after it was dark, rejoined the fhips of the fouthern divifion which had efcaped the purfuit.

G, M. BOUGAINVILLE, with the rear divifion of the enemy, crowding fail, and faft advancing to the weftward.

Plate XVIII. fig. 2. Upon the breaking of the van divifion of the enemy, the fouthern divifion, which had at firft fteered to the S. S. W. as at K, foon afterwards got with their heads to the northward, as at F, with the view of rejoining their other divifions, and forming a new line of battle to leeward, COUNT

K k   D F

DE GRASSE making repeated fignals for that purpofe; but feeing, after every pains taken, thefe fignals without effect, and, at
the fame time, perceiving, if this northerly courfe was continued, that the line of the Britifh purfuit would thereby be much
fhortened, he changed his direction again, and is now, about two
o'clock in the afternoon, with his fhips heads to the S. S. W. as
at I.

A and B, The centre and rear of the Britifh in purfuit of the
fouthern divifion of the enemy.

C, The van of the Britifh.

G, The rear divifion of the enemy advancing ftill farther to
the weftward.

H, The middle divifion of the enemy, not being purfued,
under an eafy fail repaired their damage.

Plate XVIII. fig. 12. F, The fouthern divifion of the enemy
with their heads again to the northward, at fix o'clock, at fun-fet,
having run through the dotted line of courfe H H, in which
they were outfailed, and turned from their foutherly direction,
by the Britifh fhips in purfuit, as at A.

During this purfuit, five fhips were taken from the enemy. The
Glorieufe having loft her mafts by the fire which fhe received in
the morning, while ranging paft to windward, ftruck to the
fleet at 12 o'clock, upon their bearing away large for the purfuit.
The Cæfar ftruck to the Centaur at four o'clock.—The Hector,
at half paft four, ftruck to the Canada and Alcide.—The Ardent,
a little after five, ftruck to the Belliqueux and Prince William.—
And the Ville de Paris, COUNT DE GRASSE, at fix o'clock,

about

about fun-fet, ftruck to the Barfleur and Canada.   At this time,
COUNT DE GRASSE had got above five leagues to the weftward
and leeward of the field of battle ; and, night immediately coming on, Admiral RODNEY thought proper to give over further
purfuit *.

By

---

* LORD RODNEY'S NARRATIVE *continued.*

' COUNT DE GRASSE, in the Ville de Paris, having behaved moft bravely, and
' his fhip being entirely crippled, and three Britifh Admirals being very near him,
' ftruck his flag about ten minutes after the fun had fet.   Admiral RODNEY made
' the fignal for a night battle ; but looking about him, and obferving that his fleet
' were greatly difperfed ; that two of his 90 gun fhips were totally difabled ; his
' own (the Formidable) greatly damaged ; that his van and centre were much
' hurt ; that none of the prifoners from the captured fhips were taken out ; that a
' very dark night, of twelve hours, was come on, he thought it moft prudent to
' make fure of the victory, and not run the rifk of a reverfe of fortune, or the
' danger of a night battle, wherein his own fleet might receive more damage from
' one another than from the fhips of the enemy ; that, by running to leeward in the
' night, the enemy might deceive him by ordering fome of their frigates to hoift
' the lights of their Admirals, and fteer a courfe to lead him (RODNEY) a different
' courfe from them ; and as the night was extremely dark, being the firft day of a
' new moon, they might have hauled their wind to the north, or to the fouth, with-
' out being feen ; at the fame time they moft carefully had hid all lights whatever.
' The Britifh fleet, by purfuing, might have found themfelves far to leeward in
' the morning, without a poffibility of their getting to windward, by the crippled
' condition they were in.   Thefe reafons, and his experience of a night battle, in-
' duced the Admiral to fecure the victory, and not to hazard a reverfe of fortune.
' He therefore made the fignal for the Britifh fleet to bring to, on the ftarboard
' tack, then fo dark that one fhip could not fee another.   Day-light the next morn-
' ing proved the wifdom of that fignal ; for notwithftanding it was the duty of
' every fhip to obey it, thirteen made fail, yet not one of them fired a fhot, or
' came up with an enemy.   This was a convincing proof of what might have
' happened had the whole fleet gone to leeward, and the enemy have hauled
' their wind ; not only the captured fhips might have been re-taken, but fome
' of the Britifh crippled been taken.'

K k 2

By faying that thefe fhips of the enemy ftruck to particular fhips of the Britifh, is meant only, that thofe of our fhips mentioned were engaging the prizes clofe at the inftant of hauling down their colours, while the whole of the fleet was furrounding them at the time.

G, Monfieur BOUGAINVILLE, with the rear divifion of the enemy, advanced now above ten leagues to the weftward and to the leeward of the field of battle.

I, The middle divifion of the enemy, confifting of feven fhips, having waited for, rejoined the fhips of the fouthern divifion, which afterwards effected an efcape *.

LINE

---

* LORD RODNEY's NARRATIVE continued.

'On the morning of the 13th, frigates were difpatched to St Chriftophers ' and Euftatia, to fee if any of the enemy's fhips had fheltered themfelves in thofe ' roads. Upon the report returned, that none were there, but that fome fhips had ' paffed thefe iflands in a crippled ftate, Rear Admiral HOOD and his divifion were ' fent to intercept fuch fhips as might go to the fouth fide of Porto Rico and St ' Domingo, while Admiral RODNEY took care of the prizes and his own fhattered ' fhips; and, fo foon as he was enabled to put his fquadron in a condition to bear ' away, he got to St Domingo, where Admiral HOOD foon joined him with two ' other enemy's fhips of the line, which had been taken in the Mona Paffage.

' On the Britifh fleet arriving off Cape Tiberoon, the weft end of St Domingo, ' Admiral HOOD was fent with a fleet of 25 fail of the line to blockade the ifland ' of St Domingo, while Admiral RODNEY himfelf bore away for Port Royal, ' Jamaica, with the prizes, and thofe of his fhips which were moft fhattered, ' with the view of having the whole put in repair. The enemy's fhattered fhips, ' in the mean time, made their efcape to the Havanna, fome to America, and ' fome even to France; and the Britifh fleet, within a month, were completely ' refitted, ftored, and manned. The van was gone out of harbour; the centre ' going; and Admiral RODNEY himfelf, with the whole fleet, in purfuit of the ' enemy to America, was ready to leave Jamaica the next day, when Admiral ' PIGOT arrived from England, and took the command.'

LINE OF BATTLE *of the* BRITISH FLEET *under the command of* SIR G. B. RODNEY *(the Royal Oak to lead on the ſtarboard tack, and the Marlborough on the larboard tack), with the Liſt of the Killed and Wounded in both the battles of the 9th and 12th of April. The damage which the ſhips in the van ſuſtained in the battle of the 9th, made it neceſſary that this order of the line ſhould be reverſed; and* SIR FRANCIS DRAKE'S *diviſion becoming the van, the Marlborough, as the headmoſt ſhip, led the fleet on the 12th of April.*

Ships.	Commanders.				Guns.	Men.	Killed.	Wounded.
Royal Oak,	Capt. Burnet,	-	-	-	74	600	8	30
Alfred,	—— Bayne,	-	-	-	74	600	12	42
Montague,	—— Bowen,	-	-	-	74	600	12	31
Yarmouth,	—— Parry,	-	-	-	64	500	14	33
Valiant,	—— Goodall,	-	-	-	74	650	10	28
Barfleur,	{ Sir S. Hood, Bart. }{ Capt. Knight, }	-	-	-	90	767	10	27
Monarch,	—— Reynolds,	-	-	-	74	600	16	33
Warrior,	—— Sir James Wallace,	-	-	-	74	600	5	21
Belliqueux,	—— Sutherland,	-	-	-	64	500	4	10
Centaur,	—— Inglefield,	-	-	-	74	600	-	-
Magnificent,	—— Linzee,	-	-	-	74	650	6	11
Prince William,	—— Wilkinſon,	-	-	-	64	500	-	-
Bedford,	{ Commodore Affleck, }{ Capt. Graves, }	-	-	-	74	617	-	17
Ajax,	—— Charrington,	-	-	-	74	550	9	10
Repulſe,	—— Dumareſque,	-	-	-	64	500	3	11
Canada,	—— Hon. W. Cornwallis,	-	-	-	74	600	12	23
St Albans,	—— Inglis,	-	-	-	64	500	-	6
Namur,	—— Fanſhaw,	-	-	-	90	750	6	25
Formidable,	{ Sir G. B. Rodney, Commander in Chief, }{ Sir Cha. Douglas, firſt Captain, }{ Capt. Symons, }{ —— Lord Cranſtoun, }	-	-	-	90	750	15	39
Duke,	—— Gardner,	-	-	-	90	750	13	61
Agamemnon,	—— Caldwell,	-	-	-	64	500	15	22
Reſolution,	—— Lord Robert Manners,	-	-	-	74	600	5	34
Prothée,	—— Buckner,	-	-	-	64	500	5	25
Hercules,	—— Savage,	-	-	-	74	600	7	19
America,	—— S. Thomſon,	-	-	-	64	500	1	1
Ruſſell,	—— Saumarez,	-	-	-	74	600	10	29
Prudent,	—— Barklay,	-	-	-	64	500	-	-
Fame,	—— Barber,	-	-	-	74	550	3	12
Anſon,	—— Blair,	-	-	-	64	500	3	13
Torbay,	—— Gidoin,	-	-	-	74	600	10	25
Prince George,	—— Williams,	-	-	-	90	750	9	24
Princeſſa,	{ Francis S. Drake, Eſq. }{ Capt. Knatchbull, }	-	-	-	70	577	3	22
Conqueror,	—— Balfour,	-	-	-	74	600	7	23
Nonſuch,	—— Truſcott,	-	-	-	64	500	3	3
Alcide,	—— C. Thomſon,	-	-	-	74	600	-	-
Arrogant,	—— Corniſh,	-	-	-	74	600	-	-
Marlborough,	—— Penny,	-	-	-	74	600	3	16
					2704	21,361	230	759

37
1 Deduct the Prudent not with the fleet in the action, — 64
36 — 2640

FRIGATES.

Preſent in the Action.		Not Preſent in the Action.	
Champion, to repeat.	Andromache.	Lizard.	Pegaſus.
Zebra.	Flora, to repeat ſignals.	La Nymph.	Salamander.
Alecto.	Alert.	Convert.	Germain.
Endymion.	Triton.	Fortune.	Blaſt.
Alarm.	10 Eurydice, to repeat ſignals.	Sybil.	10 Santa Monica.

LIST

LIST OF THE FRENCH FLEET.

Ships.	Guns.
La Ville de Paris,	110
L'Augufte,	80
Le Duc de Bourgogne,	80
Le Languedoc,	80
Le Neptune,	80
Le Zele,	74
La Glorieufe,	74
Le Citoyen,	74
Le Souverain,	74
Le Magnanime,	74
Le Cæfar,	74
Le Hector,	74
Le Pluton,	74
Le Hercules	74
Le Scipion,	74
Arrived with the Breft convoy, { La Couronne,	80
Le Dauphin Royal,	74
Le Magnifique	74
Le Bourgogne,	74
Le Bien Aimé,	74
Le Sceptre,	74
Le Northumberland,	74
Le Conquerant,	74
La Marfeilloife,	74
Le Palmire,	74
L'Ardent,	64
L'Eveille,	64
Le Caton,	64
Le Jafon,	64
Le Fier, armé en flute,	64
Le Minotaur, ditto,	74
Joined at St Kitts, { Le Brave,	74
Le Triomphant,	80
Out of repair, { Le St Efprit,	80
Le Deftin,	74
Le Reflechi,	64
Le Sagittaire,	50
L'Experiment,	50

Thirteen Frigates,
Seven armed Brigs,
One Cutter.

Total, 36 of the line, two 50 gun fhips, 13 frigates, 7 armed brigs, 2 fire fhips, and 1 cutter.

OBSER–

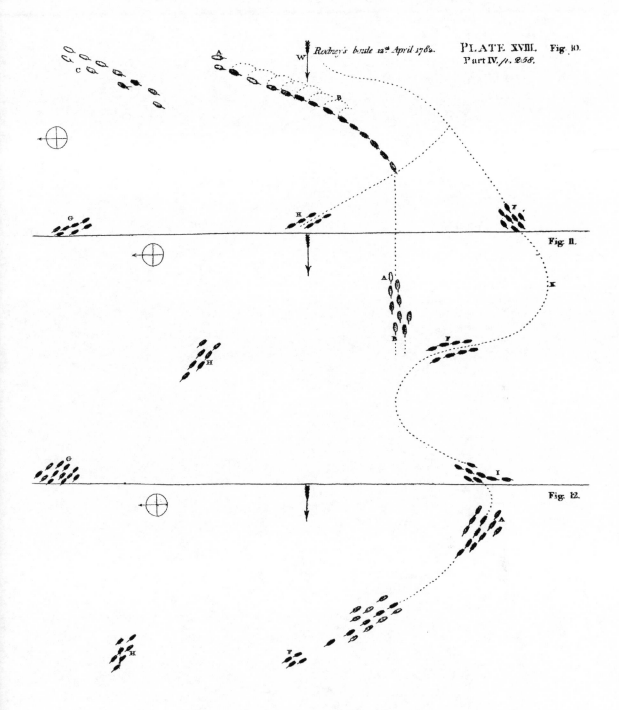

Rodney's battle 12th April 1782.   PLATE XVIII.   Fig. 10.
Part IV. p. 258.

Fig. 11.

Fig. 12.

OBSERVATIONS ON THE BATTLES OF THE 9TH AND 12TH
APRIL 1782.

*In the courfe of thefe Actions, there will be found a complete Il-
luftration of the following particulars :*

1. The difficulty which an enemy's fleet will find in making
an efcape to windward.

2. That the crippling of fome of his fhips will be a neceffary
confequence of the efforts made to effect this efcape.

3. That the protection given to fhips crippled in confequence
of thefe efforts, as it was the caufe of bringing on the actions of
both the 9th and 12th, and had nearly produced an action on
the 10th,—will alfo be a caufe of bringing on an action on all
future occafions of the like nature, or in like circumftances.

The attack made by the Britifh in the action ot the 9th, may
be confidered as an example of the fimple attack, and fhows how
little may be expected from any rencounter between two fleets
on the fame tack, when an attempt fhall be made from the leeward.

The judicious movement made by the Britifh fleet, from a
northerly courfe to a foutherly one, on the night between the
11th and 12th, as it fhows the advantage that may be made by a
change of wind, at the fame time fhows the neceffity of attention
to fuch periodical changes.   For it was by this means only that
the

the Britiſh fleet got within reach of the enemy on the morning of the 12th April.

The little loſs ſuſtained by fleets, while ranging paſt an enemy's line, particularly exemplified in the caſe of the leading ſhip, the Marlborough, in this battle, as well as in others, viz. the three battles formerly mentioned,—the 27th July 1778, the 15th and 19th May 1780,—ſufficiently and incontrovertibly ſhould eſtabliſh how little can be effected by the rencounter of two adverſe fleets paſſing on oppoſite tacks, without having ſomething more important in view than the ſimply effecting the ſaid paſſage.

From the facility with which the Formidable, the Admiral's ſhip, kept her wind, and forced her paſſage through the line of the enemy, and the neceſſary conſequence that the headmoſt ſhips of the rear diviſion muſt thereby be forced and driven to leeward, ſhould with certainty eſtabliſh, that breaking or cutting an enemy's line, by an attack rom the leeward, is not only a practicable manœuvre, but a manœuvre attended with little additional danger, or riſk of ſhipping; and that, with the ſame facility, and with equal probability of ſucceſs, it might have been attempted, in former rencounters, as already mentioned *. And although Admiral RODNEY, in either of his former rencounters of the 15th or 19th of May, had not then been convinced of the importance of this manœuvre—ſtill, having been the firſt to put it in execution, as on this occaſion of the 12th April, he has acquired a name renowned over the whole world, as well as among his countrymen,

---

* KEPPEL's engagement of the 27th July 1778, and RODNEY's two engagements of the 15th and 19th May 1780.

countrymen, who muſt ever remember this eſſential effort of ſervice with the utmoſt gratitude.

The glorious conſequences, from having cut and divided the
enemy's line on this occaſion, as they may be admitted to be il-
luſtrations of the foregoing demonſtrations, may alſo be admitted as a proof of what ought to be expected in future on every
ſimilar occaſion.

The hurry and precipitation with which the rear diviſion of
the enemy made their eſcape through the gap in the Britiſh line,
as it ſhewed their apprehenſions, ſhould alſo be a proof of the
danger of their ſituation.

The effort to eſcape, made by the van diviſion of the enemy,
as it confirms the general poſition, their deſire of evading a con-
flict, confirms alſo the idea of that ſuperiority of Britiſh ſeamen,
which ſeems, indeed, to have been inconteſtible from the beginning of the whole affair to the end thereof.

The manner by which the van of the Britiſh was rendered almoſt without effect, ſhews that the rear diviſion of the enemy,
and not the van, ought to have been the object of purſuit *.

The proximity of the rear of the Britiſh to the rear diviſion
of the enemy, ſhould ſufficiently point out the object of purſuit
they alſo ſhould have choſen. *

Therefore the Britiſh line, van and rear, not having been prepared to take advantage of their neceſſary mutual proximity to the
rear diviſion of the enemy was a loſs. *

Again, the rear diviſion of the Britiſh, by having been obliged
to put about ſhip, in purſuit of the van of the enemy, already

L l

got

---

* *Vide* Attack with the Centre, Part II, pages 180, 181, 182, and 183.

got some number of miles diftant, is a full confirmation of the hypothefis laid down, That the purfuit of a rear divifion, cut off from the van of an enemy's fleet paffing on contrary tacks, ought in general to be preferred.

Laftly, The facility with which the rear of the Britifh came up with the flying van of the enemy, after confideration had to all the foregoing circumftances, without doubt fhews, that neither was there any inferiority of failing in the Britifh fhips on this occafion.

BATTLES

BATTLES BETWEEN THE ENGLISH AND FRENCH SQUADRONS IN THE EAST INDIES, 1782.

EXTRACT OF A LETTER FROM SIR EDWARD HUGHES BART. TO MR STEPHENS, DATED ON BOARD THE SUPERBE, AT SEA, OFF THE COAST OF COROMANDEL, 4TH APRIL 1782.

I SAILED on the 31ft of January from Trincomalé for Madras Road, in order to get a fupply of provifions and ftores, of both which the fhips were then in want.

On the 8th of February I anchored in Madras Road; and the fame day received advice from LORD MACARTNEY, the governor of that place, that a French fquadron, confifting of thirty fail of fhips and veffels, was at anchor about twenty leagues to the northward of that port. In the afternoon of the 9th, Captain AIMS, in his Majefty's fhip Monmouth, with the Hero, Ifis, and the armed tranfport Manilla, joined me in the road. I continued to ufe all poffible diligence in getting the neceffary ftores and provifions on board the feveral fhips, until the 15th of February, when the enemy's fquadron, confifting of 12 fail of line of battle fhips, 6 frigates, 8 large tranfports, and 6 captured veffels, came in fight to the northward, ftanding for Madras Road; and, about noon, the fame day, anchored about four miles without the road. In the mean time, I placed his Majefty's fhips in the moft advantageous manner to defend themfelves, and the other fhips in the road, with fprings on their cables, that they might bring their

L l 2

broad-

broadfides to bear more effectually on the enemy, fhould they attempt an attack.

At four in the afternoon, the enemy weighed and ftood to the fouthward, when I immediately made the fignal to weigh, and ftood after them, having received on board a detachment of 300 officers and men of his Majefty's 98th regiment, who were dif-tributed to the fhips of the fquadron that were worft manned. I ftood with the fquadron, as per margin *, to the fouthward all that night under an eafy fail; and in the morning, at day-light, found the enemy's fhips had feparated in the night; their 12 line of battle fhips and a frigate bearing eaft of me, diftant about four leagues, and 16 fail of their frigates and tranfports bearing fouth-weft, diftant about three leagues, and fteering a direct courfe for Pondicherry; on which I inftantly made the fignal for a general chafe to the fouth-weft, in order, if poffible, to come up with and take their tranfports, well knowing the enemy's line of battle fhips would follow to protect them all in their power.

In the courfe of the chafe, our copper-bottomed fhips came up with, and captured fix fail of fhips and veffels, five of which were Englifh, taken by the enemy, when to the northward of Madras, out of which I ordered the Frenchmen to be taken, and the vef-fels to proceed, with their own crews, to Negapatam; the fixth was the Laurifton, a tranfport, having on board many French officers, and 300 men of the regiment of Laufanne, and laden with guns, fhot, powder, and other military ftores. This fhip, fo valuable to us, and of fo much confequence to the enemy, was taken by Captain Lumley of his Majefty's fhip Ifis.

So

---

* Superbe, Exeter, Monarca, Hero, Worcefter, Burford, Monmouth, Eagle, Ifis, Seahorfe, Combuftion.

So foon as the enemy's fquadron difcovered my intention to chafe their tranfports, they put before the wind, and made all the fail they could after me; and, by three o'clock in the afternoon, four of their beft failing line of battle fhips were got within two or three miles of our fternmoft fhips; and the fhips in chafe were very much fpread, by the enemy's fhips they were chafing fteering different courfes, fome to the fouth-eaft, others to the fouth, and feveral to the fouth-weft. I therefore judged it neceffary to make the fignal for the chafing fhips to join me, which they all did about feven o'clock in the evening; and I continued ftanding to the fouth-eaft, under an eafy fail, all that night, the enemy's fquadron in fight, and making many fignals.

At day-light, in the morning of the 17th, the body of the enemy's fquadron bore north by eaft of ours, diftant about three leagues, the weather very hazy, with light winds and frequent fqualls, of fhort duration, from the north north-eaft, the enemy crowding all the fail they could towards our fquadron.

At fix in the morning, I made the fignal for our fquadron to form the line of battle ahead; at 25 minutes paft eight, our line a-head being formed with great difficulty, from the want of wind, and frequent intervals of calms, I made the fignal for the leading fhip to make the fame fail as the Admiral, and made fail, formed in the line ahead, intending to weather the enemy, that I might engage them clofely. At ten, the enemy's fquadron having the advantage of the fqualls from the north north-eaft, (which always reached them firft, and in confequence continued longeft with them), neared us very faft; and I made the fignal

for

for our line to alter the courfe two points to leeward, the enemy then fteering down on the rear of our line, in an irregular double line abreaft. At half paft noon, I made the fignal for our fqua-dron to form the line of battle abreaft, in order to draw the rear of our line clofer to the centre, and prevent the enemy from breaking in on it, and attacking it when feparated.

At three in the afternoon, the enemy ftill pufhing on to our rear in a double line abreaft, I again altered my courfe in the line, in order to draw our rear fhips ftill clofer to the centre; and at forty minutes after three, finding it impoffible to avoid the enemy's attack, under all the difadvantages of little or no wind to work our fhips, and of being to leeward of them, I made fig-nal for our fquadron to form at once into the line of battle a-head. At four, the Exeter (which was the fternmoft fhip in our rear, when formed in line of battle ahead, on the larboard tack), not being quite clofed to her fecond ahead, three of the enemy's fhips in their firft line bore right down upon her, whilft four more of their fecond line, headed by the Hero, in which fhip M. Suffrein had his flag, hauled along the outfide of the firft line, towards our centre.

At five minutes paft four, the enemy's three fhips began their fire upon the Exeter, which was returned by her and her fecond ahead. At ten minutes paft four, I made the fignal for battle; and at twelve minutes paft, the action became general from our rear to our centre; the commanding fhip of the enemy, with three others of their fecond line, leading down to our centre, yet never at any time advancing farther than oppofite to the Superbe, our centre

fhip,

ſhip, with little or no wind, and ſome heavy rain during the engagement.

Under theſe circumſtances, the enemy brought eight of their
beſt ſhips to the attack of five of ours.   As the van of our line,
conſiſting of the Monmouth, Eagle, Burford, and Worceſter,
could not be brought into action without tacking on the enemy ;
and although the ſignal for that purpoſe was at the maſt-head
ready for hoiſting, there was neither wind ſufficient to enable
them to tack, nor for the five ſhips of our centre and rear, then
engaged with the enemy, hard preſſed, and much diſabled in
their maſts, yards, ſails, and rigging, to follow them, without an
almoſt certainty of ſeparating our van from our rear.

At ſix in the afternoon, a ſquall of wind from the ſouth-eaſt
took our ſhips, and paid them round ahead on the enemy to the
north-eaſtward, when the engagement was renewed by our five
ſhips, with great ſpirit and alacrity, from our ſtarboard guns ; and
at twenty-five minutes paſt ſix, juſt before dark, the enemy's ſhips
engaged with ours, having viſibly ſuffered ſeverely, the whole of
them hauled their wind, and ſtood to the north-eaſt.

At this time the Superbe had loſt her main-yard, ſhot into two
pieces in the ſlings, had five feet water in her hold, which continued
for ſome time to gain on all her pumps, until ſeveral of the largeſt
ſhot-holes under water were plugged up, and neither brace nor
bow-line left entire ; and the Exeter, reduced almoſt to the ſtate
of a wreck, had made a ſignal of diſtreſs.   The other three ſhips
in our rear, the Monarca, Iſis, and Hero, had ſuffered leſs, as the
enemy's fire appeared plainly to be directed principally againſt the
Superbe and Exeter.

DESCRIP--

DESCRIPTION OF THE BATTLE BETWEEN THE FRENCH AND
BRITISH SQUADRONS ON THE COAST OF COROMANDEL,
17TH FEBRUARY 1782, TAKEN FROM THE FOREGOING
LETTER.

Sir Edward Hughes having left Trincomalé the 31ft of January 1782, came to an anchor in the road of Madras the 8th of
February; and, the fame day, he received advice, that a French
fquadron was at anchor about twenty leagues to the northward of
that place; and, all diligence being ufed in getting the neceffary
ftores aboard the feveral fhips, the enemy's fquadron, on the 15th,
came in fight from the northward; and, at noon, anchored about
four miles without the road. In the mean time, the men of war
were placed in the moft advantageous pofture of defence, with
fprings on their cables, that they might bring their broadfides to
bear more effectually on the enemy, fhould they attempt to make
an attack.

Plate XIX. fig. 1. The Britifh fquadron at anchor in the road
of Madras, the 15th of February, at A, with fprings on their cables, prepared to receive any attack.

F, The French fquadron come to an anchor likewife, the
morning of that day, and about four miles diftant, without the
faid road; but not finding it convenient to attack Sir Edward
Hughes, as he was then fituated, they got up their anchors that
fame afternoon, and ftood away to the fouthward. The Britifh
fquadron

fquadron foon after weighed, and ftood after them, carrying an eafy fail all the night; and, in the morning of the 16th, at day-light, the enemy's fhips having feparated during the night-time, the pofitions of the different fleets lay as follows :

B, The Britifh fquadron ftanding to the fouthward.

G, The enemy's line of battle fhips, fuppofed to be 12 in number, with one frigate, bearing eaft from the Britifh fquadron, and diftant about four leagues.

H, The enemy's tranfports and frigates, 16 fail, bearing S. W., diftant about four leagues, and making for Pondicherry.

The Britifh fquadron being thus fituated between the enemy's men of war and their tranfports, fignal for a general chafe to the fouth-weft was inftantly made, in the hope of taking fome of their tranfports, not doubting that their line of battle fhips would fol-low and endeavour to protect them.   In the courfe of the purfuit, the copper-bottomed fhips came up with and captured fix of thefe tranfports ; but by this means the Britifh fquadron was much fe-parated.

In the mean time, the enemy's fquadron, fo foon as they per-ceived the danger their fleet of tranfports were in, having put before the wind, fome of their beft-failing coppered fhips had got within three or four miles of the fternmoft of the Britifh, about three o'clock in the afternoon ; upon which, a fignal was made by Sir EDWARD HUGHES for the chafing fhips to join the fquadron, which they all did about feven o'clock in the even-ing, when, afterwards, he continued, all the following night,

M m   ftanding

ftanding to the fouth-eaft, under an eafy fail, as at C, while the enemy ftill kept in fight, as at I, making many fignals.

Plate XIX. fig. 2. A, The Britifh fquadron, on the 17th, at 10 o'clock forenoon, extended in a line of battle ahead, on the larboard tack; at this time the fhips in the rear of the line were too far aftern, particularly the Exeter, B, the fternmoft, occafioned by the light irregular breezes of wind.

F, The enemy having the wind more conftant, fteering down on the rear of our line in an irregular double line abreaft, and nearing us faft.

Fig. 3. The fhip B, the Exeter, in the rear of the Britifh, from the irregularity of the wind, continuing ftill to be far feparated; at half an hour paft noon, a fignal was made for the fquadron to form a line of battle abreaft, as at A, to give an opportunity for each fhip in bearing away, particularly thofe in the rear, to clofe with the centre, as at the points C C C, which, if accomplifhed, would prevent F, the enemy, from taking the rear at a difadvantage.

The enemy, F, ftill pufhing on for the rear. At three in the afternoon, the courfe of each fhip in the line was attempted to be ftill farther changed, and with the intention to draw the fhips in the rear ftill clofer to the centre, as from D to E.

Plate XX. fig. 4. At 45 minutes paft three o'clock, finding it impoffible to avoid the enemy's attack, a fignal was made for the Britifh fquadron to form at once into the line of battle ahead, as at A.

B,

B, The Exeter, the sternmost ship, not having been able to close with the next ship ahead,—

G, Three of the enemy's ships of their first line bore right down to attack her, while four ships of their second line, headed by the Hero F, in which ship Monsieur Suffrein had his flag, hauled along the outside of these three ships which were firing on the Exeter, intending to attack our centre, the Superbe with her seconds, at A.

Plate XX. fig. 5. G, The enemy's three ships began to fire on the Exeter at five minutes past four.

B, The Exeter and her second returning the fire.

F, The Admiral's ship, Monsieur Suffrein, with three others of the enemy's second line, having led down on our centre A, the engagement commenced from our rear to centre about 12 minutes after four.

In this manner Monsieur Suffrein had it in his power to bring eight of his best ships to make an attack on five of the British only ;—the wind at N. N. E.

Fig. 6.   At six o'clock in the afternoon, the wind having changed, a squall from the south-east, as at Z, took our ships, and paid them head round on the enemy to the north-east, viz. from the first position A, to the position B ; that is, from a larboard tack to a starboard tack, when again the engagement was immediately begun with fresh spirits from the starboard guns of our five ships.

Fig.

Fig. 7. At twenty-five minutes paſt ſix, juſt before it was dark, the enemy's ſhips which had been engaged having ſuffered ſeverely, the whole of their ſquadron hauled their wind, and ſtood off to the north-eaſt, as at F; and the Britiſh ſquadron being on a contrary tack, ſtanding to the north-weſt, as at A, the two fleets were ſoon ſeparated.

LIST

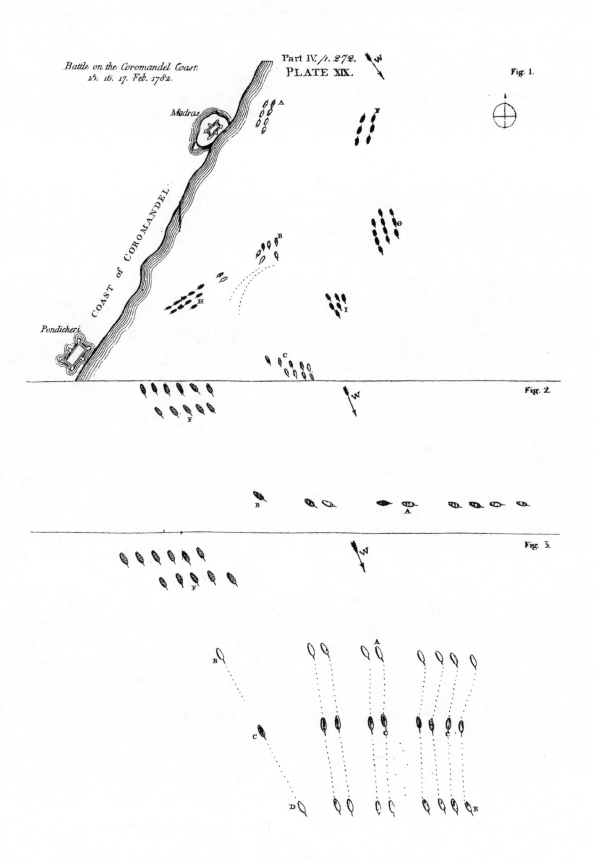

Battle on the Coromandel Coast
15, 16, 17, Feb. 1782.

Part IV, p. 272.
PLATE XIX.

Fig. 1.

Madras

COAST of COROMANDEL

Pondicheri

Fig. 2.

Fig. 3.

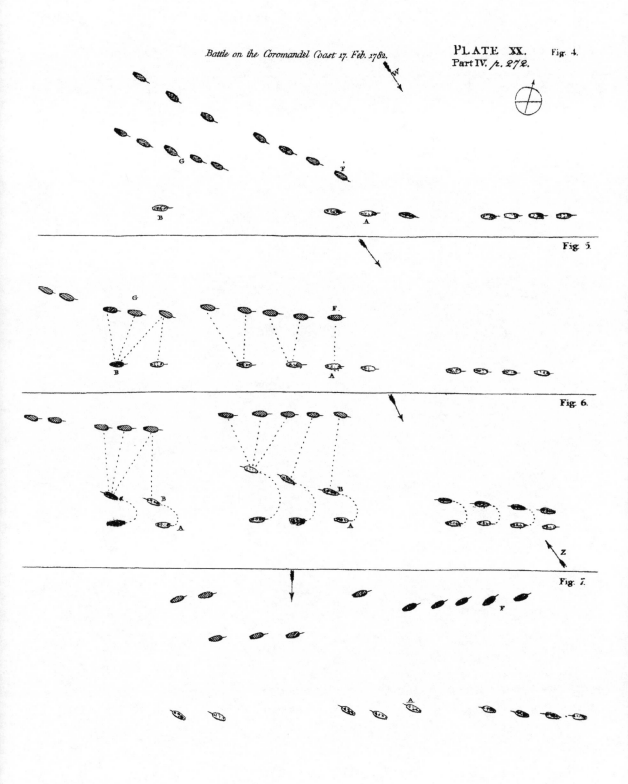

Battle on the Coromandel Coast 17. Feb. 1782.

PLATE XX.
Part IV. *p. 272.*

Fig. 4.

Fig. 5.

Fig. 6.

Fig. 7.

LIST *of the* BRITISH SQUADRON, *with the Killed and Wounded, in the Battle of the* 17*th February* 1782.

				Killed.	Wound.
Superbe,	-	-	-	11	25
Exeter,	-	-	-	10	45
Monarca,	-	-	-	1	5
Hero,	-	-	-	9	17
Worcester,	-	-	-	0	0
Burford,	-	-	-	0	0
Monmouth,	-	-	-	0	0
Eagle,	-	-	-	0	0
Isis,	-	-	-	1	3
Seahorse	-	-	-	0	0
Combustion,	-	-	-	0	0
				32	95

Officers Killed and Wounded.

Superbe, Captain Stevens wounded (since dead).
    Lieutenants Hughes and Newcombe wounded.
Exeter, Captain Reynolds killed.
    Lieutenant Charles Jones wounded.

LIST *of the* FRENCH SQUADRON *now on the Coromandel Coast, and of the Land Forces embarked in it, and the Transports at the Mauritius, the* 7*th December last, and now landed to join* HYDER ALI.

	Guns.		Men.
L'Hero, -	74	{ M. D. Suffiein, } { Chef D'Escadre, }	625
L'Orient, -	74	Cap. Du Pallaire,	625
L'Annibal, -	74	Tromelin, -	625
Le Brilliant, -	64	St Felix, -	516
L'Ajax, -	64	Bouvet, -	516
Le Severe, -	64	Sultier, -	516
Le Sphynx, -	64	Duchaleau, -	516
L'Artesien, -	64	L'Alandrois, -	516
Le Vengeur, -	64	Forbin, -	516
Le Flamand, -	50	De Queberville,	430
Eng. Hannibal, -	50		

FRIGATES.

La Purvoyeuse,	50	Cap. Du Galle,	400
La Fine, -	40	Perier de Salvert,	400
La Bellona, -	36	Bovard, 1st Officer,	350
La Subtile, -	22	De Beaulieu, -	140
La Silphide, -	18	- - -	200
La Diligente, -	8	- - -	80

FLUTES AND TRANSPORTS.

Lauriston, Bon Ami, Maurepas Brison, Deux Amis, Fille Unique, St Anne, Duc de Tuscany.

LAND FORCES.

Regiment D'Austrasie,	-	-	659
—— D'Ile de France,	-	-	800
De Legion de Lausanne,	-	-	455
Volontaires de Bourbon,	-	-	139
De Regiment d'Artillerie,	-	-	200
Caffres of the Islands,	-	-	1157
Sepoys,	-	-	47
			3457

OBSER-

OBSERVATIONS ON THE BATTLE OFF THE COAST OF CORO-
MANDEL, 17TH FEBRUARY 1782.

As the Britifh navy has hitherto afforded fo few examples of an
inclination to evade or avoid battle, our object has hitherto been
confined to treat of the mode of attack only, not that of defence.
On this occafion, however, it muft be admitted, that M. Suffrein, the commander of the fquadron of the enemy, has given
us fomething new, not only by obliging Sir Edward Hughes
to act on the defenfive, but by having, in his mafterly feamanfhip,
attempted a change, and put in practice a new mode of attack
from the windward. He is alfo the firft of an enemy, for this
century at leaft, who will be allowed the honour to have made an
attack upon a Britifh fquadron.

In the courfe of this action, there will be found an illuftration
of the following particulars:

1. That the fwift-failing veffels of the fquadron in purfuit were
coming faft up with, and would have cut off, the flow-failing veffels of the fquadron endeavouring to make off.

2. That to prevent the lofs of thefe flow-failing veffels, and to
protect them from the enemy, Sir Edward Hughes was induced to abide an engagement, which otherwife he was inclined
to have avoided.

3. That M. Suffrein, by carrying down his fquadron in two
divifions; fending three of his headmoft fhips to force an attack
upon two fhips in the rear of the Britifh, at B, fig. 5. Plate XX.;

bringing

bringing up the remainder of his fquadron in fupport of thefe three fhips; hauling paft them to windward, fo as to attack, and confine himfelf to the attack of the Britifh centre, the Superbe and her feconds, has put in practice a new mode; and it is alfo an illuftration of that mode which we have formerly demonftrated and endeavoured to recommend.

Though the full effect of·this admirable difpofition of attack made by M. Suffrein, was in the end prevented, by the Britifh fquadron being brought round on the ftarboard tack, and thereby enabled to get all its fhips into action by the change the wind made; yet nothing but a confcioufnefs of inferiority fomehow in his feamen can excufe M. Suffrein, or account for the retreat he made, or why he drew off his fuperior number of fhips, after once having had the merit of bringing up his fquadron to fo mafterly and advantageous an attack, where in one place he had three fhips oppofed to one, and in another place had brought five fhips againft three; and after having had the additional advantage, when the Britifh fhips might have been much hurt by his raking fire, while they were forced, with their heads round, by the change the wind made in the heat of action.

SIR.

SIR EDWARD HUGHES'S ENGAGEMENT IN THE EAST INDIES
WITH M. SUFFREIN, THE 12TH APRIL 1782.

EXTRACT OF A LETTER FROM SIR EDWARD HUGHES TO MR STEPHENS, DATED
ON BOARD THE SUPERBE, IN TRINCOMALE BAY, 10TH MAY 1782.

In my laſt I mentioned the junction of his Majeſty's ſhips Sultan and Magnanime with the ſquadron on the 30th of March. Both ſhips were then very ſickly, and much reduced by the ſcurvy; but as I had on board the ſquadron a reinforcement of troops for this garriſon, and a quantity of military ſtores, I judged it moſt for the public ſervice, eſpecially as I knew the enemy's ſquadron was to the ſouthward, not to return to Madras to land the ſick and ſcorbutic of theſe two ſhips, but to proceed directly for Trincomalé, and there to land the reinforcement and military ſtores, as well as the ſick of the Sultan and Magnanime, without either ſeeking or ſhunning the enemy.

In purſuance of this reſolution, I ſtood with the ſquadron to the ſouthward; and, on the 6th of April, fell in with a French ſhip, laſt from Mauritius, having on board diſpatches from France for their Commanders in Chief by ſea and land: This ſhip was chaſed on ſhore, and burnt near Tranquebar, the officers and men eſcaping with the diſpatches.

On the 8th, about noon, I came in ſight of the enemy's ſquadron,

dron, confifting of 18 fail, in the N. E. quarter ; and continued my courfe for this place, on the 9th, 10th, and 11th, the enemy ftill in fight ; on the 11th, having made the coaft of Ceylon, a-bout 15 leagues to windward of Trincomalé, I bore away for that place. On the 12th, at day-light, the pofition of the enemy's fquadron being altered by my bearing away, fo as to give them the wind of ours, I difcovered them crowding all the fail they could fet after us ; and their copper-bottomed fhips coming faft up with the fhips in our rear, I therefore determined to engage them.

At nine in the forenoon, I made the fignal for the fhips in our fquadron to form the line of battle ahead on the ftarboard tack, at two cables length diftance from each other. The enemy then bearing N. by E. diftant about fix miles, and the wind at N. by E., they continued manœuvring their fhips, and changing their pofitions in their line, till fifteen minutes paft noon, when they bore away to engage us ; five fail of their van ftretching a-long to engage the fhips of our van, and the other feven fail fteer-ing directly on our centre fhips, the Superbe, the Monmouth her fecond ahead, and the Monarca her fecond aftern.

At half paft one, the engagement began in the van of both fquadrons, three minutes after I made the fignal for battle. The French Admiral in the Hero, and his fecond aftern, the L'Orient, bore down on the Superbe within piftol-fhot. The Hero con-tinued her pofition, giving and receiving a fevere fire for nine minutes ; and then ftood on, greatly damaged, to attack the Mon-mouth, at that time engaged with another of the enemy's fhips, making room for the fhips in his rear to come up to the attack

N n   of

of our centre, where the engagement was hotteſt. At three, the Monmouth had her mizen-maſt ſhot away, and, in a few minutes after, her main-maſt, and bore out of the line to leeward. At forty minutes paſt three, the wind unexpectedly continuing far northerly, without any ſea-breeze, and being careful not to entangle our ſhips with the ſhore, I made the ſignal for the ſquadron to wear, and haul their wind in a line of battle, ahead, on the larboard tack, ſtill engaging the enemy. At forty minutes paſt five, being in fifteen fathom water, and apprehenſive leſt the Monmouth might, in her diſabled ſtate, drift too near the ſhore, I made the ſignal for the ſquadron to prepare to anchor. At forty minutes paſt ſix, the enemy's ſquadron drew off in great diſorder to the eaſtward, and the engagement ceaſed ; their Admiral having ſhifted his flag from the Hero to the French Hanibal, on account of the Hero's diſabled ſtate ; and ſoon after I anchored with the ſquadron, the Superbe cloſe to the Monmouth, in order to repair our damages, which, on board the Superbe and Monmouth, were very great in the hulls, maſts, ſails, and rigging ; and almoſt all the ſhips had ſuffered conſiderably in their maſts, ſails, and rigging.

Much about this time, the French frigate La Fine, being ordered, I ſuppoſe, to tow and aſſiſt their diſabled ſhip the Hero, fell on board his Majeſty's ſhip the Iſis, and had actually ſtruck his colours to her ; but taking advantage of the darkneſs of the night, and the ſtate the Iſis was in, juſt come out of action, in which ſhe had a number of men killed and wounded, and otherwiſe ill manned, the frigate got clear of the Iſis and eſcaped.

An

An account of the officers and men killed and wounded, on board the feveral fhips of the fquadron, is herewith enclofed.

On the morning of the 13th, at day-light, I found the enemy's fquadron had anchored about five miles without us, in much diforder and apparent diftrefs, but they had loft no lower mafts.

Both fquadrons were bufily employed in repairing damages, drawing into order for defence, the enemy feeming to apprehend an attack from us ; and I myfelf uncertain if they would not renew the engagement in order to get hold of the Monmouth.

In thefe fituations, both fquadrons continued at anchor till the 19th, in the morning, when the enemy's got under fail with the land wind, and ftood out to fea clofe hauled ; and at noon tacked with the fea breeze, and ftood in for the body of our fquadron, as if with intent to attack ; but after coming within two miles of us, finding us prepared to receive them, they again tacked, and ftood to the eaftward by the wind ; and I have not fince been able to learn certainly where they are gone. Having refitted the Monmouth in the beft manner our fituation would admit, with jury, main, and mizen-mafts, I failed with his Majefty's fquadron for this place on the 22d, and anchored here on the evening of the fame day, immediately landing the reinforcement and military ftores deftined for the garrifon, and the fick and wounded.

In this fituation of the fquadron and its men, I thought it beft for his Majefty's fervice, to remain at anchor here, and to fet about the repairs of the hulls, mafts, and rigging of the feveral

N n 2

fhips,.

fhips, while the fick enjoy every benefit of frefh meat, vege-
tables, and wine, on fhore for their recovery.

I have the fatisfaction to inform their Lordfhips, that I fhall
be able to re-maft the Monmouth by the end of this month, from
the fpare ftores on board of the feveral fhips; and that the damage they fuftained in the laft engagement will be every way
made good about that time.

ABSTRACT OF THE OFFICERS AND MEN KILLED AND WOUNDED ON BOARD THE
SEVERAL SHIPS OF THE BRITISH SQUADRON.

					Killed.	Wounded.	Total.
Superbe,	-	-	-	-	59	96	155
Exeter,	-	-	-	-	4	40	44
Magnanime,	-	-	-	-	—	7	7
Monmouth,	-	-	-	-	45	102	147
Monarca,	-	-	-	-	7	28	35
Worcefter,	-	-	-	-	8	26	34
Burford,	-	-	-	-	6	36	42
Eagle,	-	-	-	-	—	22	22
Hero,	-	-	-	-	2	13	15
Sultan,	-	-	-	-	—	9	9
Ifis,	-	-	-	-	6	51	57
					137	430	567

Among the killed were the following Officers :
Superbe, two Lieutenants,—Mafter.
Monmouth, one Lieutenant of Marines.
Worcefter, one Lieutenant.
Burford, one Lieutenant of Marines,—names not mentioned.

DESCRIP-

DESCRIPTION OF THE BATTLE OFF CEYLON, THE 12TH OF APRIL 1782.

THE FRENCH SQUADRON, CONSISTING OF TWELVE SHIPS AND FRIGATES, COMMANDED BY M. SUFFREIN; THE BRITISH SQUADRON, CONSISTING OF ELEVEN SHIPS AND FRIGATES, COMMANDED BY SIR EDWARD HUGHES.

SIR EDWARD HUGHES, in his letter of the 10th May, acquaints us, that while he was on his way down the coaſt of Coromandel, from the northward to Trincomalé Bay, he came in ſight of the enemy's ſquadron, confifting of 18 ſail, in the north-eaſt quarter, about noon, on the 8th of April: That he continued his courſe; but the enemy following, kept in ſight of him during the 9th, 10th, and 11th; and having made the coaſt of the iſland of Ceylon on the 11th, about 15 leagues off Trincomalé, he bore away for that place.

On the morning of the 12th of April, at day-light, perceiving that the enemy had got the wind of his ſquadron, by reaſon of his bearing away during the night; and perceiving alſo that, by crowding every ſail, their copper-bottomed ſhips were coming faſt up with the ſhips in his rear, he therefore came to the reſolution to wait for and engage him.

At nine in the forenoon, a ſignal was made for the Britiſh ſquadron to form the line of battle ahead, on the ſtarboard tack,

at

at two cables length diftance from each other; the enemy being directly to windward, diftant about fix miles, and the wind N. by E.

The enemy continued manœuvring their fhips, and changing their pofitions in the line, till fifteen minutes paft noon, when they bore away to engage us; five fail of their van ftretching along to engage the fhips of our van, while the other feven fail fteered directly on the fhips of our centre.

Plate XXI. fig. 1. A, The Britifh fquadron on the ftarboard tack, formed in line of battle ahead, at two cables afunder.

F, The enemy right to windward, bearing N. by E. diftant fix miles, by crowding fail faft coming on.

Fig. 2. B, The van of the Britifh, confifting of four fhips.

A, The centre, confifting of three fhips.

C, The rear, confifting of four fhips.

G, The van of the enemy, confifting of five fhips, ftretching along to engage the four fhips in the van of the Britifh.

F, The French Admiral, with the other feven fhips of their line, fteering directly on to the centre of the Britifh, confifting of the Superbe and her two feconds, viz. the Monmouth ahead, and the Monarca aftern.

Fig. 3. F, The French Admiral in the Hero, with the L'Orient his fecond aftern, bearing to attack the Superbe. It is faid the Hero came within piftol-fhot.

H H,

H H, The other five fhips of the enemy fupporting the Hero in the attack of the centre.

A, The Britifh Admiral, in the Superbe, receiving the fire of the Hero, within piftol-fhot, as it is faid.

B, The four fhips in the van of the Britifh, fuftaining the attack from the five fail of the enemy.

C, The four fhips in the rear of the Britifh which feem not to have been much engaged.

G, The five fhips in the van of the enemy attacking the van.

Plate XXII. Fig. 4. F, SUFFREIN in the Hero, after having been greatly damaged by the fire of the Britifh Admiral, A, ftood on to the attack of the Monmouth, E, who was engaged with another of the feven fhips; making room at the fame time for others of the fhips in his rear to get up in fucceffion to the attack of the centre, and where it is faid the engagement was the hotteft.

C, The Monmouth, about three o'clock falling out of the line, after having loft her mizen-maft and her main-maft.

B, The four fhips in the van, fuftaining the attack from the five fhips of the enemy.

Fig. 5. At forty minutes paft five, the wind unexpectedly continuing far northerly, without any profpect of a fea breeze, and careful therefore not to entangle our fhips with the fhore of Ceylon, Sir EDWARD HUGHES made fignal for the fquadron to wear and haul their wind in a line of battle ahead on the larboard tack, the engagement continuing all the while.

At

At forty minutes paſt five, being in fifteen fathoms water, and apprehenſive leſt the Monmouth, in the diſabled ſtate ſhe was, might drift too near the ſhore, the ſignal was made for the ſquadron to prepare to come to an anchor.

At forty minutes paſt ſix, the enemy's ſquadron drawing off to the eaſtward in great diſorder, the engagement ceaſed. M. Suf-frein, on account of the diſabled ſtate of the Hero, ſhifting his flag from that ſhip to the French Hannibal.

A, The ſhips of the Britiſh ſquadron in the act of wearing, and while expoſed to a raking fire from the enemy, after having quitted their ſtarboard poſition, B B B.

F, the enemy's ſquadron.

W, The wind at north.

Fig. 6.   The Britiſh ſhips having wore, and withdrawn to leeward, in manner like the ſyſtem of defence already obſerved to have often been practiſed by the enemy, are now with their heads to the eaſt at A, when the action was renewed from the larboard guns, and continued above an hour; but the apprehenſion of the Monmouth's getting aſhore ſtill continuing, the ſignal was made for the ſquadron to come to an anchor.

F, The French Admiral not chooſing to renew an attack, which, according to the above mentioned ſyſtem, might have been attended at this time with much loſs, drew off his ſhips in great diſorder to the eaſtward, after having quitted their ſtarboard poſition, G G; but whether this was effected by wearing or tacking the ſquadron, is not mentioned.

REMARKABLE

PLATE XXI. Part IV. p. 284.

Fig. 1.

Battle off Ceylon 12.th April 1782.

F

Fig. 2.

5 Ships
G

7 Ships
F

B

A

C

Fig. 3.

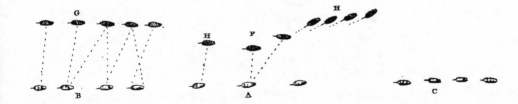

G

H

H

F

B

A

C

REMARKABLE PARTICULARS OF THE BATTLE OFF CEYLON,
12TH APRIL 1782.

THAT it was on the fame day in which LORD RODNEY fought
and beat COUNT DE GRASSE, in the battle between Dominica
and Guadaloupe, in the Weft Indies, the oppofite quarter of the
globe.

That the protection of his flow-failing veffels, who were in
danger of being overtaken by the fwift-failing veffels of an enemy
who had been in purfuit of his fquadron for four days, was the
reafon which induced Sir EDWARD HUGHES to abide an engagement, which otherwife (in this cafe as well as in his former
battle) he was inclined to have avoided ; and it fufficiently illuftrates the difficulty and danger, not to fay impracticability, of a
fleet making off to leeward, as has been before demonftrated.

M. SUFFREIN not having had the hoped for fuccefs in the attack upon the rear of the Britifh fquadron the 17th February, his
attempt upon the van, equally well concerted on this occafion,
evidently proves him to be an officer of genius and great enterprife.

If M. SUFFREIN had wind enough firft to bring down the van
of his fleet to the attack of the Britifh, and afterwards to bring
up the rear divifion to fupport it, even within piftol fhot of the
Britifh centre ; and if the fhips in the Britifh rear could not in
time get up to annoy a crippled enemy, this the more particularly

O o   illuftrates

illuſtrates the propriety and practicability of bringing up and directing the whole, or any part of a force, againſt a ſmaller part of the force of an enemy ; and that the effect ought to have important conſequences, in battles at ſea, as well as in battles at land.

But at the ſame time that it proves the above, it alſo proves this, that though the Britiſh ſquadron was at firſt inclined to avoid battle, yet thoſe ſhips which were attacked, being once engaged, ſhewed no inclination to quit the field to a ſuperior force, or to give room to the freſh ſhips aſtern, even though they could have got up to their aſſiſtance.

The apprehenſion of the danger of a lee-ſhore, though it may excuſe Sir Edward for wearing with his ſquadron while under the attack, and in the face of the enemy, as in fig. 5. ; and though he renewed the action on the contrary tack, as in fig. 6. ; yet the enemy may ſay, (as many Britiſh commanders on the like occaſion have ſaid of the enemy), that Sir Edward was beat, as his fleet had been completely driven out of their firſt line.

To which it will be anſwered : If Sir Edward, from the impending danger of a lee-ſhore *, was forced to this manœuvre of wearing, he did thereby renew his line of battle in ſtrong poſition to leeward, and in the ſelf-ſame manner which the French fleets have done on every former occaſion, whenever they have been attacked from the windward ; and, as it was in M. Suffrein's option, and he did not think it fit to come down and renew the action, it may be admitted that this may be called a drawn battle. But in another view, if it is conſidered that the Britiſh ſquadron came to an

anchor

---

* The iſland of Ceylon.

anchor on the fpot, that they kept poffeffion of the field of battle, and that M. Suffrein fairly drew off his fhips; by the laws of war, the victory fhould be adjudged to Sir Edward Hughes, the Britifh Admiral. Again, to return to M. Suffrein's firft battle, that of the 17th February: By the Britifh fquadron putting about their fhips heads to the enemy, and thereby forcing him to go off when he might have continued the engagement; the victory, therefore, on this occafion, alfo ought to be determined for the Britifh fquadron.

In confidering the power of cannon fhot, and bringing to our recollection the little effect fometimes of a cannonade, after having been kept up for above three hours, we cannot help remarking, on this occafion, the cannonade, of nine minutes duration only, which fo much difabled the Hero, M. Suffrein's fhip. Her opponent, the Superbe, the Britifh Admiral, during the engagement, had 59 men killed and 96 wounded; and the Monmouth, her fecond, 45 men killed and 102 wounded.

FINIS.

D. Willifon, Printer, Craig's Clofe, Edinburgh.

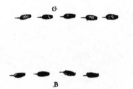

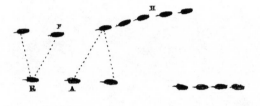

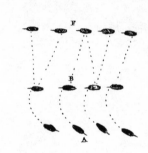

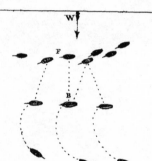

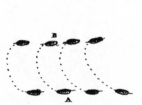

Fig. 5.

Fig. 6.

29150815R00257

Made in the USA
San Bernardino, CA
14 January 2016